*Dear Helen*

# *Dear Helen*

## Wartime Letters from a Londoner to Her American Pen Pal

*Edited by*

Russell M. Jones and John H. Swanson

—ɱ—

UNIVERSITY OF MISSOURI PRESS
COLUMBIA AND LONDON

5   4   3   2   1      13   12   11   10   09

Library of Congress Cataloging-in-Publication Data

Swallow, Betty M., 1915–1969.
  Dear Helen : wartime letters from a Londoner to her American pen pal / edited by
Russell M. Jones and John H. Swanson.
     p. cm.
  Summary: "In letters written between 1937 and 1950 to her American pen pal,
a working-class Londoner offers accounts of the Blitz and of wartime deprivations and
postwar austerity, interweaving descriptions of terror with talk about theater, clothes,
and family outings, providing a unique view of daily life during World War II"—Provided by publisher.
     Includes bibliographical references.
     ISBN 978-0-8262-1850-6 (alk. paper)
     1. Swallow, Betty M., 1915–1969—Correspondence. 2. World War, 1939–1945—
Personal narratives, English. 3. World War, 1939–1945—England—London. 4. Pen
pals—England—London—Correspondence. 5. Young women—England—London—
Correspondence. 6. Working class—England—London—Correspondence. 7. London (England)—Biography. 8. London (England)—Social life and customs—20th
century. 9. Bradley, Helen, 1890–1979—Correspondence. 10. Pen pals—Missouri—
Kansas City—Correspondence. I. Bradley, Helen, 1890–1979. II. Jones, Russell M.
(Russell Moseley), 1927– III. Swanson, John H., 1938– IV. Title.
     D811.5.S924 2009
     942.1'084092—dc22
     [B]
                                                                    2008051321

Designer and typesetter: Kristie Lee
Printer and binder: Thomson-Shore, Inc.
Typefaces: Adobe Caslon and Mistral

*This book is happily dedicated to*

Pamela Swallow Coulter

*grandmother of six (so far), mother of three,
daughter of Jack Swallow, niece of Betty
and the oomph girl of 1960!*

# Contents

# Acknowledgments

The editors gratefully acknowledge the following individuals and organizations for the essential help they provided, enabling us to complete the Betty Swallow letters project: Director Rob Havers, Assistant Director Sara Winingear, Curator-Archivist John Hensley, and Education and Public Programs Coordinator Mandy Crump of the Winston Churchill Memorial and Library; Amy Fluker, a senior history major at Westminster College who transcribed the letters for the manuscript; D. Jennifer Dawson for her critical editing assistance in formatting the manuscript; David White and Joel Starr, history majors at Westminster College, who based their senior theses on the letters of 1940–1942; Angela Gerling, Head Librarian of the Reeves Library at Westminster College; John E. Marshall, for hours of patient proofreading and sound editorial advice, as well as research into the background of Helen Bradley. Our special thanks to R. Crosby Kemper III for his interest in this project.

We also wish to thank the Bureau of Vital Statistics of the Missouri Department of Health and Senior Services, the Reference Department of the Kansas City Public Library, and the General Register Office, UK. Special thanks to Marie Thompson, MLS, St. Luke's Hospital, Health Sciences Library, Kansas City, for referring us to John Barnard, MD, who worked with Helen Bradley at the Dixon Diveley Clinic, and Dawn McMinnis, Director of the Kansas University Medical Center, Kansas City, Kansas. We are grateful for the opportunity to read the M.A. thesis "The Swallow Letters: Bridging Interpersonal and Mass Communication in WWII," by Barbara Friedman (University of Missouri, 1999).

We are also grateful to Britisher John Digby, writer, poet and noted collagist, who shared his knowledge of London and cricket, helping us tremendously.

Our deepest gratitude is to Beverly Jarrett, Editor in Chief of the University of Missouri Press and Jane Lago, Managing Editor. Beverly's enthusiasm for this book was an inspiration to us, and her initial question: "Tell me more about what went on between these two women," became the central theme of the introduction.

The unflagging patience and professionalism of our editor, Jane Lago, made this book much better than it would have been otherwise. Despite the excellent preservation work of archivists at the Winston Churchill Memorial and Library, the originals of these letters were in some instances in chronological disarray. Helen Bradley apologized for this disarray to Virgil Johnston, then Director of the Winston Churchill Memorial and Library, upon presenting the letters, explaining that she had tried to organize the continuity of the letters. But this was difficult. Most often Betty did not date her letters—particularly after the Blitz began—but Helen often saved the envelopes they came in with their postmarks. We and, years earlier, Helen also tried to use internal evidence from the letters to establish the logical progression of this correspondence.

When Jane Lago joined us with the task of producing this book, she elevated the job of getting the time sequence of the letters right with her questions and suggestions and in doing so preserved intact Betty's "voice from England," as the editors of *Picture Play* dubbed her letter written so long ago. The result is that readers today can hear that voice more clearly.

# About the Text

We have attempted to reproduce Betty's typing accurately. Although her spelling is remarkably correct, she often omitted apostrophes, leaving blank spaces in contractions such as "we're" or "he's." Those eccentricities as well as the occasional misspelling have been retained. Obvious typos, of which Betty made very few, have been silently corrected. The majority of Betty's letters were typed, with her signature handwritten. In the few cases when Betty handwrote a letter, she indicates so in the letter itself. Betty seldom dated her letters. When a date is evident from a postmark or other evidence, it has been added in brackets.

In identifying movies and actors in the footnotes, our guideline has been that even though contemporary readers will be familiar with many of the films and actors mentioned, the information provided adds to the reader's understanding of how these movies provided respite to the strain the Blitz caused Betty and, by inference, Helen also. There are many excellent encyclopedias of movies and their stars. We have used the Internet Movie Database (www.IMDb.com), easily available on the Web, for our information.

*Dear Helen*

# Introduction

These letters introduce us to two remarkable women: Betty Swallow, a youthful Londoner, and her pen pal, Helen Bradley, who lived in Kansas City, Missouri. The letters cover the period from 1936 to 1950 and with two exceptions were written by Betty. Betty and Helen became pen pals because of their mutual fascination with the movies, which at the time were a enormously popular cultural force. Betty wrote a letter to the editor of *Picture Play,* and it was published in that New York movie magazine in 1936. Helen apparently contacted Betty through the magazine. The correspondence began as a lighthearted exchange centering on the two women's shared passion for the silver screen, but the focus rapidly changed to an ongoing commentary by Betty on the events leading up to the outbreak of World War II, the devastation of the London Blitz, the privations she personally suffered, and the loss of her health as a result of the Blitz. However, the letters are not all about gloom and doom. Betty was, to say the least, resilient, ironic, and humorous, as well as angry and sometimes almost overwhelmed by her frustration with the world.

In the beginning, Betty reveals herself as a bright, twenty-two-year-old living in London with her mother and working as a stenographer/secretary for the shipping department of the Great Western Railway. Betty immersed herself in the pursuit of entertainment, friends, holidays, and work—what we would expect of a young middle-class single woman in one of the richest, most sophisticated cities in the world.

As the reader will perceive, she was a gifted writer who honed her talent with innate skill from the start to the end of her correspondence with Helen. She interwove the serious topics of the war and postwar austerity with vignettes of her daily life—the office, friends and beaus, holiday trips, family, hospital stays—which she executed with clarity and dramatic interest. Even though these vignettes were not always cheerful, they had the effect of brightening her style.

More than once she mentioned her desire to be a writer. But she was not in the right place at the right time to realize that ambition. Her discussions of movies and the theater reveal a dedication to the dramatic arts. She sought contact with leading actors in the London theater such as John Gielgud; perhaps, if she had reached adulthood in the years after the war, with her health intact, the literary community in London would have provided encouragement for a young woman with such talent and desire.

During the course of this correspondence, we learn practically everything about Betty. About her pen pal, Helen Bradley, we know less, but a portrait of her does emerge, that of a patient and caring woman who had a lot to give a friend, even one met through the somewhat artificial convention of a "pen palship."

We know from letters that Helen wrote in 1969–1971 to Virgil Johnston, director of the Winston Churchill Memorial and Library in Fulton, Missouri, as well as from her obituary, that she was trained as a nurse and physical therapist. She attended the Kirksville College of Osteopathic Medicine in Kirksville, Missouri; the University of Southern California in Los Angeles; and Harvard University Medical School. She was a pioneer in the then relatively new profession of physical therapy. She lived most of her adult life in Kansas City, Missouri, and became the chief therapist at the Dickson-Diveley Clinic, at the time one of the leading centers in the country for physical therapy. She was born in 1890, in Kansas City, before birth certificates were issued. But we do not know much about her family, other than that she had a cousin, Mrs. Barbara Runyan, who supplied information for her obituary printed in the *Kansas City Star* on September 5, 1979.

Helen carefully saved the letters, cards, and snapshots she received from Betty, although, as the letters reveal, some of their wartime correspondence seems to have wound up on the bottom of the Atlantic. We do not have any of the letters Betty received from Helen, however, and therefore we have to rely on inference to get a sense of Helen's side of the dialogue. As the reader will see, there is plenty to go on; Betty related personally and energetically to Helen as she portrayed the events that surrounded her during these years.

The correspondence diminished and then ceased in 1950, seemingly Helen's doing more than Betty's. In one last piece of the correspondence, a letter written in 1969 that was returned undelivered, Helen makes a dramatic confession: "I quit writing to you because I could not take any more of your criticism of the U.S."

So a rupture in their relationship occurred, but it is not easy to find in the letters themselves. During the thirteen years of the correspondence, Betty did not refer to any sharp break between the two, although she often registered differences of opinion with Helen: about their favorite movie stars and actors in the early letters, and then, as the war began to develop and finally burst out, in response to what apparently were increasingly strong differences of opinion about American isolationism and criticism of Britain's conduct of the war in U.S. newspapers. In the postwar letters the differences centered on such political issues as socialism and the cold war. Throughout the letters, these differences of opinion are both explicit, when Betty refers to something Helen has said, or implicit, as Betty seems to be addressing something Helen might have said. In fact, Betty sent Helen a number of newspaper clippings, most of them in letters written in 1940 and 1941 when Britain was involving herself in the conflicts in Finland, Norway, Denmark, Holland, and France. These clippings focus primarily on the British reaction to American isolationism and American criticism of England's role in these campaigns. They indicate that Betty's criticisms reflected the prevailing climate in the British press rather than an actual conflict between her and Helen. They also show that Betty borrowed many ideas as well as words and phrases about America's position from these newspaper articles. For instance, one article that she sent, headlined "It's Your War, Too," contained a passage Betty echoed several times: "President Roosevelt can hardly open his mouth . . . without pronouncing a condemnation of Nazi methods . . . mustn't he, if he's honest with himself, realize that America is in this struggle with us up to the neck—only she isn't paying her share?" Walter Winchell defend~ ¹ American isolationism in a broadcast and drew a re~~ *day Dispatch* from which Betty picked up another p. is no comfort to the average Briton . . . to be told tha war.'"

During the German invasion of Belgium, the newspapers were full of eyewitness accounts and pictures of the effects of the Blitzkrieg on civilians. Betty sent pictures from newspapers and included details from an article in the *Daily Express:* "Between thirty and forty high explosive bombs were dropped . . . into the narrow streets where 20,000 refugees were pouring toward France."

A statement in the *Sunday Chronicle* from an American apparently rankled Betty: "It was suddenly discovered that Britain and France had finally gone to war purely for selfish motives." This seems to have stung so much that Betty confessed her resentment to Helen in a letter dated May 8, 1940: "How anyone in the World could say that Britain is fighting a selfish War beats me. What in God's name *can* we gain by it? All this affair in Norway!" She also sent a clipping from the *Sunday Pictorial* in February 1941 titled "Why Don't They Come Home?" featuring famous British athletes, night club entertainers, movie actors, and writers who were staying in the United States during the Blitz. Although this was not an instance of anti-Americanism, she registered anger about the attraction the American theater and movie business had for British actors, writers, and entertainers. She was not as chauvinistic when it came to her own rejection of English weather in favor of "balmy" Kansas City and, of course, the sunshine of California.

The implication of these articles is that in discussing the issues drawn from the newspapers Betty was attempting to objectify her sentiments by showing Helen the sources of her information. One clipping included a photo of a British soldier saying good-bye to his infant son. It seems to have been sent at about the time that British forces were still in France after the evacuation at Dunkirk. This must have been an iconic image for Betty, who mentioned it in a context laden with her intense feelings of pain over the death in World War I of the father she never knew. In her letter dated January 11, 1940, she wrote: "Every day I go to Victoria station on my way to work, and there are hundreds upon hundreds of boys and men leaving for France, after their brief home leave. It always makes me want to howl that their father fought like mine did, in the last War thinking they'd finished it all, and now their children are left to start the whole terrible business again!"

But often Betty's criticisms of America came as sharp tirades that indeed can trouble readers. In almost every case, these tirades are surrounded by a helpless and frustrated tone as Betty accounts for the events that are taking place—international developments, the frightening course of the war at its start, the bombing itself, the privations she experienced, the destruction of London, her severe health problems. One can see from what Betty describes in these letters that she was in fact the helpless victim of war. The loss of her father left her a fatherless child. World War II took her beloved city, her childhood friends, and her health. But she was not hopeless. She was, without a doubt, the epitome of English pluck, irony, and humor.

The haven she and Helen shared in the ideal world of movies became a frequent counterpoint to the stress of the war in Europe and the Blitz. Another ideal Betty often asserted was her intense desire for peace. Her father was lost to her in the fruitless effort of World War I to create a lasting peace. He had written idealistically about that to his wife while he was stationed in France. Betty idolized Neville Chamberlain for his diplomatic efforts to achieve peace. She distrusted Winston Churchill, even more intensely after the war, because of his warlike tactics in pursuit of peace. In the immediate aftermath of the war, she made the transition from a "true blue Tory" to a socialist because she felt that socialism and, with some reservations, communism held out hope for the working class and for peace. She consistently expressed anti-American opinions because she did not feel that attitudes in the United States or the policies of the American government such as prewar isolationism and later the cold war served her and her compatriots' desire for peace.

Helen claimed that these attitudes caused her to break off the dialogue, but that may have been an overstatement. Betty's polemical diatribes began early in the correspondence and continued throughout the thirteen-year period. Throughout those years Helen remained a caring, giving person, initially sending movie magazines and, once the privations of the war took hold, providing gifts of food and clothing as well. She even enlisted friends and family members in this expression of friendship. However, other causes may have contributed to the break. On the one hand, Betty was constantly awash in her sense of helplessness. On the other, Helen had her own insecurities, including their age difference (she was twenty-four years older than Betty). In her letter of September 8, 1937, Betty brushed that concern off with youthful self-assurance: "You say in your letter you were surprised at my age. That s funny, but I would never have dreamed that you were older than me." She continued: "I happen to like older people a great deal more than younger ones. . . . As for still wanting to write to you—of course, I do. And I hope you'll feel the same about me." In another letter, written in November 1938, Betty chided Helen for not wanting to send her picture: "Thank you for your charming compliments on my appearance. Let me assure you I have a million faults. . . . As for saying you could never send your photo—You must have an awful inferiority complex. I think I shall be one of those young ladies who 'fade' quickly. When I'm in me forties, I've a firm feeling that I shall be enormous, with three or four chins, and a marvellous 'spare tyre'." Not the most tactful way to ask for a picture of a forty-seven-year-old woman. Such insecurities may have contributed more to Helen's decision to stop writing than did Betty's anti-American criticism, as Helen claimed nineteen years later.

Unquestionably, the tensions caused by some of Betty's outbursts could have built up by the last years of the correspondence to the point of thoroughly frustrating Helen. Betty's anti-Semitism may have been the start of such frustration. Her first expression of this sentiment comes early on in the correspondence when Betty lashes out at the Jewish immigrants from Austria. In subsequent letters her repetition of this attitude seems compulsive. Although it does not justify her display of prejudice, it is noteworthy that Betty always projected a distinct mood of helplessness preceding or surrounding these attacks. However, where such outbursts occur the mood is not all frustration and anger; Betty often goes on to discuss current movies and plays that she has seen in a chatty contrast to her dark mood about Jewish immigration to England that strikes one as insensitive.

One passage, written by hand in December 1941 near the end of the Blitz and long after the immigration of the Austrian Jews, illustrates how this mood of helplessness seems to have triggered her anti-Semitic outbursts. Betty wrote the letter after having spent months in a sanatorium recuperating from inflamed lungs: "I do hope you will forgive me, dear, for scribbling in pencil . . . I cannot go back to the Office and use the Typewriter until the New Year. . . . I am now safely home again, after just over four months in the Sanatorium—four months which seemed like four years! The country is beautiful, when you are fit . . . but when you have to lie about and just gaze at it, it's plain monotonous. London seems like heaven in comparison. However, . . . if the raids start in earnest again, I shall have to pack up and go elsewhere—no more shelters for me! Its a case of you die if you go below, and you die if you stay on top so I think I'll take the top."

Betty went on to complain about the scarcity of food under the rationing program and lamented that she and her mother hadn't sufficient ingredients for really good Christmas puddings. But her pluck resurfaced: "[U]nless I can use my wiles on the Butcher, Grocer, and what have you! Still, leave it to little Betty to keep up Ye Olde English Christmas if possible."

Then she caught herself almost forgetting to thank Helen for a Christmas package of candy, nylons, and cosmetics: "Now, I almost forgot to tell you the most important thing of all—that is, I actually received the Box. . . . Gosh! was I grateful ?? . . . I am using the Powder, and it is just the right shade." In the next sentences, however, comes this: "Some of the Cosmetics put on the Market here now, are appalling concoctions, made mostly by Jews in forbidden factories from anything they can lay their hands on. The Government have just put a Ban on them. . . . Wherever you find any dirty work afoot, there you find the Yids, and if that sounds prejudiced, I really can't help it. I hate the sight of the Jewish people, and more than 50% of the Shirkers in this country belong to that Race." Then she returns blithely to the subject at hand: "Anyway, enough of that. Many, many thanks for the Box."

Betty's criticism of America started in her early letters, when England was gearing up for war; then, as the bombing of London began and later when America entered the war, her criticisms of America ceased. They resumed once the war was over and the British suffered the extreme hardships of the postwar austerity programs. Her criticisms were often addressed directly to Helen, and each time they were preceded by a description of her frustrations. The war and the suffering were real for her and everyone else.

On November 24, 1939, she wrote: "[A]s you will probably guess, our lives have been turned upside down and everything seems changed. I have been so terribly busy in work that I've gone home feeling like a pricked Balloon." She explained, "I was on holiday the week War broke out. . . . [W]e packed up . . . and got back to London. . . . On the Sunday morning we all sat round the Radio and listened to the Premier's speech and we all cried—the young ones because they didn't know what was coming and were frightened, and the older ones because they did." She went on to say, "It seems funny but last week my mother turned out a

letter from my father dated sometime in 1916, and he says '. . . it's rumoured out here that Jerry is angling for an Armistice. But I and most
of the chaps out here feel we'd rather fight on and finish the Germans
for good and all so that our children won't have the same old battle
all over again. I don't want Jacky to grow up to anything like this. If it
means peace for our kids we'll fight till we all drop'. Prophetic, wasn't
it? And you've got it just as it was written." She was expressing her
dismay at how doomed that idealistic wish was. A few lines later, she
lashed out: "But I wish Americans wouldn't stand around doing precisely nothing but criticise and call it a 'phoney' War. After all, they are
not risking a single American life, and are only thinking of the whole
thing in terms of Newspaper Headlines and Dollars for Armaments."

Betty often tried to soften the effect of her emotional censure of
America and its policies. She frequently concluded such letters by apologizing for getting off the subject, "rambling" as she put it, and in one
of them she tried harder to soften the effect of her criticism: "I don't
mind *you* criticizing us Honey! . . . When I think of how much I talk
and how marvellous you are to me, I get thoroughly ashamed of myself.
. . . I hope you know how sincerely I appreciate everything you do." At
the same time, however, there is that underlying note of helplessness.

Beyond the suffering Betty experienced in the war, these moods may
have had their source in a deeply felt grief over the loss of the father she
never knew. When she spoke of him, she reflected the pain of a fatherless child. She seems to have idealized him as a peace-loving figure,
but she expressed bitterness that he died for such an ideal. In fact, her
complaint, in the early letters when England and France and the other
European allies were trying to avoid war, that Britain had to be "polite,"
as she put it, honoring treaties and standing up for the smaller countries, may have had its genesis in her disillusionment with idealism such
as her father's, which she felt caused her to lose him.

In her letter of April 10, 1940, she likened her brother, Jack, who
was impatient to get into the army, to her father: "My father was exactly the same. He tried three Recruiting Offices in 1914 before they
finally accepted him and then the Chief Clerk in his Office got him
out because he was a valuable man, but he got in again, and went to
France in '15. He died when I was a baby and I don't remember him
at all, though Jack has some fleeting memories of him. We've only got
one photograph of him and that's in Soldier's Uniform. He looks pretty

nice. I think he and I might have got along very well together." This last poignant thought suggests the depth of her yearning for the man she never knew.

If a profound sense of helplessness characterizes her discussion of the loss of her father, and her life during the war, one of the starkest and most disturbing self-images that recurs in Betty's letters appears for the first time in one postmarked October 16, 1940, during the Blitz: "I no longer suffer from Housemaids Knee but have developed instead 'Shelter back' due to lying flat on my back on the cold stone Platform of an Underground Railway." A similar image of helpless passivity is repeated in her letter of August 17, 1941, written from East Anglian Sanatorium, where she was trying to recuperate from tuberculosis: "Doctors say I have not been strong enough to stand up to all the hardships of War conditions last Winter. Lying about on wet and cold stone floors of Deep Shelters, breathing bad air, getting no sleep, and not the proper food have all combined to break my resistance down. Still, I am getting better now."

Describing one of her most serious, near fatal illnesses in a letter written on September 28, 1946, "in bed, propped up with umpteen pillows," Betty expressed her aversion to lying about passively awaiting death with characteristic pluck and dark humor: "I was transferred to Hospital in the middle of it, & sent home because I was lying awake all night what with women dying next to me & another Woman going mad & rushing round the Ward as though she was on a Horse!"

Helplessness and anger and fear are not the only emotions Betty showed to Helen. Despite being overwhelmed by illness and the adversities of the war, she invariably projected a tempering mood of hopefulness, and it is important to recognize that despite lashing out at Helen she always reaffirmed her affection for her American friend. A vignette in the later letters shows how deep that affection could be for both women. The Austerity Program had settled over England, and over Betty, like a lead blanket. She longed for white shoes, with stylish open toes, which she could not find at home. This produced a burst of correspondence about white shoes in which Betty asked Helen to send her some. In late May 1946 Betty wrote, "The main thing is, Helen, that the package arrived quite safely yesterday . . . and oh! I am so grateful to you. The shoes were simply marvelous."

This package contained canned goods and clothing, for which Betty thanked Helen joyfully, although there is one sobering note: "the vest is

going to be put away for Medical Exams and X-Rays, of which I have
plenty of as you can imagine." Betty's mother was caught up in the joy
and was persuaded to add a note of her own, which was sent along with
Betty's letter: "I am quite sure you would feel quite satisfied without
expressed thanks if you could only have seen both of us. . . . As for the
white shoes, well, ecstasy is the right word. . . . Betty is really one of the
war casualties. She was a lovely healthy girl before the war, but life in
shelters and lack of variety and quality of food caused a breakdown that
we have never been able to pull up."

Although there is no direct evidence in the letters of an irreparable
difference of opinion or of a threatened break in Helen and Betty's
relationship, an episode in the last letters may shed indirect if somewhat surprising light on why Helen stopped writing. In August 1945,
Betty wrote that she had broken up with her boyfriend, Chris, who
was a Coldstream Guard and a decorated veteran of the North African
campaign. He was also, as Betty put it, "a very good looking man. . . .
Women chase him around like Moths round a Candle." Apparently,
when he came back to England he deserted the army for a time. However, because of his good military record he was allowed to return without penalty. But he jilted Betty. As she said, "He seems to be a different
man—went completely mad—you know, wine, women and song—the
old story." In these letters, Betty told Helen of her disappointment, but
she also took pains to convey a stoic attitude in her acceptance of the
end of the relationship.

What complicates our understanding of Betty's discussion of this
failed romance is the fact that at some point (when is unclear) Helen
started writing to Chris herself. Apparently he was stationed at the
time in North Africa, where Betty had been sending him the movie
magazines Helen had sent her from America. He shared them with the
other men, who used the pictures of the movie stars for pinups above
their bunks.

In a letter written in August 1945 Betty said, "I should have loved
to have seen Chris's letter to you (his name's 'Chris', not Ted, honey—
you've got them mixed up) If you still have it, I wish you'd send it over
to me. I'll return it without fail." And then she went on to tell of the
failed relationship. In the next letter, written sometime afterward, Betty
said, "Thanks so much for sending Chris' letters. He and I are washed
up now, finally—and I think it's the best and most sensible thing to do.

. . . . I have tried with him, but I've lost heart now. I am giving you his address, because I know he'd be happy to hear from you—he was very grateful to you for sending him books . . . you'd better say you asked me for his address, which will adjust things from my angle."

It sounds as if Betty did not want Chris to think she had asked Helen to write him and intercede on her behalf—which may have been what Helen had done or had intended to do. Or perhaps Betty thought that writing Chris would provide a little romance in Helen's life. At any rate, Betty was resolute. "He and I are on opposite sides, Helen, and it doesn't work out," she went on to explain, as if she was cautioning Helen about trying to straighten out the relationship.

She mentioned him again in a letter dated April 1946: "Chris is 'demobbed' [demobilized] next week, I believe—so what he will be doing with his future I haven't the faintest idea. . . . Don't suppose I shall ever see much of him, even though we live in the same town." Betty wrote again about Chris a few weeks later, in the spring of 1946, perhaps from a lingering sense of hurt, or perhaps because Helen had continued to inquire: "Chris was demobbed about five weeks ago, and is causing a great stir among the females of the town. I have spoken to him on one occasion—for about five minutes, during the whole of which time he never looked at me once—just spoke with his shoulders hunched up and his face turned the other way. It was just like speaking to a stranger—not a man I'd known for four years. I was beginning to wonder if my face was pock-marked or become so distasteful that he couldn't look at it!! I see him fairly often at dances, and he ignores my existence as completely as I ignore his. . . . I have given up wondering and puzzling about such things. I only regret the loyalty and thought I wasted on him, which was obviously so little appreciated. It really doesn't seem like him at all—almost like someone else had taken his place. Unless, of course, I was seeing him through rose-coloured glasses, which often happens. Anyway, it's over and done with, now, and I have settled down to it better than I thought I would."

Betty seems to have been trying to put the subject to rest between her and Helen, but she couldn't resist a last swipe at the fickle fellow: "From what I can gather, he seems to be going from bad to worse as far as Women are concerned, and the lies and yarns he tells are fantastic. Seems to be living in a world of his own. I'm honestly beginning to wonder if he knows when he's telling the truth, and when he isn't."

Later that year, in the early summer of 1946, Betty added a characteristically ironic coda to the matter. A fellow office worker had just returned from a day off to meet her boyfriend who had arrived back from overseas: "P.P.S. Joyce has just come in sporting a great big diamond ring which was just put on the third finger of her left hand at quarter past 11 last night! So *she* obviously had what it takes even if I didn't!"

Helen's interest in this failed romance may shed more light on why she stopped writing Betty than does her returned letter of nineteen years later. Helen was consistently responsive, caring, and giving to Betty throughout the years of the correspondence. Evidence of her concern and generosity is abundant. Considering Helen's steadfastness and considering the terrible wartime events Betty described, it would be hard not to think Helen was experiencing them vicariously through these letters.

Helen Bradley seems to have been shy compared to Betty. We know she was insecure about their age difference. In addition, while Betty sent quite a stream of snapshots of herself, her family, girlfriends, and boyfriends, Helen had refused to send her own picture. Perhaps Helen was loyal to Betty because she was lonely. Indeed, it seems likely that Betty's descriptions of her personal life were of vicarious interest to Helen.

In addition to describing her relationship with Chris, Betty frequently mentioned other boyfriends as well as incidents in her social life, her feelings for the father she never knew, her idealization of John Gielgud, the two women's debate about the merits of Maurice Evans's Broadway *Hamlet* versus Gielgud's London *Hamlet*. At one point Betty even thanked Helen for bothering to envision the complicated route she had to take through the suburbs to get to work in the heart of London.

Through the course of the letters, Betty described a tight-knit family: her adventurous, robust brother, Jack, whose wife was close to Betty and her mother; the couple's child, who was welcomed into the family; her mother, Gladys, who was a warm and caring single parent. Gladys got both of her children jobs with the railroad, and Betty kept hers all her life, even though she complained about it. This warm family is part of what Helen saw of Betty's life, as well as the struggle to survive the war and its aftermath. Ultimately, the human story contained in these letters may have spoken more to Helen, faithful nurturer to Betty for all those years, than did her young friend's frustrated criticism of America.

Betty wrote in a tone markedly different from her usual brash outspokenness on May 10, 1949. Helen's letters had become less frequent, and this would be Betty's last letter. It begins with a description of her health and her treatments. There are echoes of the old frustration. She had been in a sanatorium and a hospital for twenty months: "Needless to say I was pretty sick of the country life after 9 months of lying around looking at some very uninteresting railings with a flat expanse of green field beyond it." But this letter, pervaded by a tone of resolution, is also hauntingly elegiac. On a hopeful note, Betty even describes her health as improving, "I am beginning to feel a lot better now, and am certainly much brighter since I started work," before she concludes the subject with typical irony: "I'm beginning to wonder if a short life and a gay one isn't the best way to look at it!!"

This time her frustration with the world was only lingering and she did not lash out at Helen but rather reached out to her: "[H]ow are you all this time, Helen. I have wondered so often how things were with you. I always counted you, and one other American girl I know, as very dear friends of mine, and I often speak to people of your kindness to me. I always hope to hang on to individual friendships, however many international differences crop up, as crop up they will—even among allied nations. I know there is a lot of things we do that irritate Americans intensely, just as there are things in their characters utterly alien to our way of thinking, but I have always spoken of people as I found them and you, and Gwen (the girl in New York) were very good to me, and I am not likely to forget it."

She proceeded to account for their political differences constructively: "Politically, I think you and I differ Helen—I am an ardent Socialist and a great supporter of our present Government—the only one we've ever had that ever gave the workers of Britain a square deal. I am not, too, as anti-Russian probably as you—in fact I don't think the masses of Britain are violently anti-Soviet at all. I am no admirer of the Communist doctrine in its entirety, though there are many things in it, which had the party stuck to the ideals laid down by Lenin, would have made the world a pleasant place for the poorer people, but I have a mortal horror of War . . . and I cannot conceive of anything bad enough to cause nation to rise up against nation. . . . [W]e'd be wiped off the face of the earth should it happen again. And there you have the hard core of the disagreements between British and Americans. We feel that if there is another War with Russia it will be America's war, and we shall be dragged in as a buffer state for Russia to drop the bombs on."

Betty seems to have recognized that Helen had a different view. At the time, America was transfixed by the cold war. Popular opinion had it that socialism was a pale but dangerous shade of Russian communism, and Betty seemed to be trying to accommodate Helen's feeling. On a deeper level, this letter suggests that Betty had come to a fork in the road she and Helen had for a time traveled together. She seems to have come to peace with many of her old frustrations. She had resolved her conflicts at least about her station in life and her vision of a just society. And at the end of the letter she even introduced a new, "current boy friend." She sent a picture: "It's very good of Bob. . . . He has corn-coloured hair and I was always devoted to dark men. It just shows you!" She concluded: "I shall have to finish now, and will tell you more of the family history on my next letter. Do write me soon, Helen. I was so pleased to hear from you, and I hope we may keep in touch with each other now."

But that never happened. There were no more letters between them. Betty did send a Christmas card in 1950 from Ireland: "I do hope everything is well with you—Haven't heard from you for so long!" Then she added, almost matter-of-factly, "I am married now, but still living in the North of England." Betty's husband was Bob Arnold, who in 1969 signed her death certificate, on which his occupation was listed as "sheet metal worker." No doubt he was the man with the corn-colored hair. Perhaps she attached some of her yearnings for a father to him and in him found something of the peace she longed for. Helen never married.

In Betty's relationship with Helen Bradley, we see a rich skein of ambivalence, gratitude, and love. In Helen we see a person to whom Betty could bare her soul—with all of its contradictions. Helen may have felt frustration, even embarrassment over a failed attempt to restore Betty and Chris's romance. Or she may have been self-conscious about involving herself at all in the little triangle. She may not have found Betty's attempt in her last letter to resolve the political differences between them as sufficient as Betty hoped it would be. But it is hard to take Helen's statement that "I could not take any more of your criticism of the U.S." as the full story. She admitted feeling guilty for the lapse, and the tone of love for her old friend is unmistakable: "[A]fter reading again of all you had been thru I know I should have forgiven you anything."

Perhaps both women had reached a point from which their lives led them onto separate paths. The correspondence broke off, but the friendship really did not. In the end, Helen was determined to preserve that friendship, as well as the historical record it constituted, in the archives of the Winston Churchill Memorial and Library at Westminster College in Fulton, Missouri.

## Helen Bradley:
### "straight man to Betty's brilliant performance"

Today, Helen Bradley is almost a mystery woman. A few of her colleagues at the Dickson-Diveley Clinic are still alive and remember her as "very energetic"; "a person who expected a lot out of everybody, but fun at the same time"; "something of a character." Dr. John Barnard, an orthopedist with whom she worked at the clinic, noted that "she was an excellent physical therapist" and that "she certainly did not let the patients have their own way." He also remembers that she did not have any family to speak of.

In the 1940s and even into the 1960s, hospitals and medical school programs did not maintain much biographical information about students and staff. Thus, with the exception of her silent presence in the letters of Betty Swallow, we have little information from which to form a picture of Helen.

However, we do have her own words in brief letters she wrote to Virgil Johnston during 1969 and until 1971. Helen wrote to him on December 5, 1969, offering her letters to the Winston Churchill Memorial and Library. Her belated letter to Betty had been returned from England some weeks earlier. She concluded this offer by saying, "As I am 79 years old I should soon find a place for them that would be interested."

Johnston quickly accepted the gift, and Helen acknowledged this, mentioning the returned letter she had written to Betty: "I'm afraid she was another war casualty (tuberculosis). I am sorry now but I quit writing her because she became so critical of America." About six months later, on June 14, 1970, she wrote Johnston apologizing that she had been hospitalized at St. Luke's in Kansas City because of a heart attack and was still "gradually returning to normal."

She explained her relationship with Betty as "only 'straight man' to Betty's brilliant performance. She had written a letter about John Gielgud to one of the fan magazines and I sent her a letter. . . . I tried to compensate for what she was going through by writing often and sending parcels. . . . But now the war was over and with each letter she became more critical of America so I stopped writing to her. I wish I had realized . . . that the war was not over for her. I have been in England in 1956, 58 and sixty two, but have been unable to find Betty. While I enjoyed each country I visited, England is the one that enchanted me. It was like going home."

She continued to give a brief biography: "I was born in Kansas City in 1890 and my residence has been here except for years in college and working for the army as a physical therapist in World War I and with the Veterans Administration. My last professional work was with the Dickson and Diveley Orthopaedic Clinic where I served for 20 years before retiring in 1963."

Two subsequent notes to Johnston reveal Helen's continued interest in Betty Swallow's letters. In the last, she discusses her interest in David White, a history major at Westminster College whose senior thesis was on the Swallow letters.

This brief correspondence with Virgil Johnston shows a person very like the intelligent, dedicated woman remembered by her professional colleagues and evident in the correspondence of her pen pal, Betty Swallow.

# I

## The Beginning

In these nine letters (one to *Picture Play*, a movie magazine published in New York, and eight to Helen Bradley), Betty Swallow, age twenty-two in 1937, describes herself as a proud British blonde, fair-skinned, an ardent fan of films and theater. Her favorite actors include John Gielgud and Leslie Howard, while she dislikes Madeleine Carroll and Marlene Dietrich. Indeed, Betty's opinions on films and their stars dominate these letters.

Current political events receive little comment. She mentions Nazi Germany's annexation of Austria (the Anschluss), the consequent flight of Jews to England, and as a result their excessive, to Betty, influence in English business and public opinion. Opposed to a war against Germany, Betty applauds Prime Minister Neville Chamberlain's appeasing of Hitler at Munich by not going to war to prevent annexation of the Sudetenland. She is relieved at no longer having to wear her gas mask and angry at Labour and U.S. papers for attacking the appeasement policy.

By July 1939, relieved that war has been avoided, Betty describes her political heritage: her father was a communist and her mother a conservative. But Betty's immediate concern is vacations.

*Picture Play,* April 1937
"A Voice from England"

Can you spare a line or two for an English fan to pass some opinions? It's more than three years since I wrote and I feel it's time I poked my nose in again.

Firstly, I'm so glad Norbert Lusk took notice of our John Gielgud in the September issue. Mr. Lusk, you ain't seen nuthin' yet. Wait till you see him as "Hamlet." He's marvelous!

Secondly, as one of Jessie Matthew's ardent admirers, I'm so pleased that America likes her as much as we do. She's about the only one of our British actresses who can dance, sing, and act. One unbeatable combination.

Thirdly, it's refreshing to see that our pictures are making good progress in America, films like "Nine Days a Queen," "Secret Agent," and "Rhodes." They're all supers and our producers over here are concentrating on making more and more pictures like them. The trouble is we've got the directors and the actors, but our actresses—ouch! You have one of them now trying to make an actress out of her—Madeleine Carroll. You'll never do it, Hollywood. She's cultured, she's lovely, but that's about all.[1]

And as a final plea, will some kind American come and take Dietrich away from here? She's nothing more than publicity crazy. She's even taken to visiting hospitals now. This morning's paper quotes her as saying "I was born to be a nurse." Now laugh that one off!
Betty M. Swallow,
38 Raleigh Road, Shepherds Bush, London W. 14, England.

---

1. After her sister was killed in a London bombing raid, Madeleine Carroll stopped acting to work in Red Cross field hospitals. She was awarded the Legion of Honor for her bravery in France.

18A. Sinclair Gardens,
West Kensington,
LONDON. W 14.
England.
June 23rd 1937.

Dear Helen,

Forgive the familiarity but I never call people "Miss" anything. Always seems peculiarly unfriendly to me. What do you think? And as I'm anything but an unfriendly person, you must forget about the "Miss Swallow", too.

I was delighted to hear from you, and did not consider it impertinent at all. I have met very few Americans, but correspond with quite a few, and my opinion is that they must be the friendliest nation on earth. Strange to us, who are, if anything, a rather reserved nation. Although the famous British reserve isn't quite so pronounced as people would have you believe. Once the ice cracks the British are liable to become the best of pals with anyone. Speaking for myself, I don't seem to have inherited the national characteristic. I'm quite chatty with strangers, have very little self consciousness, and get along well with everyone as a result.

About myself, if it matters. I'm 22, British and proud of it, blonde, blue-eyed, with a very fair skin (can't sun-burn at all, even on those rare occasions when we do get some sun to burn with). I'm an ardent Theatre and film "fan", have been stage-struck for as long as I can remember, like reading, and drawing, and dancing, dislike sports, have a fairly good knowledge of political and international affairs, but am at my best when discussing Films and the Theatre. My mother says with gentle sarcasm, that those two subjects are all I *can* discuss, but she's a "fan" too, so we can have arguments together.

I'm a very loyal kind of fan too. I like nearly all the English actors (except Lawrence Olivier,[2] whom I cannot stand at any price), and have

---

2. One of Laurence Olivier's earliest successes as a Shakespearean actor came in 1935 when he played Romeo and Mercutio in alternate performances of *Romeo and Juliet* with John Gielgud. Gielgud got the better reviews. Olivier appeared in a special production of *Hamlet* with Vivien Leigh (Ophelia) performed at Kronberg Castle in Elsinore, Denmark, in 1937. They married in 1940, after returning to Britain from Hollywood, where they both made hit movies in 1939, he *Wuthering Heights* and she *Gone with the Wind.*

no intense dislikes save, Dietrich, and Madeleine Carroll, and Wendy Barrie.[3] But I have only one prime favourite, and that's Gielgud.[4] He's been the one and only for the past five years, and looks like holding the same position until I'm an aged old woman. Mother says I'm not quite sane on the subject of John—I'm not quite as bad as that, but with several thousands of other young London females, I am practically incurable. You haven't seen him at his best, although I like him in "Secret Agent". Did you see "The Good Companions" by any chance?[5] That was marvellous, the best British film I've ever seen, and one of John's most charming performances. I've seen all of his plays, (he's turned me into a Shakespeare maniac), and I shall never forget his "Hamlet", or anything else he's ever appeared in for that matter. He is, of course, the No. 1 Matinee Idol over here. Has an enormous following, mostly women, and the reception he gets at a "first-night" is amazing. Cheers and screams, and everything that goes with it. I go to all of them, and have the most exciting time. He is generally regarded as England's greatest actor, which isn't bad going for a man as young as he is. There are rumours about now that he intends to marry Peggy Ashcroft (the English actress who was his "Juliet" in London and was with Burgess Meredith in "High Tor" in New York).[6] She has just got her third divorce, a pretty dreadful thing in England, and I think Gielgud will lose a great deal of respect if he becomes a fourth husband. Still, that's his private life and has nothing to do with anyone, although I can't say I admire his choice much.

3. Marlene Dietrich was the highest paid actress of the early 1930s, but in the mid-1930s her films fell out of favor with the critics and the public. She became a U.S. citizen and toured for the Allies during World War II; after the war she was decorated by the United States and France for her strong stand against Nazism. Wendy Barrie, a British actress of the 1930s, is best remembered as Jane Seymour (wife number three) in *The Private Life of Henry VIII* (1933).

4. John Gielgud was the first English actor under forty to play Hamlet, which established his career at the Old Vic in the 1929–1930 season. In the following season he played the title role in *Richard II*.

5. *Secret Agent* (1936; UK), directed by Alfred Hitchcock, is based on stories by W. Somerset Maugham and stars John Gielgud and Madeleine Carroll as British agents assigned to assassinate a German spy during World War I who become conscience stricken about the mission. *The Good Companions* (1933; UK), a musical comedy based on a J. B. Priestley novel, stars John Gielgud.

6. Peggy Ashcroft, later a Dame of the British Empire, was a legendary stage and film actress whose work included the plays of Shakespeare, in England and later in the United States.

As for the campaign you spoke about. English fans, Producers, Film Magnates and the rest, have been breaking their necks for three years to get him signed up on a Picture Contract, but its just a waste of time. I rather wish he had gone to Hollywood. There's been dozens of parts suggested for him, but he's turned them all down. The only plan now is that "Richard of Bordeaux" *may* be made in the Spring, in Colour.[7] I should think it would be a lovely film, and I wish they'd have Merle Oberon as his wife, Anne.[8] I always wanted to see those two together, and John is supposed to be Merle's favourite actor, but I don't see much prospect at the moment.

By the way, if it isn't too much to ask you, would you let me have just a tiny peek at that reply he sent you, if you have it that is. I promise I'll send it straight back, Cross my heart. Only I should love to see it, And if you ever see anything about him in any Books or papers, would you send it to me. We can't get hold of many American Books here, and I'm always trying to get copies of the "Theatre Arts Monthly"—but they don't seem to sell it much round here. If there's anyone you want clippings of over here, I'll scout around and get 'em for you.

I like Leslie Howard very much,[9] and was in a bit of a mess when the famous "Battle of the Hamlets" was raging on Broadway. I wanted John to win, yet I felt sorry for Leslie. I think he intends to make a picture of some sort while he's in England, and "Bonnie Prince Charlie" was suggested. But then, it was suggested for Fairbanks Jr. too, and nothing came of it. The latest plan for Howard, according to our Film writers, is that he intends to play the part of Shakespeare on the screen, That

7. Inspired by Gielgud's acting, Elizabeth Macintosh wrote the play *Richard of Bordeaux* under the pseudonym Gordon Daviot. It was a smash hit and made Gielgud a celebrity. Its success provided him with the financial means to produce classics in the West End, pioneering the theater company system. Among the new generation of actors that resulted were Olivier and Peggy Ashcroft. Betty mentions this play and the rumors that it would be made into a movie frequently in the early letters. It was clearly a subject of interest in the movie and theater world of England.

8. Merle Oberon played Anne Boleyn in *The Private Life of Henry VIII* (1933). She was successful in films both in the United States and in Britain, starring with Laurence Olivier in *The Divorce of Lady X,* a romantic comedy (1938; UK).

9. After being shell-shocked while serving in the army in World War I, Leslie Howard took up acting as therapy. He was successful in London and New York theaters as "the perfect Englishman." Very active in England's war effort, he died when the airliner on which he was traveling was shot down over the Bay of Biscay by the Germans.

incidentally, is causing a minor riot amongst the Gielgud supporters, who contend that John is better able to play Shakespeare than Leslie is. And so it goes on.

I like Walter Huston very much. He strikes me as a man who is sincere about everything he does. I thought he was grand in "Rhodes".[10] Peggy Ashcroft was in that too. She was Anna Carpenter, the novelist. She's not a bit pretty, but has a lovely voice, and is a good actress, but. Oh! those three husbands. Ruth Chatterton is over here now, playing in the "Constant Wife".[11] We saw her one night after the Show. She seems very charming, We saw her again, together with practically every celebrity of the English stage, at the Theatrical Garden Party in Regents Park last week. That was a day for Autograph hunters. Everywhere you went you tripped over some "celeb" or other. I spoke to Charles Laughton,[12] in broad Yorkshire, and he answered me in even broader Yorkshire. He was so good-tempered, and jovial looking that I got quite a shock. He's such a beast in all his films. Noel Coward and I did a bit of back-chatting, when he stood up to autograph a photo of his.[13] Two guineas was supposed to be the lowest bid (that's about 10 dollars in your money). Said he "What am I bid for this masterpiece" So I chirped up "fourpence-hapenny", somewhere in the region of 10 cents. Was his face red.

Nobody here seems to like Dietrich much. She bores me stiff. There's absolutely nothing to the woman, except a pair of false eyebrows, and a flat nose. I don't suppose she'll be any better in "Knight Without Ar-

---

10. Walter Huston was one of the most respected American actors of the 1930s. Confirming Betty's judgment of him as sincere, he once said, "I was certainly a better actor after my five years in Hollywood. I had learned to be natural—never to exaggerate. I found I could act on stage in just the same way . . . using my ordinary voice." He appeared with Peggy Ashcroft in *Rhodes of Africa* (1936; UK), a biography of Cecil J. Rhodes.

11. American actress Ruth Chatterton began her career as a chorus girl on Broadway at age fourteen. Her reputation from the theater made her a major film star of the 1930s. The play *The Constant Wife* was written by W. Somerset Maugham.

12. Although educated at Stonyhurst College, British actor Charles Laughton enlisted as a private in World War I. Following theatrical training at the Royal Academy of Dramatic Art, he became one of the most successful actors and drama teachers in film and stage.

13. Noël Coward—dramatist, actor, writer, composer, lyricist, painter, and wit—is considered to have virtually invented Englishness. In the 1920s he injected the fast pace of Broadway shows into the staid British drama and music.

mour" and I'm not particularly smitten with Robert Donat, so I don't know if I shall bother to see it.[14] Its the picture scheduled to open our new super-luxury cinema in Leicester Square in September. According to all reports this Cinema is going to be *the* Acme of perfection. Let s hope so—Our Theatres and Cinemas could do with a great deal of improvement. So could some of our films, and as aforesaid our actresses. With the exception of our Jessie, and Gracie Fields,[15] and Merle Oberon, I don't think there's one of 'em I'd give you tuppence for. Still, I'm about the most patriotic Briton there ever was, and what makes me boil is when some of our stars go over to America, and forget they were ever English and start calling us very uncomplimentary names. The Americans who come over here don't do it. They never start all this bilge about "I think England is far nicer than America and I want to live here all my life". Don't mistake me, I'm not saying that our stars don't owe a tremendous lot to America and the Americans, and if they love the country, there's nothing to stop them saying it, but they shouldn't degrade their own country at the same time. Some of our young actresses just go completely "Hollywood" when they get out there, and it makes me sick. Still there's one consolation, as you say, Hollywood isn't America. Otherwise we should think it a very funny country altogether.

I saw Henry Wilcoxon and his wife when they were in England. He's just finished the lead in "Jericho" with Paul Robeson, and it should be shown soon.[16] I see Wilcoxon is divorcing his wife, or is it the other way around. I never can get straightened up on these divorce tangles.

14. *Knight without Armour* (1937; UK), a Russian spy movie, stars Dietrich and Robert Donat. The British-born Donat worked as a Shakespearean actor in repertory companies in England in the 1920s and 1930s and appeared in *The Private Life of Henry VIII.* He was contracted to Hollywood studios but insisted on working for them in England after appearing in the hugely successful *39 Steps* (1935), directed by Hitchcock. He won an Academy Award for best actor for *Goodbye, Mr. Chips* (1939) and stayed in England during the war.

15. Jessie Matthews was a 1930s film star, dancer, and singer. Gracie Fields, a comedienne and singer, was the highest paid female star in the world in 1937. She developed a very popular northern working-class-girl character. Ironically, considering Betty's prejudice against British actors who went to the United States during the war, Gracie was one of them. She never regained her prewar popularity.

16. In *Jericho* (1937; UK), Henry Wilcoxon played a friend to the main character, Jericho (Paul Robeson), who is sent to prison for an accidental murder, escapes to Africa, and becomes the leader of a tribe. Wilcoxon played Marc Antony in Cecil B. DeMille's *Cleopatra* (1934; U.S.) and was involved with many of DeMille's movies.

We in England were very sorry to hear of the death of Jean Harlow.[17] She was a native of Kansas City, wasn't she? I was not a "fan" of hers, exactly, but I thought it was terribly tragic that one so young and vital should have to die. And when the news came to us over the Wireless I couldn't have had a worse shock if it had been someone personally dear to me.

I must close now, Helen, as I have rather a lot to do this evening. Please do write soon, I enjoyed your first letter so much.

Sincerely,<br>Betty

P.S. We have changed our address as you will notice from the heading of the letter.

18A. Sinclair Gardens,<br>Kensington. W 14.<br>England.<br>[September 8th, 1937]

Dear Helen,

Many thanks for your very interesting letter, which I received two days ago. I am so glad you had an enjoyable holiday—it certainly was marvellous reading about it, made me wish I had been there. I have been working rather hard lately, and have had two bad bouts of Summer 'fluenza, and a very nasty sore throat. I've been feeling the strain of all of it. Its a pity my holidays came before it—I felt fine when I came back, but all the work and colds have put me back again.

I went down to the Gower Coast in Wales for my holidays. I believe I told you that my native county is Monmouthshire, which is on the borders of Wales (although it is definitely an English county. You can't annoy a Monmouthshire person more than by calling her Welsh.) Anyway, I went down to see my relatives and friends, and then went on from there to the Gower. I did a lot of swimming, although I can swim like a fish, I'm not really keen on it, and for once we had a heat wave and I was able to sun-bathe. All I could manage, however, was a

---

17. Jean Harlow, America's blonde sex symbol during the 1930s, died in 1937 of uremic poisoning during the filming of *Saratoga* with Clark Gable.

blister and a freckle or so. I can never tan, because I am so fair. I go a dreadful shade of brick-red, and my skin comes off like wood shavings. I'm always bleating about it. My brother is as fair as I am, but he went to Ireland and came back a glorious copper bronze, and his wife looks like a cross between a Chinaman and a Nigger (female gender). John lives down by the river in Windsor, and spends half his time bathing in the Thames, and all his Sundays in Maidenhead, Eton, or Runnymede. Delightful places, but too quiet for me. I like noise and bustle and everything that goes with the town life. My brother is exactly the opposite—he lives in the open air, and getting him into a Cinema is the toughest job on earth. He continually tells me that I'm crazy going to the Theatre on a warm day, and spends his time attempting to convert me to the "back to Nature" movement. I swear he'd become a Nudist, only he knows we'd all laugh at him. However, we share one thing in common, a liking for warm weather and sunshine—and as [I] get very little of either we can grumble together at least.

Talking of weather—its been so cold this past week, we've had to go back to fires, and woollen jumpers. Yesterday we had a terrific storm—the sky was absolutely pitch black and the Lightning played havoc with some of the houses around here. The Office next door to us was flooded out—things were floating about, and meeting you through the door. It's a little better to-day, although I think we're in for some more rain. The clouds look very ominous and threatening. Yet some people over here say we've had a good summer. I can't imagine why. The Sunny days put together, would only make up about a month of the year. However, English people are notoriously easily satisfied.

You say in your letter you were surprised at my age. That s funny, but I would never have dreamed that you were older than me. I've always dabbled about in writing. I've written things for film and Theatre Magazines, and once tried my hand at short story writing. I always wanted to be a Journalist, but I was brought up in the wrong place for it. I haven't really got a great deal of patience, and have a terrible slap-dash way of writing letters. Mother thinks I ramble too much, so it's a great comfort for me when you say you think I write well. I give myself credit for being able to discuss a variety of subjects, and as a result I try to cram them all in. The resulting mixture isn't too good, always. Give me a listener in sympathy with my views on something, particularly the Theatre and Cinema, and I'll yapp for hours. I've never been shy in my life, never feel the slightest bit awkward with strangers, and can make friends remarkably easily. Yet if I walk down the street, or sit in a Bus and think people are looking at me, I go a rich red colour, and fidget, and suffer tortures, if I'm on my own. That must be what they call "Self consciousness". I never could make it out, because I'm usually so sure of myself. Blushing is a dreadful habit, and I'm doing my best to break myself of it. Anyhow, to get back to the age business—I happen to like older people a great deal more than younger ones. Some of the very young creatures, in their teens, get on my nerves—though I'm not much older myself. As for still wanting to write to you—of course, I do. And I hope you'll feel the same about me.

I've had a young cousin staying with me this week. She has come up from Monmouthshire. And what a handful she is. Shes eighteen, a very pretty child, with a passion for London and terrific "mash" on John Gielgud (worse than me, if that's possible). Of course, we took her to the first night of John's new play "Richard II" on Monday, and she nearly chewed her gloves up in her excitement. It was a lovely performance of a lovely play—and John gave one of the finest shows I've ever seen him give. His Richard is absolutely remarkable. You may think I'm prejudiced, but that's everybody's opinion. When he was giving the famous "For God's Sake let us sit upon the ground, and tell sad stories of the death of Kings" speech, you could hardly hear the people breathing in the house, and when he finished it the crowded house broke in with bursts of applause. It was one of the most exciting theatrical moments of my life. I've seen Maurice Evans "Richard" that New York is making such a fuss about, but believe me, it doesn't come within hailing distance of Gielgud's.[18] I wish John would take it to America, but he won't. He's doing three classical plays after this "The School for Scandal" "The Three Sisters" and "The Merchant of Venice". Peggy Ashcroft is his leading lady in all of them. She's a remarkably talented young actress and even though the Queen in "Richard" is such a negligible part, she made it into a vital, living thing. The marriage rumour, by the way, was denied vehemently by John on the opening night of "Richard". He says

18. Gielgud starred in *Richard II* in London, and Maurice Evans played the same role in New York. As is clear from Betty's letters, a rivalry developed between the New York and London productions of Shakespeare plays starring these two actors. Although Evans was enormously popular and critically acclaimed in the United States, Gielgud and, later, Olivier were considered the better Shakespearean actors.

he has no intention of marrying her. Other people have different ideas though—and it is whispered in Theatrical circles that Miss Ashcroft is very upset over the whole affair. It does make it rather unpleasant for her. They say, too, that John Gielgud's mother, who is a very charming, but very puritanical lady, is horrified at the idea. Still her divorce isn't final yet, so we shall see. It's a pity her moral character is so rotten—and with a thrice divorced wife, his chances would be practically negligible. Divorced women are not allowed at the English Court. And since the terrible Windsor-Simpson mess, they're even stricter than they used to be. And English divorces are such mucky things—so much dirty linen washed in the Courts. It's only now that they're beginning to ease up on the Divorce laws at all. Before it was only misconduct that was grounds for divorce, at all. Now they're including desertion over a period of five to ten years, and Insanity. Nothing mentioned of cruelty, or habitual drunken-ness. As for some things that certain American states grant divorces on, such as incompatibility and reading at the Breakfast Table—well! Our Judges would drop dead. Yes! I read in the "Daily Mirror" that "Richard of Bordeaux" is to be commenced next month, although I don't believe that—I thought it was next Spring they were doing it. Anyway, if I read anything about it, I'll send you the clippings, and if you see anything about John in the American mags you'll send it over to me, won't you? They haven't started to cast "Richard" yet—I wish it were possible for Merle Oberon to be the Queen. I'm very keen on Merle. So if you see anything about her, clip it out for me. By the way, you ask me what American mags I see in England. The answer is, hardly any. I want very much to get John's autobiography, which has been running the "Theatre Arts" Book. I've got the first part, which is I think, the May issue, and I can't get the others. So if you have any spare copies, perhaps you can put me out of my misery. A friend in Massachusetts sends me "Picture Play", though I can buy that occasionally on our Bookstands. Perhaps you would like a copy of the Theatre Book, with the "Richard II" pictures in? The "Theatre World" or the "Play Pictorial" nearly always publish a souvenir of John's plays. There is rather a nice photograph of him in the Programme, and I will send you one. I will keep my eyes skinned for any information about Henry Wilcoxon, though he seems to have faded out a little of late. "Jericho" hasn't been shown here yet, but when it is, I will get the reviews and forward them to you for your friend. Also, I forgot to thank you for the envelope of clippings you sent. Believe me they were very welcome, especially, the Life story from COLLIERS which has been perused, chewed and inwardly digested by a large number of Gielgudites.

Y'know, I seem to have rambled on and said exactly nothing in this letter. I've been typing it under difficulties, with the eagle eye of the Boss upon me, and he has a most profoundly disapproving look upon his face. Probably he will give me enough work this afternoon to last me for the rest of the week. However, I really can't blame him for the shocking typing in this epistle, nor for the scrappy way in which it's written.

I'm enclosing a snap of my sweet self—I look very miserable, but I never smile in a photograph. My mouth seems to stretch right across my face.

Please write soon. I enjoyed your letter so much,

Sincerely,<br>Betty

18A. Sinclair Gardens,<br>Kensington.<br>London. W 14.<br>England.<br>[June 9, 1938]

Dear Helen,

Am making a belated attempt to answer my correspondence, and have just realised the fact that I have about eight letters to answer. I believe it's about six weeks since I had your letter, and I'm only just finding time to answer it. Trouble is, I've always got plenty to say, but no time to type it in. We've been working so hard lately, that I can't squeeze a spare half hour anywhere, and I have no Typewriter at home, so I hope you'll forgive me this time, even though I know it's darned rude not to answer people when they take the trouble to write you nice letters.

I have a terrible cold in the head, and have been sniffing for about a week now. The weather has been so terribly cold through April that it seemed like December (as a matter of fact the temperature was lower than it was all through the Winter.) I nearly froze to death, and had to type with my gloves on and with a duster wrapped around my feet.

They had a snow storm in the Midlands in early May! And we've had no rain for two months, and the country is up in arms about it. Farmers go to Church and pray for the rain, because what with the drought and the frost, the whole of the early Plum Crop has been lost, and nearly all other Produce. Vegetables are terribly dear. Actually speaking, I cannot make out why in a country like England, which is probably the wettest in the world, they can't store the water properly. Still I Suppose it will rain in torrents over the Whitsun, just to celebrate. Outside now the sky is nearly black, and promises a lovely downpour. All the Clerks are crossing their fingers and hoping it will, because of their darned gardens, and the one sitting next to me is rubbing his hands and chortling gleefully of the marvelous effect it s going to have on his 10 inch patch of rhubarb and his amazing Lavender Bush, which grew two whole sprigs last year. My brother qualified for the great Gardener stakes last season by raising a large crop of weeds of every description and three magnificent Cauliflowers of which he was so proud, he left 'em in the Garden till they went to seed. For myself, I have a Hyacinth Bulb in a Pot, and a couple of Peas sprouting in a Saucer. London Flat Dwellers rarely own gardens. I shall have to wait until I can afford a Country Cottage—though when that will be, the Lord only knows. We've been trying the English National Gambling Game—Football Pools—for the past year without success. However, when I *do* win some money, I am coming to America. This year s holiday is being modestly confined to a tour of Belgium, either we shall stay on the Coast, or in Brussels. I rather want to see the Battlefields. My friend wanted to go to the South of France, but I couldn't afford it, and she can't go without me, because I speak French and she doesn't. Actually I shall need my bit of French in Belgium, because they aren't very good English speakers over there. All I hope is that we get a good Channel Crossing. When I went to Jersey and Normandy in 1936, I nearly died of sea-sickness.

I should rather like to go to Germany some time, too, although my friend will never go there. She and I disagree violently over the German question. Y'see Helen, I don't know what your religion or your political opinions are. There s plenty to hate Hitler for, but there s a great deal I admire him for, and admire him intensely. The trouble over this business with Austria is, that people refuse to see that the Austrians welcomed Hitler. They aren't unhappy or miserable about going over to the German Reich: It s only the Jews that are bleating about it. And now we shall get thousands of Austrian Jews pouring in here.[19] I'm thoroughly fed up with it. England is overrun with Jews of all nationalities—they have a stranglehold on our Industries, they own our Shops, they're in our Parliament, they rule us, and the English people are so darned silly they refuse to see the Menace they're becoming. I don't advocate persecution, or cruelty of any sort, but I do think that England needs a minor Hitler who will put down this Jewish influx before it s too late. As for Hitler and Mussolini dragging the world in War, we have just signed a new pact with Italy which will ensure peace, I think, and while we keep our noses out of the European stew, I think we shall be all right. But do we ever keep our noses out of it? We're pledged to join with France to attack Germany if Hitler's troops enter Czechoslovakia. What do we care about the Czechs and why should our people fight for them, similarly if an attack is made on Belgium, we have to protect her. Our Communist party sends ammunition and Money, and troops to Spain, which makes things difficult again. Still, I'm mighty glad Eden got out when he did, otherwise I'm convinced we should have been at War with Italy. Eden was full of the "England can beat anyone" idea. He wanted to use Brute force, instead of tactful diplomacy, which is so much better. I went to the London Communist Theatre last night to see Irwin Shaws Anti-War play "Bury the Dead". It was a magnificent illustration of the "War is Hell" theme, and though I'm a true blue Tory, I forgot my sentiments because the play was so marvellously acted. A friend of mine was acting in it—she's been a pal of John Gielgud's for fifteen years—was his first "fan" I believe, and gets special privileges accordingly. Anyways, she s a lovely actress.

I had America on the Radio (we call it wireless) last week. I think it was the Columbia Co, broadcasting from Schenectady (I knew I should make a mess of that word). It was the "Princess Pat" programme, or

---

19. At this time there was a popular acceptance of Germany's annexation of Austria on the grounds that Austria was a "German" nation. The anti-Semitism Betty espouses had deep roots in England going back several centuries. Polls taken three or four years after the war "suggested that extreme anti-Semitism was confined to a small minority, but that about half of the population, working class and middle class alike, were capable of making anti-Semitic statements; and this probably underestimated latent anti-Semitism" (Angus Calder, *The People's War: Britain, 1939–45*, 2d ed. [London: Panther, 1971], 576.). Relentless propaganda by the Nazis had also exposed the British to anti-Semitism.

something like that.[20] The announcer had a very American accent, and sounded just like the men on the pictures. We don't have any sponsored programmes in England. Our Broadcasting Corporation is known as the B.B.C. and is a very conservative body, indeed. We get fairly well balanced programmes—all the best Orchestras, Operas relayed from Covent Gardens Music Hall, Variety and Musical Shows, Talks, Symphony Concerts, all sorts of Sport, and Plays and Dramatic Programmes; John's good-looking brother, complete with little black Beard and Monocle, and rejoicing in the name of Valdemar superintends the Dramatic Department, and is as famous in England as John is. He's been to Hollywood and New York recently, I believe. He's an awful crank, but very clever and has a devastating effect on the ladies. Sad but true! In fact I think the whole of their family has a devastating effect on the ladies; I can't think why. Must be the fault of the ladies.

I saw "The Divorce of Lady X" again last week, and must say Olivier is getting better and better Still, however, I refuse to like him in Shakespeare. The Oberon film is, in my opinion, one of the finest comedies we've ever made, and the colouring is marvellous, particularly the shots of the Red London Buses in Piccadilly, shining through one of our Pea Soupers, and an English Hunt.[21] In fact the colour is the finest I've ever seen; Do try and see it, if it s shown your way. Have also seen "Snow-White" which I think was marvellous. "A Yank at Oxford" very enjoyable, though I cannot stand Robert Taylor usually, and two first class new British films "The Drum" and "Owd Bob".[22] I don't think the new

---

20. Princess Pat was the name of one of the most successful makeup lines of the 1920s. Produced in Chicago, the program of that name was the brainchild of M. Martin Gordon and his wife, Frances Patricia Berry. "She managed promotion and sales . . . broadcasting as 'Beauty Editor of the Air'" (Kathy Peiss, *Hope in a Jar: The Making of America's Beauty Culture* [New York: Metropolitan Books, 1999], 107).

21. Given her dislike of Olivier, Betty calls *The Divorce of Lady X* the Oberon film.

22. *Snow White* (1937; U.S.) was Disney's first full-length production. In *A Yank at Oxford* (1938; U.S.), a brash American comes to Oxford and overcomes his difficulties in getting along with the English by coxing the Oxford crew to victory over Cambridge. Also starring Maureen O'Sullivan (discovered by Charles Laughton), Lionel Barrymore, and Vivien Leigh, the film was Robert Taylor's biggest hit at the time. *The Drum* (1938; (UK), produced by Alexander Korda, one of Britain's premier producers whose movies starred most of Betty's favorite actors and actresses, is a tale of Indian revolt against the British Raj in which one loyal Indian uses a drum to tap out messages to the British. *Owd Bob* (1938; UK) is a story about Cumbria's sheep farmers and their dogs. These films were wholesome, sentimental entertainment, less intellectual than Betty's preferred fare.

Play crop is so good, though I enjoyed "Idiots Delight" without seeing why critics waxed *so* lyrically over it.[23] I saw a grand farce last week called "Banana Ridge" with Alfred Dayton and Robertson Hare,[24] and the Komisarjevsky production of "Comedy of Errors" at the Stratford. I went to Shakespeare's Birthplace over Easter, and had some snaps taken of myself outside the house where he was born. If they're any good, I'll let you have copies.

"Amphitryon 38" with the Lunts arrives at the Lyrica on Wednesday,[25] and the new C.B. Cochran Show "Many Happy Returns" with Beatrice Lillie,[26] arrives the night after. We're all particularly keen on seeing this show, because they've included a modified version of Moss Hart's Broadway skit "Mr. Gielgud passes By". They've had to be careful of course, because the aforesaid Mr. G. is very touchy about people impersonating him, but I believe they've got over the difficulty, by leaving out some of the expressions Hart used including "Blast the Old Vic" which upset John's feelings very much. Tough! They also have a skit on the "Three Sisters", which strangely enough was London's biggest success. Anyway, I think the Cochran Show is going to be fun.

"The Merchant of Venice" which opened on April 21st. is a lovely production, beautifully balanced, without a bit of ranting. For that reason some of the critics have torn it to bits, and said that John shouldn't have made Shylock a part of the play. He should have *been* the play. Taken by and large, the general consensus of opinion, however, is that he's the finest Shylock of our time. At least he is one that you believe in; I've seen everything he's done since 1933, and I've never seen him give a more magnificent performance. And I liked the production much better than the much patronised "Three Sisters" which I thought was an abominable bit of drivvle, and bored me stiff.

Regarding your question of our Film Producers making your folks say "sure" (Gosh. What a mouthful). D'you know, whenever I see an American film, one of the characters always says "Sure", and whenever

23. *Idiot's Delight*, starring Alfred Lunt and Lynn Fontanne, was written by Robert Sherwood, a major U.S. playwright who worked extensively on movies with Alexander Korda.

24. *Banana Ridge* was made into a movie in 1942, but Betty saw it several years earlier as a play.

25. A play starring Lunt and Fontanne.

26. Considered Britain's greatest comedienne in the 1930s, 1940s, and 1950s.

I speak to any in London, they also say "Sure". So that s where we get it from. Anyways, it s the perpetual question of English filmgoers as to why your Producers think Englishmen always say "Yes, old boy! Topping, old fellow! Bai Jove." and so on. English people do *not* talk like that, even the aristocracy. It seems that when an Englishman has to be represented in a film, he must be either a "Gorblimey" Cockney, or a "Huntin' Shootin' and Fishin'" peer. So you see while you have your little moan, we have ours. Actually I can imitate most of the English dialects, but am not so good at American. I did try one sentence (spoken by a very American juvenile (could it have been Tom Brown?)[27] and he said something like this "Gee. Papp, poor Tam cayunt have done ut. He'd never do a theyung like thayut" Which is probably all wrong, but that s how it sounded phonetically. I mastered that speech beautifully, and was getting quite expert at it. I can also say tomayhter and skeddule, and all the other American expressions such as the famous "Oke, Sez You and You're tellin' me" which I think are vivid and expressive. We have no slang to match them.

Yes we are taught at school that we had a couple of Wars with you, though I don't remember so much about the 1812 ones, except that the Americans were on the side of Napoleon and we weren't, so that was that. We were taught quite a bit about the War of Independence though. We learned European history more, with our own, and when you consider we have over two thousand years to get through I think British History was enough for us poor little blighters. I always remember my favourite Kings were Richard II (prophetic!) Henry V. and Charles I, with a warm place in me heart for Bonnie Prince Charlie.

I still cannot persuade myself that Maurice Evans is six times better than John, but I wish him luck in his Shakespearian ventures. A pal of mine was speaking to Gielgud a week or so ago, and he said that he rather thought he would be going back to America in the Autumn. However, "Richard of Bordeaux" is being started in early June, and will take about 12 weeks to make, after which he now says he is going to take a holiday, Other rumours current in the West End are that he will

27. Prolific Hollywood actor appearing in movies and television shows from the 1920s through 1960s. Betty may have been referring to *Navy Blue and Gold* (1937; U.S.), a football movie set at the Naval Academy. Brown was thought to look too young to play a twenty-two-year-old, even though that was his actual age at the time.

have another season like this present one, that he'll be in a modern Comedy, and that he s found a new play written for him by a new Author about Sir Thomas More. The main thing is that he's promised me personally (believe it or not) that he's not going to have another Beard for a long time. The "Richard of Bordeaux" film publicity will be trickling across the Pond now they're actually starting the thing, but if I see anything interesting, I'll send it to you, if you like. Please thank your friend for promising me the "Theatre Arts Monthly" clippings. I shall dance at her wedding for that, though I'm afraid she'll have to come over to England to be married, or perhaps she's already married?

The typing in this letter is appalling. Please try and forget it, also the long time I took to answer you. Don't follow my example will you.

Love,
Betty


GREAT WESTERN RAILWAY

Goods Department,
South Lambert Station,
London S.W. 8
[July 21, 1938]

18A. Sinclair Gardens
Kensington
London. W 14.


Dear Helen,

Please forgive the "Office" paper, but I've run out of "Rice", and I'm typing this in work, and with the letter-head uppermost in the Machine it sort of allays suspicion, if the Boss gets nasty. We have a new Chief here, my last one was transferred to our Head Station, Paddington, and the new bloke is a bit of a mystery. Looks like the strong, silent, man type. Seems a bit scared of me—heaven knows why, I'm a harmless individual, if a bit high-spirited. Anyway, I'm not moaning about it, because he writes out his letters, and that saves me the trouble of taking 'em down,—also I don't have to be his memory like my last Boss. Joe couldn't do a thing on his own, and he could hardly remember what day it was. The poor blighter's on his holidays this week, and went with a faint hope of being able to paddle in the Rock Pools at Dorquay to cure his rheumatism, but by the look of the weather I hope he's taken his Blankets and a mackintosh. It's as cold as ice to-day, and has been raining solidly since seven oclock. July has been the most terrible month, and during the latter part of June we were rocketed by the awful gales which tore down trees, wrecked Seaside Beaches and played hell with shipping. The wind has died down a bit now, and it's just chilly—described in the papers by our tolerant British press as "cool", Heaven forgive 'em—with drizzling rain, and the skies are as grey as your next door neighbour's Sheets in the Fels Naptha adverts. Honestly the British climate is enough to make an Angel weep, and all you get if you grouse about it is "Look what a lovely March we had" or "Well! It's early yet!" Early, in July!

At all events, if the Weather prophets can be believed, which they never can be—we are to have our summer in the later part of the year. My holidays are due the second and third weeks in September, and as I invariably get an Oilskin and Umbrella vacation, I am reconciling myself to the inevitable. I do long to get a respectable sun tan, but I shall have to have a tropical blaze and a couple of barrels of Oil to coax it. I usually go red and look like a cross between the Sunrise, the Sunset and a boiled beetroot, and come home with either (a) a thousand or so large Banana shaped blisters or (b) large numbers of brown freckles, which make me look ridiculous. I've decided that I won't go to Belgium this year—why should I waste my time going on a sea voyage when the weather'll probably be lousy anyway. So some kind chap who knows my sister in law has offered the use of his modernized cottage in Devonshire, free of rental etc, Methinks I will hide myself there. My pal has got the hump decidedly about it because her original wish was to go to the South of France. Saw herself draped in a couple of linen squares and a string of Beads reclining lazily on the sun kissed Sands of Juan les Pins, or something of the sort. (Which reminds me Mr Gielgud has a Villa at Juan les Pins, at which he is now resting. Praps if he'd lend me the Villa for nothing I might have considered it). Anyway, Frances doesn't like the idea of taking a holiday at home, but I'm afraid she'll have to lump it. I want a quiet holiday this year and the Belgian Coast is far from restful—also my mother has maternal qualms about the males over there. Thinks I might, in my golden haired innocence, pick up with a bad French man with designs on my virtue. When we went to Jersey, I went with a very nice youth, who was very respectable and had another very respectable brother for Frances, so luck smiled on us. We went to a Hotel, which cost a heck of a lot, but had a rotten reputation—we were invited to approximately four Bottle parties a night, but stuck close to our Bodyguards and slid out through Side entrances, and bribed the Porter not to tell the number of our rooms, and as a result, we got along fine. You don't need to go haywire if you don't want to. I had a grand time in Jersey and lovely weather, but the journey over, 80 miles on a rough Sea was too appalling to describe. I honestly thought I was dying! I should also have liked to go to Scotland this year. The Empire Exhibition is on in Glasgow, and when we went to Edinburgh last year I was tremendously impressed with the City, I have a boy friend there with a Car who took us around the lower Borderlands, but we could only stay two days, and the journey is so long—nine hours—it doesn't seem worth it. My brother and his wife are on holiday this week in Londonderry, Northern Ireland. They went to the South last year. They were going to Paris, but Muriel has a nasty feeling she's going to have a baby, and if that s true they'd better start saving their money for a more extravagant couple you never knew. They live near Windsor, mainly because Jack is an open air fiend and must live in what he terms "God's fresh air", London, of course, is far too cooped up for him. He drives you insane after you've lived with him for a week, though why he should want to bury his wife in the country miles from anywhere is beyond me. I love the country for a day or two, and the districts surrounding London are lovely, Berkshire and Essex, and Buckinghamshire. I'm not so keen on the Southern Counties, though some people rave about the Chalk Cliffs of Kent, and the Sussex Downs, and can't stick the Thames Valley at any price. Essex is all flat country, with a fairly low population. Most Theatrical stars have country cottages there. John has what he fondly terms a cottage—you know a small place with 12 bedrooms, three tennis courts, an open air swimming pool, acres of fields and an Orchard—at Finchingfield. Name of the place is "Foulslough"—God knows why, and we're always trying to go down and see it. One of these days we shall land there and I'll have a snap taken of myself leaning on the Gate, if the Gardener doesn't come down and throw apples at me. Laurence Olivier has a small place somewhere near Maidstone, I believe, Leslie Howard's House is in Dorking, in Surrey (ditto Charles Laughton). I have no country place as yet, and the only garden we possess is a couple of peas sprouting in a saucer, and a Bulb, which should bloom next year unless it gets temperamental. I'm glad you've got some Cherries out in your garden. Over here the crops have been ruined by the drought, and the frost, and Cherries are now a shilling a pound (that s 25 cents) at the height of the season when they should be somewhere in the region of fourpence. And Strawberries are still terribly dear. As for our green grass—they can keep all that for a few hours sunshine. I'm sick and tired of rain and gales, and cold.

Yes! I'm afraid I shall have to wait until I win a lottery before I can get to America, but if I do get as far as New York I shall come and see you in Kansas even if I have to walk there. The only alternative to the Irish Sweep is that I'm going to have a shot at writing a novel this winter (Now you can laugh) and if it does even get written, and more miraculous, get sold, I shall certainly come to the States if I have to travel steerage. Anyway, I've had these grand ideas of writing before. It was a play a few years ago, though I admit, I still have hankerings to write a play.

Some of these days I'm going to get a little record made of my voice, and send it to you, and you can see then whether I'm talking "Oxford" English. Actually, I can't make out why they couldn't understand "The Divorce of Lady X" as the voices in it weren't particularly affected, and Oberon's voice is beautiful I think. There's lots of American I can't say I think particularly easy to understand ("Dead End"[28] was the most puzzling) but I've always managed to make out what they were saying. Most Americans seem to say "natt" for "not" and of course they Brr-r-r their "rs" and to our ears speak through their noses, but we've got so used to it, we take no notice and don't have much difficulty with it. I expect you'd have a grand time listening to the Cockney twang, which I can imitate standing on my head. Actually my voice used to have a slight Welsh sing-song about it, till three years ago but after listening to Cockneys so long, I lost it, and now my voice is practically accent-less, except for a few Cockneyisms which I've picked up. But to go back to the "Divorce of Lady X" I thought it was most amusing, and am going to see it again when it comes to the suburbs. I have always

28. In the drama *Dead End* (1937; U.S.), starring Joel McCrea, Humphrey Bogart, and Claire Trevor, a gangster, street gangs, and a struggling architect all revisit an East-side New York slum on the edge of Park Avenue.

liked Oberon (Did I tell you that she's a Gielgud "Fan" too?) I like her because she hasn't gone Hollywood and doesn't indulge in giving a lot of tripey interviews like Madeleine Carroll; who has gone absolutely balmy since she's been out there—trying to impress on everyone that she's really French Irish, and doing this Hollywood's Ambassadress in Europe stunt. Ugh! She makes me sick. I'm no flag waver, but can't see why you have to go so darned hysterically effusive over one country, and call your own names while you're doing it. If I thought Carroll had everything to thank Hollywood for I'd forgive her, but after all she got her start here, and our producers and the British Public were darned good to her, though she appears to have completely forgotten it.

Yes! It's strange about American and English humour. Many an American play has been put on here and flopped hopelessly because an English audience sat stonily through the Jokes. I saw one called "You Can't take it with You" and thought it absolutely terrible. And there's those short stories by Dorothy Parker, supposed to be witty and humourous, and they don't go over here at all. Personally, I think the whole spirit of England lives in our Music Halls, and I hope they will never be eclipsed altogether.

I'm glad someone else isn't religious. I was brought up Church of England, but I don't attend Church now because I feel like a hypocrite if I do. It's useless to say you believe if you don't. I only wish I could. Faith, and religion, must be tremendously comforting, and the thought that you're going to a higher plane when you die, would make your life worth the living, but I can never force myself to believe it. Perhaps it's because we moderns have such questioning minds.

In politics, I follow my Mothers way of thinking. Our family are all Conservatives on my mother's side, and Socialists, verging to Communism on my fathers (Sorry it's the other way round, I didn't notice). Anyway, Mother and I vote for the National Government (which is a sort of Coalition, a mixture of the two). I believe in the National Government because I always wanted Tariff reform. When the Labour Government were in England was a Free Trade country, and the Dumping Ground for everyone. Since we've had the Nationals they've pulled the country back up, trade is better, Unemployment is less. If it wasn't for the War Clouds, we wouldn't be so bad.[29] However, Mr Chamberlain is still

29. Since 1935, when the government first issued a directive concerning air raids,

relentlessly pursuing his Non-intervention policy, and refuses to get all het-up if they bomb a British ship in Spanish waters. Most of those ships are taking guns and food to Spain,[30] things the Government are trying to avoid, Why plunge a country into war for the life of one of these Law breakers. I don't belong to the "Britain's right is Britain's might" gang. I want peace, and to hell with our national prestige!

As for the Jews, we are getting thousands of them in here now from Austria. It's terrible to stand by and watch our country being turned into a little Jewry. I'm convinced that one day Britain will see the menace, too. It may not come in my lifetime, but come it will. And they'll turn the Jews out of England just as they've turned them out of Germany. I don't want persecutions, but something must be done to stop the influx into England. And don't believe that Germans are starving to buy arms. I have met Germans over here. They're jovial, happy people, who literally idolise Hitler, and the stories of the dreadful things that happen to them are mostly a lot of Newspaper twaddle. I liked the Lunts in "Amphitryon" though I thought the piece a little weird. Saw a marvellous comedy last week called "Spring Meeting"—quite the funniest play I've ever seen—and it s interesting to note that it was written by John Perry, the young man that John has lived with for about eleven years. They look so alike its hard to tell them apart.

John is coming back after his trip to France to appear with Marie Tempest in a new play by our most popular author—Dodie Smith (who wrote "Call it a Day"—it's a comedy I'm told, and it's the first modern part John's had for ages. He has a play about Sir Thomas More to appear in after, and Noel Coward has written a piece for him—He intended to bring his classic plays to America, did I tell you?—but when the new play came up he had to cancel it. Also, I'm afraid there's bad news in connection with "Richard of Bordeaux". When we went to the last night of the season of the Queens, the audience of course, nearly went insane and screamed and shouted and yelled every time he walked on, (I don't think Americans can have any idea of how popular he is over here—they

---

England had been gearing up for war. By the end of 1938, sandbags were appearing at important buildings all over the country.

30. In Spain's civil war, England's left wing aided the Republicans (communists), and the right wing supported the Fascists. Chamberlain's government steered a course of nonintervention; however, squadrons of the German Air Force did participate in the conflict.

very nearly treat him like a God) anyway in his curtain speech he said that as he had so many commitments to carry out the film would probably be postponed till next June. Can you beat it? Anyway, I'm watching for news about it, and if I see anything stirring, I'll send you the clippings. Also kiss your friend on both cheeks for me and thank her for saving me the photograph. I think I should like her very much. And you won't forget to send it will you? By the way, the Company that's making "Richard" is Jack Buchanan Productions, Ltd, Pinewood Studies, IVER, Bucks. Why don't you write to their Publicity Manager, at that address, and ask him when they're going to start it?

I haven't read G.J. Nathan, and after what he said about John's nose I don't want to read him.[31] The big stiff. I see Maurice Evans is copying John's idea and having a season in New York. I've seen his "Hamlet" and didn't think much of it, but I suppose the N.Y. critics will go into raptures over it, particularly Mr. Watts. Curse him. The coming young man of British films is Michael Redgrave—Watch out for him. He's very good. He was a member of the Company at the Queens.

Darling! Take heart when you read this letter. The typing is ten times worse than yours could ever be and typing is supposed to be my job! I've been typing so quickly though, I suppose there's an excuse.

Hope you can read this letter. It s a bit rambling, but its all done with the best of intentions, and written the *day after* I received yours!

Love,
Betty

18A. Sinclair Gardens
Kensington
London. W 14. Eng.
[September 2, 1938]

Dear Helen,

Received your very welcome letter a few days ago, and am going to make a full-blooded, British attempt to type one page this morning. It s now about eleven a.m. on a cold, frosty, morning—I am feeling fed-up with nothing in particular and everything in general—indeed I am so

31. George Jean Nathan, considered the greatest American theater critic of the twentieth century, apparently commented unfavorably about Gielgud's nose.

bored I really think I shall have to search around for a nice old gentleman and marry him—anyway, I feel absolutely unfit to tackle any work.
I care not if the Railway stops. Trade has been going down shockingly
lately, so we'll probably get the sack anyway. Curse it! I wish I'd been
born with a set of silver spoons in my mouth or some unknown relative
would die in Australia or points west, and leave me Bags of shekels. It's
always the favourite pastime of our family, when they're not discussing international affairs, my bigoted views on the Drink question, or,
in my brother's case, how he bowled the finest Batsman in Middlesex
for a paltry six,[32] to plan what we'd do with thirty thousand pounds
if we had it. We have thought about the most blasphemous, unprint-
able words we're going to use in our final farewell speech to the various
Bosses, Mother is going to purchase yards of mink and miles of Sable,
and I am going to sit in the Royal Box at a Theatre on a first-night,
and tour America in a Motor Car, dress myself up and try my wiles on
Robert Taylor. (I regret to tell you that I actually *like* Robert Taylor.[33]
I stuck out against it as long as I could, but I saw "Yank at Oxford"
last night, and as I've said before, I now like Robert Taylor) anyway,
I'm determined, money or no, to visit New York if I have to stowaway
in the "Queen Mary". The Worlds Fair is in 1940, and they may run
some cheap trips You know—a week to get there, twenty-four hours
there—and a week to get back, if you're still alive by that time. I suppose if I do ever get to New York you couldn't come up from Kansas
(Oh! pardon, me, Missouri) to see me. Or perhaps if they gave me two
days I could come down to Kansas (Missouri) to see you. On the other
hand, maybe we'd better meet half-way, though I haven't the slightest
idea (a) where Missouri is, (b) where half-way is, or (c) When I'll be
able to save enough to go to New York. If Mr. G. starts doing any more
Shakespeare on Broadway, there's six of us coming over to stand in the
Gallery and cheer our heads off with a British accent. I, personally, am
coming over to strangle Richard Watts. Jr. and Geo. Jean Nathan.[34]

32. Betty is being sarcastic. The phrase would mean that her brother delivered such
an easy pitch that the batsman hit the ball so far into the field that his team was able to
score six points while her brother's team was retrieving the ball.

33. Robert Taylor played romantic leads during the 1930s and was considered by
some to be too handsome to be taken seriously as an actor. One of the most prolific
movie actors in Hollywood, he served in the U.S. Air Force as a flight instructor during
World War II.

34. The U.S. movie critic Richard Watts Jr. was particularly critical of Gielgud.

*Next Day.*

It has rained all night, and outside it is still raining. It's cold (Maximum temperature this week has been 67 degrees minimum 45) and windy, and so miserable. Gosh. Don't you ever let me hear you grumbling about the heat—for heaven's sake. I'd give anything just to see a bit of sunshine. London has had an average of 1 ½ hours Sunshine a day for weeks, and we haven't had more than two weeks warm weather (added up in days and half-days) since *May*. Now you grumble about your 90 in the shade after that. I've got a wardrobe of summer things I haven't been able to wear, and Autumn is starting now, before we've had any summer. Honestly, I don't know how English people remain so cheerful about it. I'm nearly driven to suicide over the climate, but if you mention it to some people they say "Ah. Well, we don't get Earthquakes, and it s never *too* hot, and it s been drier than usual." It was dry for exactly two months (known in England as a dreadful drought) and I believe the temperature once reached a staggering total of 78 degrees (known in England as a Heat-wave)—then a week ago the temperature dropped in some districts to 37 (known in England and described in the papers as 'cool'). I've been thinking of clearing off to South Africa or summat[35]—where I can go about in shorts with a hanky on my head, and where I know when the rainy season is due, and can plan accordingly. Do you get it very cold in the winter in Kansas, Missouri, and do you think if I got out there some kind Missourian would give an English cousin a job? I can do Office work, after a fashion, and I can cook good plain, serviceable fare—I'm very bright and industrious, and adaptable, and if anyone wants more than that they'll have to go and fish for it. Someone here has just raised my hopes to soaring point, by suggesting that there's an Electric fire in one of the Warehouses, if we could pinch it, and fix it to the light. My arms are very nearly blue with the chill and I probably shan't last the day out. Aint life wonderful??

It's my holidays next week, so my hopes of getting that coppery sun tan are fading far into the distance right out to Africa in fact. We are going to the quietest spot on earth—its called Gwithian, and its just a typical Cornish farm in a typical Cornish village with one little Inn, patronised by the oldest inhabitant, an old gent with a long beard, and some of the Fishermen around—and they all play Darts (ever heard of

---

35. The island of Sumatra, in Indonesia, is practically on the equator.

Darts? It's a most instructive game, everyone in England plays it and I'm a little marvel at it) Anyway theres this little Inn, and a Post Office, and general Shop, a couple of Cottages, and a Church. Its near the Beach—and in Cornwall the coast is so rugged theres hundreds of little Beaches which would be lovely to bathe in if the waves weren't so fierce. I was hoping to laze on the Rocks, and sun-bathe. I should have known better, having been brought up in a country where sun-bathing is practically impossible. I'm staying in Cornwall for a week, then going home to Monmouthshire for a few days, and travelling back to London on the Wednesday to go to the first night of Mr G's new play "Dear Octopus" which will probably be as weird as it sounds.[36] I shall have done some travelling by that time. It's a ten-hour journey to Cornwall, and I'm going from there to Monmouthshire via Bristol another six or seven hours, and back the same way. I hate trains, too. Would much rather travel by Bus. When we went to Scotland last year it took eight hours, and that bored me stiff, especially as on the way back the train broke down at Newcastle and we had to sit outside the station for two hours at three oclock in the morning. It was the London-Edinburgh Streamline train, too, and its very rarely it breaks down. It usually breaks all records when it starts. I want to go to Glasgow this year, to see the Empire Exhibition, but I don't know when I'll get the time. Its shut on a Sunday, and it would mean getting a Saturday morning off, and travelling up Friday evening, so maybe I won't get there after all. I expect they'll manage without me. I didn't get on with the Scots too well last time and have a distinct memory of scrapping heartily with a gent and his wife about a packet of Cigarettes out of a Machine. We'd put in the sixpence and got nothing in return, so we marched into tell the Proprietor about it. Of course, he said he "wasna going to give us the Ceegarettes until he got the sixpence". Anyway, he turned out all the Cigarettes from the Machine—Hundreds and hundreds of packets—it took him half an hour, and found the sixpence had rolled down the back of the slot—and by that time the woman (his Mrs. presumably) was calling us cheats, Thieves, Swindlers, and all sorts of names in a choice Scots brogue, and I was answering her back with fierce English gusto, and trying to prevent my sister-in-law from scratching her eyes out, and my brother from socking the Scottish gentleman(!) right on the nose. Afterwards

---

36. *Dear Octopus*, a play by Dodie Smith.

we cheered ourselves up by visiting a Waxworks (you know, exhibitions of wax models of famous men, famous women, famous murderers, ad lib and so on) laughed ourselves sick in the Distorted mirrors, drank lemonade out of the bottle, and then went into the Chamber of horrors and saw Tableaux of executions—World known Cut-throats sitting in darkened cells, skeletons stretched out in coffins, the preserved bodies of two headed rats—three legged Cats, and (in a bottle) a two-headed baby, of all things. And one very gruesome exhibit I'll always remember—a funny, black, charred looking object, propped up in a Box, with a notice underneath that it was the body of Jenny something or other who was hanged at Edinburgh in 1804 for poisoning babies. After all this, we went home and ate a darned good supper of Fish and chips.

Someone has just saved my life by lending me his blazer and I now feel somewhat warmer. All I need now is a couple of Rugs, and some hot Cocoa, and a fire to toast my feet on. Then I shall feel all right. Talking of Rugs reminds me—I went to the Open Air Theatre in Regents Park Saturday. We have a brave soul in this country called Sydney Carroll who defies the British climate and puts on Shakespearean and other plays in the open air.[37] I went to see "Tobias and the Angel" and was it cold![38] We had a big Travelling Rug, and wrapped it round our shoulders—put cushions over our feet, and trusted to the Good Lord to hold off the rain. He did, but now hes making up for it with a vengeance. Its going to teem down again in a minute—We have all the lights on, because it's as dark as pitch, and I should be surprised if it doesn't snow later. I am sad, but resigned.

I'm glad you think about the way I get to work in the morning, because to know that somebody sympathises with you goes a long way. I have to get in and out of three different Trains and then catch a Tramcar. I spend my time running down steps, running up steps, and chasing after Tramcars. All the Railway officials know me, and open the Gates for me to burst through, waving a paper in one hand and my Season ticket in another, with a look of concentrated determination on my face. Except on Monday mornings, when the look is one of abject gloom. I detest Mondays. Especially rainy ones. As for my mother, shes one of

37. Sydney Carroll is not to be confused with the Hollywood writer Sidney Carroll.
38. The comedy *Tobias and the Angel* was made into a film in 1938 (UK).

the best. Shes Head Fitter in a West End Gown shop, modern, with a sense of humour, and a great deal of patience. Shes had to have the latter quality, having been possessed of two children who are peculiar to say the least of it. She disapproves a little of my chasing about to Films and Theatres, but has got quite accustomed to it. My brother is a fresh air fiend, whose life consists of Football, Cricket, Football again, with Tennis and Swimming thrown in for good measure, and then more Cricket. The times we've been dragged down to the Cricket Ground on the promise that hes going to make a couple of Centuries, but every time we're down there it puts him off his stroke,[39] and he manages to get bowled clean out.[40] I've just heard from an Office colleague who watched him play yesterday that he's done the extremely sensible thing by having one of his finger nails torn completely off on the Wicket—so theres something else for my mother to worry over. Anyway, I love Cricket myself, in moderation. The test matches over here cause so much excitement that no-one is able to do any work while there on.[41] Excited little Office Boys rush in and out of the Office giving the latest scores, and the men moan or cheer, according to the reports. We won the last Match, but strange to say the Aussies keep the Ashes.[42] It all seems ridiculous to me—but there, do I matter??

I still do not agree with you over Maurice Evans, and I hope his "Hamlet" flops—but I don't think it will, and theres nothing we can do about it anyway. I've seen Evans' "Hamlet"—we are taken to see it at the Old Vic—and it isn't in the same street as John's. Of course, he may

39. The batsman's swing.

40. Failure to hit the pitched ball, allowing it to knock the bail, or crosspiece, off the wicket, which consists of three wooden stumps across which the bail is laid horizontally.

41. The test matches are play-off games between two countries in which the winner takes three of five matches from the opposing team.

42. The "Ashes" refers to test matches between England and Australia. There are two distinct versions of how these test matches came to be called "the Ashes." Some say that during the 1890s the English beat Australia and some Australian women burned a wicket and presented the ashes in a can as the victor's trophy. Others say that near the same time England lost the test matches to Australia, and because the British had such a superior attitude toward Australians, whom they considered transported convicts, they burned their bats and the wickets in anger before giving the trophy cup to the Australians—with the ashes inside. Henceforth the ashes have remained in the cup, which resides at Lords, a major London cricket ground that is the headquarters of the Marylebone Cricket Club. Betty here is referring to the most recent test match. Australia apparently won the majority of the matches.

have improved. He's afraid to come over here for us to see his precious "Richard II" and pass judgment on it.

I'm going to see "The Rage of Paris"—chiefly because I am very keen on Fairbanks Jr.[43] I cannot understand why Americans jeered at him and said he'd gone British. Lord knows, we've got enough stars in Hollywood who've gone completely American, and don't mind gushing all over the place (that abominable Madeleine Carroll for one—and Cary Grant, and Wendy Barrie, and Binnie Barnes, and theres dozens and dozens of 'em.[44] I use to like Patric Knowles at one time, but the last time I saw him he's tried to adopt a cross between a California accent, and a Brooklyn scrape, and I think when English players try to adopt an American accent, the result is terrible.[45] Why Madeleine Carroll should now find it necessary to say "bin" for "been" and various other things is beyond me. Also, her interviews with the Press about this absurd "America's Ambassadress in Europe" business makes me feel sick at the stomach. The only American player I like, despite his awful accent, is John Beal. I saw him last week in "Port of Seven Seas and like his face.[46] And of course, as I said before, I like Robert Taylor, though I must keep the dreadful secret from my Theatregoing friends, who would die of shame at the awful thought. Please thank Julia for promising me that photograph I really think that Julia and I would get along very well, together. I've already warned the Gielgudites that a friend of mine in Kansas, Missouri, is going to send me a photograph, so tell Julia all depends on her. I think its very considerate of her to take "Theatre Arts Monthly"—after all theres often little bits and pieces in it, that wouldn't interest Julia at all, but would be very interesting to a certain group of wild and woolly English gals, who like receiving bits and pieces.

I am very sorry about "Richard of Bordeaux" and have decided that the cause of it must be poor John's artistic conscience. He gave up the

---

43. *The Rage of Paris* (1938; U.S.), comedy starring Douglas Fairbanks Jr.

44. British-born Cary Grant went to the United States at age sixteen and remained there. British actress Binnie Barnes, one of the wives in *The Private Life of Henry VIII*, went to Hollywood in 1934 and was active as a second lead in movies of the 1930s and 1940s.

45. Patric Knowles, a romantic lead as a British actor, went to Hollywood and became a successful second lead there.

46. John Beal, U.S. actor from 1930s to 1990s, with more than ninety film credits, including the drama *Port of Seven Seas* (1938; U.S.).

part of the Emperor Maximilian in a film called "The Phantom Crown" because the film would have to be made in Hollywood, and his artistic soul revolted at the thought of going to a Canned Film Factory. The part is to be played by Paul Muni, now, they say, and Betty Davis is to play Carlotta. And Mr. G. is appearing in "Dear Octopus" by a dreadful, sentimental author called Dodie Smith, and all he has to do is play a very untuneful second fiddle to Dame Marie Tempest—for which he was rewarded with two lines in the "Newcastle Chronicle" (the play opened in Newcastle last week).[47] This "love of the Theatre" twaddle baffles me. I never know whether it's a pose or whether they really think they do love the place. If that's being an artist, thank the Lord, I'm a mere common, low-brow, creature said she getting furious. Anyhow, I suppose its no business of mine, but I think the Emperor Maximilian would have been a fine part.

*Next day.*

How'm I doin'? Theres nothing like getting down to a job. Couldn't finish this epistle yesterday, owing to a sudden influx of telephone calls from anguished people who had sent packages, parcels, cartons, and boxes away to various points of the British Isles that mysteriously have not been received by the people they sent them to. I now have to send wires to all the stations, asking when they were delivered and who signed for 'em. Half the Firms that come on complaining of nondelivery have had the stuff all the time. They just want to make work. Theres a wintry gleam outside that looks exactly like the sun trying to break through the clouds, which are a very unhealthy misty grey this morning, but looking a little more athletic than the heavy black affairs that prowled around the sky yesterday. Its still very cold—this morning's paper tells us that yesterday's temperature was the coldest of the summer. maximum 55 degrees, minimum 43. Terrible isn't it? And me going on holiday in five days time. Ah. Well! I shall have to go back into my red flannel "undies"—wear pantaloons or something—anything to keep the cold away.

I'm taking two playsuits (very abbreviated) two pairs of shorts and a couple of blouses away with me, so I shall send you a Postcard tell-

47. Paul Muni, born in the Ukraine, made films in Hollywood from the 1920s through the 1960s but did not make any titled "The Phantom Crown." Marie Tempest, named a Dame of the British Empire for her contributions to the arts, was active in British theater and films from 1900s through the 1930s.

ing you whether I'm frying or dying in the climate. I think I'd better take a couple of woollen jumpers and a heavy coat to be on the safe side—although when I went to Jersey, I took a lot of frocks and didn't wear any of them. We just lived in shorts all the week, and I got sun poisoning in a frantic effort to acquire a tan. I couldn't lie on my back for a week—went to the colour of a Boiled Lobster, and raised a bunch of blisters as big as bananas, and a freckled nose. Me for the Oil Bottle this time. Jersey is so much warmer than Cornwall though. Its just off the coast of Normandy.

Also see in this morning's paper that Hitler is patrolling the French frontier, preparatory, I suppose to marching on Czechoslovakia. Well if that happens, we're in with France and Russia. For some peculiar reason we are bound by treaty to protect the Czechs. I suppose the idea is that Germany won't attack if she knows that the World powers will unite against her. Anyway, I don't personally think that Germany and Britain will come to blows again. The papers are trying to stir up the old hatred against the "Huns" and its not fair. I don't hate the Germans. Why should I? most of our papers are Jewish-owned, and they think its their chance of getting back on the Nazis. A party of German Policemen came to play football at Brighton last week, and a crowd of misguided idiots booed them at the station, and told them to go back to Germany. What a grand, British, welcome. And the trouble is its probably a crowd of Yiddishers that did it. Anyways, you're lucky to be out of it . . . We're so darned close to all of it, we get it in the neck all the time. My Mother is always saying that she'd rather shoot my brother than let him go. My father died through the War service he did, and all my Uncles and relatives were in the last lot. Daddy joined up in 1915, just after I was born. My pal's father was killed the day she was born, and the day war broke out. Aug. 5th. 1915. Mother's brother was seventeen when he joined up, and got a smashed foot as a reward. Daddy died through Food poisoning caused by eating so much tinned, and rotten, Beef.

Am still cold, and am being watched by the Boss. So I'd better close, I've said enough anyway. And I've just been thinking, if any of your friends read my letter, I ought to try to write some sense. I hope they'll forgive me, and realise I'm more to be pitied than blamed.

Bye for the present.

Love,
Betty

P.S. Determined to stop this Robert Taylor business so went to see the old tear jerker "Camille"[48] Last night. Regret very much to report that I still like Mr Taylor. Shall have to keep it a deep dark secret from my Theatre friends but am going to take it out on my poor boy-friend who is being dragged much against his will—to see a ["]Yank at Oxford" again tonight. Boyfriend states without enthusiasm, that if he has to pick out of the two of 'em, he would prefer to see John Gielgud. Shall report more on this international crisis later, but am afraid Mr Taylor won't last very long.

PSS Temperature is up to 62°. Whoopee!

18A. Sinclair Gardens
West Kensington
London. W 14.
[November 1938]

Dear Helen,

Sorry to be so long in answering your letter, Its been ages I know, but what with one thing and another obligingly turning up, I haven't had time, to turn round. Don't know if I've even written you since I went on holiday, apart from sending you a Postcard of the Rose covered cottage (entirely lacking in modern conveniences) where I stayed.

As you know I went to Cornwall during the first week in September, and the place was so far off the beaten track, We had little or no time to look at papers, if there ever were any papers—I didn't see a Clock the whole time I was there. The village consisted of one Inn, ten houses, half a dozen farms and a Post Office—oh. And of course a Church, dating back to William the Conqueror, and when we got tired of it in the evenings we went barging into Redruth, or St. Ives, to the Pictures, and believe it or not always had to walk home. A matter of some eight miles or so, at one oclock in the morning. I never walked so much in my life—but I'm proud of the fact that I kept up with the three boys, and didn't hop skip and jump kinda thing. I borrowed a pair of the Boys flannel trousers to walk about in, and tried to be as manly as possible, though I admit my feet hurt like hell, and every time we sat down by the Roadside to rest, I was terrified that a Frog or a Cricket would crawl

48. In *Camille* (1926; U.S.), Robert Taylor stars opposite Greta Garbo.

over me. Those damned Crickets kept me awake half the night, and we had a sweet little Field Mouse in our Bedroom. I may say right now, that I have a morbid horror of mice and am a nervous wreck when I see one. I slept with my sister-in-law, one of these lucky souls who are not cursed with insomnia, and it used to infuriate me to hear her sleeping soundly, while I stared miserably out of the window at the Cornish moon. However, apart from mice, crickets, frogs, bad sanitation, and Beds like a Stone slab, we had a lovely holiday, and the air did marvels for me. I'd been ill off and on for months before going away, but the minute I stepped off the train at Cornwall, I felt better. Needless to state, all my old complaints returned with a vengeance when I arrived back in London.

Trouble met us with a plop when we landed back home with the news of the Crisis.[49] Never in my life have I been through such a ghastly time. My mother seemed to be on the verge of insanity, because she lost my father through the last one, and the thought of my brother going nearly finished her. No one could bring themselves to talk of anything else and the tension was terrible. Things got worse and worse, and the night that Mr. Chamberlain made his speech over the Radio, will live in my memory as the worst of my existence. Mother and I had had to queue up for four hours the night before for our Gas Masks, and dreadful things they are, too. All the Parks and Commons were being dug up for Trenches—it was pouring with rain, and the men were working by flares. The Pavements had been painted in long, white, lines, Anti-Aircraft units were fixing up Guns on the roofs of Buildings (We had about twenty Machine Guns on the Roof of our Office, and the Yard was full of Soldiers. We were so busy we couldn't breathe, owing to the thousands of people leaving London for the country—all the School children were got out the day before—and life looking so miserable, I cursed the day I was ever born in England, and wished I'd had enough

---

49. During September 1938 Chamberlain made three separate visits to Hitler concerning his demands to annex Austria and the German-speaking parts of Czechoslovakia. In the meantime, Britain began preparing for war, digging trenches for air raid shelters in the parks in London, fortifying buildings with machine guns, and issuing gas masks. There was also a flood of hasty marriages. Finally, on Chamberlain's third trip to Munich, the English and the French capitulated to Hitler's demands for Austria and Czechoslovakia. Hitler signed an agreement renouncing warfare, and Chamberlain proclaimed "peace for our time," ending the "Crisis" to which Betty refers.

money to get out of it. I was scared of staying in London, and was on
the verge of contemplating marriage to someone I didn't love in the
slightest, because he had a good job, wouldn't have to fight, and could
send mother and I away. I kept thinking of my two boy friends that I
was on holiday with—both of 'em are young, in their very early twenties,
and the thought of them going to fight nearly finished me. Of course,
the one that I am most fond of seemed to think it a glorious adven-
ture, and assured me he would most certainly come back, because all his
family came back from the last War, and I was aching to howl my head
off when he was saying it, but wouldn't make an exhibition of myself.
However, as I am not the emotional type, I tried to laugh it all off, and
also tried to conjure up a picture of myself knitting socks, and sending
them off with a smile on my face, and a broken heart, but I couldn't knit
socks anyway, and if I was feeling miserable I'm darned sure I couldn't
smile. Mother was constantly calling me names because I was worried
about the boys, and not in the slightest about Ernie—a boy friend much
favoured by Mother, but not by me. However, when it was announced
next day that Chamberlain and Musso and the rest were to meet Hitler, I said a prayer for the first time in my life. I'm not religious—I
have no faith of any sort—but I went into Westminster Abbey, to the
Tomb of the Unknown Warrior and knelt down there, and said nothing in particular to no-one in particular, but just a vague sort of 'Thank
You' to Mr Chamberlain. Of course, the Labour party here, and a large
number of Americans criticised his actions with full force. "Britain has
lost prestige" they shriek all over the place. I don't give a damn for the
prestige we had or hadn't. If we had worried about prestige—if we had
antagonised Germany, fought for the Czechs, and so on, we would have
lost all our men for a futile struggle, out of which would come nothing
but disaster. They say we could have beaten Hitler—we probably could,
but while we are beating him, we lost a million men, and for nothing.
Why should Britain be constantly called upon to defend other countries? France was pledged to aid the Czechs and France backed out. We
were pledged to fight, if France fought. For a strip of country, of which
I, nor thousands like me know nothing we were to drag an Empire
into a War. My creed is that until Hitler attacks a British colony, we
should keep out of the European Boiling Pot, depend on Armed Isolation as America does, and refuse to be involved in Arguments. Because
England is the Worlds leading Power, doesn't mean that she should be

called upon to aid everyone and everything regardless of cost. I am not, however, in favour of giving Hitler an inch of British territory, and if we fight then, we fight for something that belongs to us, not a couple of chunks of Alien soil. Why in the heck we should have to pay for a loan of ten million to the Czechs is beyond me, and baffles me. There are thousands of children in the Distressed areas of this country who are literally starving, and are not helped—yet when the Lord Mayor opens a fund for Jewish and Czech refugees—the money pours in. England is cluttered up with foreign Jews, with many thousands more to come. Soon the country will belong to them. Trouble with the British race is that they're the darndest, sentimental, soft-heart crowd you ever knew, and they'd allow the Bread to be pinched out of their mouths. Its a pity they don't learn about 'Charity beginning at the home' and 'Britain for the British'.

Anyway, now that its all over and things are getting back to normal—our Gas Masks are reposing carefully in Containers in the Spare room, for future use—people are criticising right and left and saying we paid too big a price for peace. And now that darned lunatic with the Swastika is making himself even more unpopular through this new purge of Jews.[50] I shouldn't waste your sympathy on them though. If they've got no home to go to, they'll settle in England. Sanctuary No. 1. they ought to call us.

Now to get back to pleasanter subjects. I still like Robert Taylor, though not so much as I did in "The Yank [at Oxford]." Have now summed up my film likes and dislikes, on the credit side with Gielgud, Fairbanks Jr, Taylor, Wayne Morris, Melvyn Douglas, Errol Flynn, Leslie Howard, and a new one—Richard Greene, and Don Ameche.[51] Females Jessie Matthews and Merle Oberon. And my pet hates, George Brent, John Boles, a newcomer called Dick Baldwin with *the* most appalling American accent I ever heard, Joan Crawford, and I regret to

50. Krystallnacht—the pogrom against Jews throughout Germany and parts of Austria—took place on November 9–10, 1938.

51. U.S. actor Wayne Morris starred in numerous U.S. and UK movies in the 1930s. Melvyn Douglas was one of the most acclaimed U.S. film actors. Errol Flynn, born in Australia and raised in England, established his career in Hollywood as a swashbuckler, starring as Robin Hood in *Adventures of Robin Hood* (1938; U.S.). The handsome British actor Richard Greene debuted at the Old Vic and played in *The Hound of the Baskervilles* (1939; U.S.). Don Ameche was a dapper U.S. leading man in 1930s and 1940s.

state, Maurice Evans.[52] I'm sorry about the last one, but I can't help it.

We heard an American Radio programme on the Short Waves last night—one was the "Princess Pat" house of something. Had a couple of playlets, with a very soft-voiced actress in it. Oh! and before I forget—they made a sort of a special gift offer of some liquid Lip Varnish and said whether you were blonde, brunette or red-head, they'd send you a sample. Now we've been wanting to get some lip varnish over here for some time, but can't. I was wondering if as a very special concession to a conceited English pal, you'd send to this Princess Pat Woman for me, and see if you could get a sample over here, and if I sent 'em sixpence, I don't suppose they'd accept it. She just said address your envelopes to Princess Pat, Chicago—no street address was necessary, refer them to the Radio Offer, say your colouring (I am very blonde, blonde, by the way) and presto, the Varnish would be sent you. Just as simple as that. Oh! and before that we heard a man from some Coffee Manufacturers, but he spoke so quickly I couldn't get a word of what he was saying. And the week before we had a sort of a Spelling Bee from the NBC. but the words were so simple I could have answered 'em standing on my head. You should hear some of the Spelling Bees they give over here. Some of the words would take up a whole sheet of paper to write. We don't get any sponsored programmes at all—our entertainment is picked out for us by a very conservative body of gentlemen, and Dance Music is not allowed on the Sabbath—in fact Sunday's programmes are the most deadly dull things you ever heard.

Funny thing—when I tuned in to Ben Bernie from America last week he was playing our most popular Song and Dance number "The Lambeth Walk".[53] Everybody "Lambeths" over here—my brother and

52. George Brent, who appeared in more than fifty films in the 1930s alone, played a doctor in the romance *Dark Victory* (1939; U.S.), which also starred Bette Davis, Humphrey Bogart, and Ronald Reagan. John Boles, a U.S. actor discovered by Gloria Swanson, was in more than thirty films in the 1930s. Dick Baldwin, considered an inferior actor, appeared in *The Joy Parade* (1937; U.S.), a film about an American Indian football player that was ostensibly a comedy and would be considered racist today. U.S. film star Joan Crawford was in top form during the 1930s with films such as *Grand Hotel* (1932; U.S.) and *Love on the Run* (1936; U.S.) with Clark Gable.

53. A popular Cockney dance performed to a song by that title from the musical *Me and My Gal* (1937) about a Cockney lad who inherits an earldom and almost loses his Cockney girlfriend. The dance involves side-by-side steps, linking of arms, and slapping of knees but no "close" dancing. The musical was made into a movie, *The Lambeth Walk*, in 1940 (UK), also known as *Me and My Girl* in the United States.

I entertained the citizens of Gwithian, by performing the Dance right down the Beach. Where I work isn't far from the real Lambeth Walk. We are what is affectionately called South Lambeth.

I saw 'Three Comrades' and loved it, but the audiences here seemed to think it was all very funny and roared.[54] I haven't seen Hedy Lamarr, yet, I wanted to see "Ecstacy" but couldn't pluck up enough courage to go in, and I didn't want to go with Ernie.[55] Am aching to see "Marie Antoinette" which is now showing in London at the Empire Leicester Square.[56] I wanted to go last Saturday but the boys wanted to go and see "Men with Wings"—Result—we went to see 'Men with Wings'.[57] There are two of the boys and only one of me. Unfortunate part of it was that Roy had a celebration in the afternoon, and got a bit 'canned' and though he tried to keep his eye open during the film it was too much, so he just flopped on my shoulder and that was that. He seems to be fond of using me for a pillow. On the way back from Cornwall, I had one of 'em asleep on my shoulder and Roys head in my lap with his feet on the Luggage rack. Motto, does it pay to be too maternal?

Weather here is surprisingly mild for November—usually the 'pea-souper' month., but we shall suffer for it, believe me. I bet we'll have one heck of a January. Only six weeks now to Xmas, and I am determined to break out and get a bit squiffy on Xmas Eve. Have never drunk more than two glasses of Wine in my life, and on the other hand maybe I'd better not break out as I shall have all my work cut out stopping Roy from falling in front of a Bus and Harry from fighting a Policeman or something. I hope to be able to write you again before Christmas anyway.

My John is marvellous in "Dear Octopus", just like his own, normal self, minus beard and blank verse. The King and Queen, Queen Mary,

---

54. *Three Comrades* (1938; U.S.), a love story centered on three German soldiers after World War I, stars Robert Taylor, Franchot Tone, and Robert Young.

55. *Ecstasy* (1933; U.S.), one of Hedy Lamarr's earliest films, is considered a classic. The romantic film about a young wife with an older husband contains many sexual images and spare dialogue reminiscent of the early talkies.

56. *Marie Antoinette* (1938; U.S.) stars Norma Shearer, Tyrone Power, and John Barrymore.

57. *Men with Wings* (1938; U.S.), about early aviation and starring Fred MacMurray and Ray Milland, may have been the first color film.

and Duke and Duchess of Kent have all paid visits to the play, which is a great success and making thousands a week. Please thank Julia for letting me have that Magazine and thank yourself for sending it.

I see Evans' "Hamlet" is doing fine with the Critics who didn't like Johns. I, personally, think they're all nuts. But who cares, anyway.

I hope the King and Queen get a good welcome in your country.[58] Its a pretty marvellous diplomatic move—far better than the supposed 'Slumming' expedition of the precious Duke of Windsor, and his Woman.[59] They're supposed to be coming home now, but I'm quite sure we can do without them.

Must close now, as I've worked an hour overtime typing this. Please let me hear from you soon, and forgive me for being so long-winded.

Love,
Betty

18A. Sinclair Gardens
Kensington
London. W 14.
[November 1938]

Dear Helen,

I am snatching a few precious moments from work to write this. Christmas is on its way, and don't we know it—the work is simply awful. Piles and piles of letters to answer, innumerable phone calls from agitated people who are sending their Xmas stuff down the Lines early. And to make matters worse, there was some sort of a strike here yesterday—a "go-slow" strike, which means that the men work at half time pressure, and as a result the Platforms are simply choc full of goods which cannot be loaded. Great Scott! Why did my family ever work on the Railway. My mother is so pleased at the job she got me, but I've always detested it, and will never be happy until I get out of it.. The trouble is, as I said just now—we're a Railway family, and Mother

58. King George VI and Queen Elizabeth were the first English monarchs to visit North America. Their tour helped popularize the British cause in the United States as war with Germany loomed.

59. King Edward VIII, who abdicated in 1936 to marry Wallis Simpson, "the woman I love," lost the affection of the British public afterward.

thinks that theres no job on earth like it. Actually we work like slaves, and are shockingly poorly paid, and we have to exist in Offices that are a disgrace to the nation.

Anyway, having had my little "moan"—its Monday morning, so its only to be expected—I must thank you for the clippings you sent me. Your letter didn't arrive until some days afterwards, so I missed the point of a lot of them—although they were all interesting and didn't need much explaining. I was glad to get the piece about John's "Hamlet" Book—I took it to the Theatre with me the next evening, and all the Gallery Girls read it. We are anxiously awaiting the publication of the Book in England now, we've been promised it for a long time—but it doesn't seem to have arrived yet. And I *do* hope you can get those other Books—I have two friends, by the way, who keep pestering me for duplicates of the Gielgud clippings, so if you ever find anyone who has anything written about John that he or she doesn't want, perhaps they'll let me have them. I have to keep an eye on my original clippings, otherwise the young ladies in question pinch 'em when I'm not looking. We all keep Scrap Books, and some of them are really magnificent records. Mine aren't very tidy, but they [are] fairly detailed. We went to the last night of "Richard II" last night (sorry, I mean Saturday, the night before). Anyhow, we had to queue up from eight in the morning to get stools. Which reminds me, do you understand the Stool system in England? You see, the pit and gallery of all our Theatres are not reservable, therefore to make sure of your seat, you pay sixpence, and the Doorman puts down a little stool for you with your name on it. Then you go away and come back an hour or so before the Show starts and sit on your stool. Anyway, the Theatre was packed with Gielgud "fans" on Saturday, and it was a sort of a reunion for us. I met dozens of girls I knew, and we were yelling "Hullos" to each other over miles of rows of seats. I think John played up and gave the most marvellous performance he has ever given in his life, and the reception he got nearly blew the roof off. He made a charming little speech, after we'd all yelled ourselves hoarse, and in short everyone was so excited they nearly tumbled flat over the Gallery rails. "Richard" has run for 10 weeks, the maximum period for the repertory venture, and it could have run for another 10 by the size of the audiences. I don't think, however, they're going to do so well with the rest. "The School for Scandal" is so terribly dated—I can't think why he's doing it—and "The Three Sisters" is by

Chekov, and I loathe that man's plays like poison. So much Fatalism with a capital "F". I don't mind "The Merchant" so much—John is doing Shylock for the first time so that should be interesting, but Ashcroft is such a rotten Portia. Too sweet and sugary—not enough strength, and volume. Portia was a character, not a clinging vine.

People in London are furious over the New York statement that Maurice Evans is six times better than Gielgud. I never heard such abominable piffle in my life—I've seen Maurice Evans, and I've heard his "Richard" and I can't see what all the fuss is about. How can New York pass judgment about John's "Richard" when they have never seen it? The guiding lights I believe are John Anderson and Richard Watts, Jr. Neither of them seem to like John very much.

I do hope you get those articles for me. Theres another life story of John's appearing in our "Womans Journal" now—some rather lovely photos of him as a chee-ild, but I want to read the "Theatre Arts" anyway. I can't get it over here much, and theres probably heaps of things about John I don't see. I'm sending you the "Richard" programme—theres rather a nice Photo of John in the front, and as its not in costume I thought you might like to have it. Thank you for your charming compliments on my appearance. Let me assure you I have a million faults, I'm fair I want to be dark, my eyes are blue and I'd like 'em brown. I'm tall, and I'd like to be one of the small, helpless variety. As for saying you could never send your photo—You must have an awful inferiority complex. I think I shall be one of those young ladies who "fade" quickly. When I'm in me forties, I've a firm feeling that I shall be enormous, with three or four chins, and a marvellous "spare tyre". Most of my mothers family are on the stout side, so I shall probably follow in their footsteps. So picture me in about 20 odd years time, going on a strenuous diet.

And though I know you well enough now, to skip talking about the weather—being a born and bred Briton, I can't avoid it. I've just got up again to put more coal on the fire. I feel frozen to the marrow—We've had the most dreadfully cold weather here, and November being a month of fogs we've had quite a number of good old London "pea-soupers". And a London fog is a fog. All the train services are wrong, Cars have to stop, and regulating traffic is a nightmare. When we have a blackout, sometimes in the middle of the day, its pitch black, like night. Anyhow, we have two of the coldest months in the year in front of us, December and January. February is always very wet and March very windy. In brief, theres nothing much to looke forward to until about July. Our summer doesn't start till then.

Our Armistice Day celebrations took place on Nov. 11th. Do you celebrate it much over there? Although "celebrate" is hardly the word. We have two minutes complete silence every Nov. 11th. at 11 o'clock. I honestly think the world seems to stop turning—it's the most impressive thing imaginable. The whole of a great city stilled for two minutes, and in the case of Britain its the whole country stilled at the same time, because being such a small island, theres very little difference in time here. When its 11 oclock in London, its not much more than three minutes past in Scotland. Over here we all wear Red Poppies on Armistice Day, and in the evening there is a marvellous Reunion of members of H.M. Forces at the Royal Albert Hall. The King and Queen and Queen Mary are present, and the men sing their old War Songs, and there is a service for those that did not come back. And at the close of the evening, they let over a million poppy petals float down from the roof, one petal for each man that lost his life for the Empire. It's a beautiful sight, and a sad one, seeing that everyone in Europe seems to be planning on another big. Bust-up. We do our best to keep out of it, but its a hard job, everyone seems to look to us to do something, although I don't see why we should.

I see they've given the Wandering Duke another smack in the eye now. Serves him right. "Studying working conditions" indeed. What tripe! Pity his wife doesn't give a bit more to the working man, and spend a little less on furs and clothes. All *she* wanted to visit America for was to show off her new title and her "fall wardrobe". Ouch! They make me sick.

I shall have to close now, as my boss is looking most wickedly at me. Sort of "I don't know if I'm right, but I think you wasting your time" look. So I shall close, as I don't want to lose my job before Christmas. Hope to hear from you shortly, or sooner.

Love,
Betty

18A. Sinclair Gardens,
Kensington
LONDON. W. 14.
[January 1939]

Dear Helen,

Received your very welcome letter last week and as my Lynx-eyed Boss
has retired gracefully for a few moments (if I know the old Blighter at
all, he'll be back in a couple of ticks to see what we're doing) I'm going
to try and answer it now. Its about time I attended to my correspondence which is in shockingly bad state of arrear. This epistle, however,
will probably be written in scraps while the Old man isn't looking, and
the telephone isn't ringing, and I am not banging out a few fairy stories on my trusty typewriter. Trouble with my boss is he will persist in
scratching around like a chicken in a Barnyard and driving everybody
crazy. But then what Boss doesn't?

Well! as you said lass, Christmas is now a memory, thank heavens.
It always seems to be one long rush to me. I went home to Monmouthshire for the holidays with my pal. I stayed with her Christmas
Eve (she's a hairdresser and lives in North London, right at the bottom of the Great North Road, and we travelled down to Newport on
Christmas Day. Left London at midday in an appalling patch of fog,
and believe it or not the darned train took five and a half hours to get
down. Went round Gloucester, which is a long winding, and totally
unnecessary route to go by. We sat in a carriage full of Jewish people, who fed us on sandwiches of Egg and Salmon. I loathe fish, and I
detest Eggs. So I had a very unhappy and hungry time, and had to
curb my ravenous appetite with a couple of apples and an orange. And
a bar of chocolate given me by a gentleman who should have known
better. Anyway, we had our Christmas Dinner at six p.m. fed-up and
weary and vowing never to travel on Xmas Day again. I had a very quiet
time afterwards—No parties, (I don't like parties anyway, because I'm a
non-smoker and teetotaler, and you're thought to be a bad sport if you
don't indulge in either vice. I can enjoy myself without). I went to the
pictures once and spent the rest of my time visiting relations, who all
say the same thing. "You're getting thinner,["] "How'd you like London"
and "Would you like to come home?".

I'm glad your Turkey was a success. I can cook most anything, but very rarely do, except Pastry. People come from far and near to taste my Sausage Rolls. They really are a masterpiece of the culinary art, though I sez it myself as shouldnt. The sausage is the nicest part of 'em. I once cooked some Cakes in School and put Scouring powder instead of Baking Powder. On another memorable occasion I fried some bacon in Cold Cream for lard, on another even worse one, I used Goose Grease. My other "faux pas" was intentional. I used Ginger (Powdered) instead of Coffee for the Headmistresses morning cup that cheers. And did she like it? No, she didn't. However, joking apart, I believe I could cook a dinner better than Mrs Beeton now, and that you know, is saying something.

Have just interrupted this letter to have a furious row with one of the Clerks on the other side of the Office. I have a terrible cold, and can't smell or taste anything, and they have the windows staring wide open with a piercing draught coming through them. Its terribly cold this morning and I've just marched over and shut the windows. They'll be opened again in two ticks, but I've won my point and that's all that worries me. Yesterday the *sun* shone all day and it was nearly as warm as June. To-day the weather has gone back to normal. It's as cold as ice, and the sky is grey, and the world looks a pretty lousy place.

I only hope it doesn't rain. I am going to a pantomime to-night (I don't suppose you've ever seen a pantomime. They're a British institution) I'm seeing "Cinderella" to-night, at the Princes. Stanley Lupino (that's Ida's father) is in it. I shall go and see "Beauty and the Beast" next week. Jill Esmond is the principal Boy in it. Jill is Laurence Olivier's missus and Pantomime is new to her.[60] Which reminds me, I saw Olivier's Macbeth last week, and didn't like it. But to be fair to him he is improving greatly, and may one of these days rank amongst our highest Shakespearean actors. His voice is the most awful thing about him, I think. I also saw him in the "Divorce of Lady X" the colour film with Merle Oberon. Go and see this, Helen. It's good. I've always like Merle, and she looks lovely in this. Another good British film that you're never likely to see is "South Riding" It s adapted from a novel by Winifred Holtby about Yorkshire life and its grand entertainment. It

---

60. Jill Esmond, British stage and screen actress, was Laurence Olivier's wife from 1930 to 1940.

won't be shown in America because its so typically British. The same thing happened with "The Good Companions". That was considered too English to appeal in America—But it was one of the finest films I ever saw. I wish the whole of America had had a chance to see it. It was shown pretty extensively in Canada and was one of the biggest successes in the history of British films.[61]

Well! as I warned you this letter is being done in patches. The first two pages were done yesterday, and now it is to-day. And my cold is worse. My nose is as red as a beetroot, and I have a sore throat. And the sun's shining again. Seems to be doing it to spite everybody. The sky is as blue as a summer day, and though it isn't hot, its warm. I think it meant to shine on Australia, but looked the wrong way and caught us. Sunshine in England in January is unheard of, it's a great rarity in the summer, much less in the winter.

Anyway, I went to my Pantomime last night. It was at the Lyceum (where Henry Irving used to declaim every evening). And it was "Beauty and the Beast". Had the best time of my life—even though it was such lowbrow entertainment. All the comedians get the audience to sing choruses with them, and there is an Old Witch and a Fairy Queen, and Trapdoors, and lovely illuminated scenery. My friend and I shouted and sang a ridiculous chorus called "Fido, Fido". "I yelled for my dog in the dark" till we were blue in the face. And when the Witch came on we yelled "Mind out. She's here!" with the rest of the audience, and all clapped vociferously when Beauty kissed the Beast and he turned into a Prince again. Well. they say we're all children at heart, and I've been to a Pantomime every year ever since I can remember, so perhaps there's some excuse for me. What will happen when I see "Cinderella" next week, I can't say.

Now to turn from lowbrow to highbrow. We all went to see the last night of "School for Scandal" Saturday. Had a marvelously exciting evening, with a wonderful audience, and at the end had the most sincerely spoken little speech I've ever heard John give. He said that "Scandal" had succeeded beyond his wildest dreams, and thanked Mr. Sheridan,

---

61. *South Riding* (1938; UK), whose cast includes Ralph Richardson and Edmund Gwenn, is a story of corruption, intrigue, and romance in a Yorkshire setting. *The Good Companions* (1933; UK), adapted from J. B. Priestley's novel about three musicians, stars Jessie Matthews, Edmund Gwenn, and John Gielgud.

the caste [*sic*], and then with arms outstretched he thanked us dear good people for coming and seeing it. All very sweet and touching. But it sounded so much better than his usual set speech on first nights. The premiere of the "Three Sisters" is on Friday. I loathe Tchekov, and John is playing the part of a middle-aged Colonel with two inches of padding in his Clothes, a moustache and beard, and a grey wig and pince-nez. The things we suffer!! And after that comes Shylock??? I think I liked his Joseph Surface as well as anything he's done. And I never realised that "Scandal" could be so lovely I wish he'd bring it to America, although the "fans" nearly sit on me every time I suggest it. Nobody here seems to want John to go to America at all So perhaps that's why he came home so quickly last time. Actually he was absent from the London stage for a year when Hamlet was in America—what with a holiday and the various rehearsals, and that was a bit too much for the fans. Personally speaking I'd like him to go over and see you in 1940 because there is a possibility of my coming to America myself in that year, and I should like to see how one of our actors goes over in your country.

The statement about the "six times better" is quite true and has been made twice by Richard Watts Jr. in the "New York Herald Tribune" (I have the cuttings if you'd like me to prove it to you) Two of our critics took it up, and said that Watts couldn't make such a statement until he had seen Gielgud's "Richard". Most of them who have been in New York say they are surprised at the reverence paid to Maurice Evans. He has, as you know, played Richard and Hamlet over here, and nobody took much notice of him. That, honey, is the reason he doesn't come home—there's a bit more competition over here than in N.Y. We have a great many young Shakespearean actors, all able to speak verse and prose, whereas in America there are not so many actors of that type. Apparently the three critics who remain loyal to Gielgud are Burns Mantle, Gilbert Gabriel and Mrs Sedgwick of the "Stage". Mrs Sedgwick, I believe, saw "Richard II" when she was in London this year.

I do hope you can get the article from the "Theatre Arts" Implore your friend not to throw it out. Say I'll never forgive her if she does, and she'll have that on her conscience all her life. I can't get hold of the "Theatre Arts" much. John's life story is appearing in one of our classy monthly Magazines the "Womans Journal". It started in November, and is very witty and amusing, and well illustrated. It was rather funny, too.

I bought the mag with the first instalment last November, and went to the Old Vic to see "Measure for Measure". I sat peacefully in the Pit, and opened my magazine to the aforesaid life story where there were lots of pictures of the famous Hamlet as a leetle chee-ild complete with brothers and sister. Out of the blue a hand came over my shoulder and a couple of chirpy voices chorused "Pardon us! But that wouldn't be John by any chance?" On my answering in the affirmative, the Book was whisked from my hand and passed to and fro around the Pit, and I did not see it until the second interval. Motto, never buy a Book and take it to the "Vic". Some of the young women there are far from backward!

There s one thing—if I do come out in 1940. I must stop away from Mr. G.J. Nathan, also Mr. R. Watts, Jr. And I am none too keen on John Anderson. By the way, do you remember Beatrice Lillie's skit on the two Hamlets in "The Show is On"? Well, they're bringing that show to London, but C.B. Cochran says he is omitting the Gielgud skit, owing to Censorship difficulties. Isn't it a shame?

Have just looked at the Clock and notice that it is twenty minutes to twelve, and I've hardly done anything. So shall close now, and do you a good turn.

Hope to hear from you soon, and excuse this patchy letter.

Love,
Betty

# II

The "Phony War"

On September 1, 1939, Germany invaded Poland. France and Britain, honoring their treaty obligations to Poland, declared war on Germany. Now began the "phony war." Although there was no military action on the Western Front, Betty and her fellow citizens began experiencing blackouts and were required to carry their gas masks. Since August 1939, Germany and Russia had been bound together in the Nazi-Soviet Non-Aggression Pact. The USSR invaded Finland on November 30, 1939. Sweden and Norway declared their neutrality. In February 1940, British naval forces captured the German supply ship *Altmark* in Norwegian waters and freed two hundred British prisoners of war. Finland, after a stubborn but futile winter campaign, without aid from Britain or France, surrendered to Russia on December 31, 1940. During the winter of 1939–1940, the American film *Gone with the Wind* opened in expensive suburban London theaters. As the European situation grew increasingly grave, Norway made peace with Germany. Betty, as she would write numerous times, hoped to come to the United States. On May 7, 1940, the House of Commons began a debate on the Chamberlain government's prosecution of the war. Three days later, on May 10, Winston Churchill, age sixty-five and out of office for ten years, succeeded Neville Chamberlain as prime minister. By the end of May 1940, German troops had overrun Belgium and Holland. Churchill, in a radio address, promised his listeners only "blood, toil, tears and sweat."

18A. Sinclair Gardens<br>
W. 14.<br>
England.<br>
[November 24, 1939]

Dear Helen,

I hope you will forgive me for the long delay in writing you. I'm really very sorry, but as you will probably guess, our lives have been turned upside down and everything seems changed. I have been so terribly busy in work that I've gone home feeling like a pricked Balloon, and after that I've had to remain on duty in a First Aid Post, for hours at a time. Everyone who is worth anything is doing National Service these days. I am attached to the Civil Nursing Reserve, otherwise known as the V.A.Ds but I can't do full time work, as I work for a Railway Company and am therefore in what is called a "reserved occupation".[1] We've been completely unable to cope with the work (most of the big concerns having been taken over by the Government) large numbers of our men have been called up, and we are hopelessly short staffed and how we manage to keep smiling is beyond me!

I was on holiday the week War broke out. I sent you a Postcard from France, which you may or may not have received, and the international situation looked pretty awful then but with the eternal optimism of youth, I didn't think it would come to anything. On the Friday, however, all British subjects were advised to go home so we packed up and caught the next Boat, and got back to London in time to see them

---

1. An act of Parliament made all men aged eighteen to forty-one eligible for military service. In November 1939 the British government published a "Schedule of Reserved Occupations"; Betty's job at the railroad was a "reserved occupation" because she filled in for men who were called up. In January 1940 every household received a handbook that listed full- and part-time essential wartime jobs. The "Schedule" was meant to check impulsive volunteering for military service by skilled workers in vital wartime industries and to help other workers find appropriate volunteer service on the home front (Calder, *People's War*, 58–59).

chalking white lines on pavements and dimming the Street lights.[2] On the Sunday morning we all sat round the Radio and listened to the Premier's speech and we all cried—the young ones because they didn't know what was coming and were frightened, and the older ones because they did. My mother's first thought was for my brother, knowing him as well as she did. He's mad to join the Army and full of great ideas of smashing Hitler and his Gang to atoms—but he never thinks that one German bullet is all that's needed to smash him. It seems funny but last week my mother turned out a letter from my father dated sometime in 1916, and he says ". . . it's rumoured out here that Jerry is angling for an Armistice. But I and most of the chaps out here feel we'd rather fight on and finish the Germans for good and all so that our children won't have the same old battle all over again. I don't want Jacky to grow up to anything like this. If it means peace for our kids we'll fight till we all drop". Prophetic, wasn't it? And you've got it just as it was written. Jack will probably be called up in a month or two, for service in France. He has applied to join one of the Railway Battalions. He is mad on the whole idea, though he is in no danger of being officially conscripted for ages. Now that he has volunteered, of course, he'll be called up with the rest of 'em.

I cannot make out why Britain is always dragged into these scraps, because we never get a thing out of them, only poverty and destruction and set-backs. We were just recovering from the last one, when this appalling thing had to happen. Now it will take another twenty years and more for us to get things straightened out. Still, I suppose it's a battle of Democracy against Dictators, and as Britain has to keep her prestige as a Democratic Country and the Policeman of Europe, in we have to go. But I wish Americans wouldn't stand around doing precisely nothing but criticise and call it a "phoney" War.[3] After all, they are not risking a single American life, and are only thinking of the whole thing in terms of Newspaper Headlines and Dollars for Armaments. Its a little upsetting to see one country gain on another's misfortunes. Still, I notice how brave and daring our Film people and other celebrities

---

2. Civilian drivers were required to mask their headlights, leaving only a small slit for the light to shine through. The white lines on the pavement served as visual guides.

3. The period between the declaration of war on September 3, 1939, and the German invasion of Holland, Belgium, and France in May–June 1940.

were. They all fled to America as quickly as their cowardly heels could carry 'em, and even if the British Film Industry (which was a thriving concern) is given permission to carry on, I don't know where they're going to find any Stars or Producers to make 'em. I love to read these stupid, inane, stories of British Stars who talk about this War and what they'd like to see other people do. It seems strange that when their own country needs them most they have to either go to or stay in America to do their "bit"! I hope when they're sun-bathing in California, they'll remember theres a War on over in Europe, the lazy devils!

We are working in a "Danger Spot" here. Its next door to a big Gas Plant, and next door but one to a [*sic*] Electric Power station, and adjacent to a Railway Line, so if old Fatty Goering's Air Force spot us, we're in for it. They've been making various attempts to do some damage, but we have good defences in London and although I have no doubt they will eventually get through, they'll be given a right good battle when they do. We've heard the Air Raid Sirens three times and a more nerve-racking noise couldn't be imagined. Still when we hear it, we proceed quite cheerfully down to the Basement, and wait for the "All Clear" whistles. They [*sic*] only thing that terrifies me is that we'll hear Rattles and that means Poison Gas and Heaven help us if the maniac of Europe starts using that! We carry our Gas Masks with us everywhere, and have got so used to them they seem like part of our Clothes, and we have different coloured containers to match our different Outfits.

The worst part of the War is the Blackout. If a chink of light shows from your Windows you're liable for prosecution and a large fine, and there are no lamps in the streets and you have to crawl about in pitch blackness, with the aid of a very dim torch. I say a "dim" torch, because if the light from it is at all bright, or shines across a Road the Air Raid Wardens swoop on you like vultures and you have to pay a nice little sum for disobeying the rules and Regulations. Cinemas and Theatres are coming back to normal now, though there is an eleven oclock Curfew everywhere, and very few people venture out of doors late at night, because its too darned dangerous. My mother worries me sick because she can't see at all in the Dark, and has fallen down several times and hurt herself, and I have to try and meet her from work every evening to fetch her home.

Everyone is hoping for a cheerful Christmas, although the circumstances are so gloomy. Its going to be an expensive business, though because the cost of living is going up by leaps and bounds! I am going down to Newport to see a friend of mine—the girl I went on holiday with. She came back from France, was taken very ill, and they've discovered that she's got Abdominal Tuberculosis, and that its just a matter of time. I've been terribly upset about it!

I don't know how much of this letter will be cut out by our Prize Nosey-Parker, the Censor. He'll probably look at some of it and immediately imagine that I am a Nazi Agent and that you are attached to the German Bund in America and going to give them this precious information.[4] They've got minds like that. If he only know how much I loved the Germans I'm sure he wouldn't worry. I had some snaps of my holidays to show you, but I don't think I'm allowed to send them as the Censor probably thinks that by looking at a Snapshot of me the Nazis will be able to tell where the British Fleet will be at eight oclock next Good Friday, or something. Anyway, I suppose even Censors are necessary!

I must close now, Helen. Please write to me soon and any interesting cutting from American papers would be very welcome!

Love,
Betty


18A. Sinclair Gardens,
West Kensington
LONDON. W. 14.
[January 11, 1940]

Dear Helen,

Have ten minutes to spare so thought I would like to write you a couple more paragraphs. I've neglected you so shockingly this year so I'll probably bore you stiff by writing yards too much in 1940. And of course we always have to take the risk that maybe some of our Ships will go down with the letters aboard, and bang goes all my efforts. So if you don t hear from me for a long while, send me a jerker to let me know, because it maybe all due to the so and so U Boats.

---

4. The German American Bund was an organization of pro-Nazi Americans during the 1930s.

Well! I wish to record for the satisfaction of the Government or the Censor or whom ever it may concern that I am thoroughly fed up with the War, and everything connected with it! Whatever our boys may be suffering on the Western Front, and God knows they have enough to put up with, we poor folks at home have been going through it with 'em. The worst of all our troubles is the Black-out—all lights must be screened or extinguished everywhere at Sunset, and if you've ever tried walking down a Street with no lights at all to guide the way, not even a chink from a House Window, you can imagine what it's like. Often I grope my way along what appears to be a solid Black wall and it's practically impossible to pick out the Curb Stones, or even see which is your own House without the aid of a Torch, and Torches are only permitted if their light is shone on the ground and is not too brilliant. My mother worries me sick, because she can't see anything at all at night, and has nearly bruised herself black and blue falling down curbs, and banging into Lamp Standards. I'm not so bad because I have more confidence, but the whole thing gets on your nerves to such an extent that you long to be anywhere where there s a bit of light. Yet despite all of it, the wonderful humour of the English people and particularly the Cockneys keeps on coming to the top every time. They can joke about the Black-out, and laugh at their troubles and still see the bright side of life, though most of them have probably got husbands, or sons, in khaki and never know when and if they'll ever see them again. I suppose I feel a bit dreary because it s winter, and an English winter is so terribly cold and bleak. Everyone I know is being called up and now, Rationing has started,[5] and we are presented with four ounces of Butter per person per week. Four ounces! and Mum and I used to eat about a pound and a half between us. The Sugar ration doesn't worry me much because I don't take sugar, and the Meat Allowance is quite good, but the Butter is just about killing me. Actually, I don't think it's so much a shortage of stuff but because they need the Ships for transport of War materials. It seems awful that I've got to eat Margarine because they need a couple of Bullets "Somewhere in France".

---

5. Rationing, not only of food but also of clothing, cosmetics, and other essentials, became increasingly severe throughout the war and even under the postwar Labour government (Calder, *People's War,* 439–45).

I don't know if you've got a Short Wave Radio Set. We have, and the current entertainment for all Britishers is to listen to the German propaganda Announcer (in English) from Radios Hamburg and Zeesen. This chap, is known all over England as "Lord Haw-Haw", probably because he speaks in a very affected "Old School Tie" voice, and he tells the most appalling (and the funniest) lies you ever heard.[6] Some of the things he says are so hilarious that you practically double up in your Seat. Of course, it's all supposed to be deadly serious and Doctor Goebbels thinks that we really take it all in, but honestly, if you want a laugh you should hear him some time. According to him Britain is responsible for everything bad that's happened on the Earth since the beginning of Time. The British Boy Scouts have (sez Haw-Haw) been blowing up factories in Yugo-Slavia, and the Girl Guides had something to do with the Graf Spee disaster.[7] Mr Churchill personally sunk the Athenian, and Mr Chamberlain personally blew up the Munich Beer Cellar. They've sunk practically every Ship in the British Navy, including some non-existent ones (a month or two ago they sunk a patch of ground in Middlesex!) and as for aeroplanes—well. every day old Haw-Haw announces that dozens of British and French planes were sent smoking, down to their doom.

I always listen to Raymond Gram Swing giving his American Commentary on Saturday evenings.[8] I know I can say this to you Helen, and I hope you won't mind, but the average Britisher doesn't think so much of the American these days. I always defend them because I've got friends in America who are and have been marvellous to me, but this "Sitting on the Fence" Business by Uncle Sam is a little galling for us. You see, before this War started, we had always heard America boosted as the Land of Freedom, the Home of Democracy and so forth and so on. We had even heard her describe herself as the World's leading Democracy, and not said anything. She was supposed to have

6. William Joyce, an Irish American Briton, was the Nazi's chief English language broadcaster throughout the war, but especially during the first six months when an estimated six million adults listened regularly to his upper-class accent—"haw-haw." His broadcasts were aimed at undermining confidence in the heavily censored news from the BBC (ibid., 73–74, 156–57, 633).

7. The *Admiral Graf Spee,* a German pocket battleship, was sunk by its own crew off Uruguay before Christmas 1939 (ibid., 60).

8. An American newsman whose weekly broadcasts from the United States analyzed the events of the week.

sympathy with little Defenceless nations, and to hate Dictatorships, and yet, when the big issues came, and even before it came (during last September's crisis) the great and powerful United States hastily retired and said in effect to Britain and France. "This is your Battle. You get on with it." All your papers say this is Europe's battle—but it isn't. And it certainly isn't England's. We could retire like America did and swear we would remain neutral and let Hitler trample every Pole, Czech, Austrian and so on, in Europe, but we knew that the World wouldn't be safe if we did. Americans say "We shall never send our boys to die on Europe's soil". But England is expected to send hers. And we will get nothing from it, not an inch of ground, nor a penny of money. We'll have a depression afterwards that will be second to none, and thousands of mothers and wives will have lost their men—and America will probably have made millions out of it, and *still* say she is the World's leading Democracy. It's this latter part that's upsetting people more than anything. We know that when Roosevelt raised the Arms Embargo he didn't do it out of any love for Britain and France, or any sympathy with their cause.[9] He naturally knew that it would mean Trade and Employment for America, for which I suppose, no-one can blame him, although it seems terrible that out of all this suffering the nations who are fighting for their principles will get no reward at all. I was reading a report from New York last week in which a Stockbroker says "Given some token of good faith, such as a major offensive on the Western front, the New York Stock market would possibly have a boom, but with the British and French playing around as they are we can do nothing." A token of good faith! to kill off thousands of men! Gosh. it makes me feel sick. America calls this a phoney War. It won't be phoney for long, believe me! We, over here have probably got no idea of the things that will come to us before we can find Peace again. Every day I go to Victoria station on my way to work, and there are hundreds

9. The U.S. neutrality legislation of 1935–1937 established strict control over shipments of munitions abroad, prohibited the export of arms to belligerent nations, and forbade private loans or credits to nations at war. Thus, when war broke out in September 1939, British and French orders from U.S. firms for airplanes and "other instruments of war" could not be delivered. In November 1939, Congress revised the Neutrality Laws so that Britain and France could buy as much war matériel as they could pay for and transport in their own ships. U.S. ships, by this legislation, were forbidden to sail in combat zones (William L. Langer and S. Everett Gleason, *The Challenge to Isolation, 1937–1940* [New York: Harper, 1952], 14, 232).

upon hundreds of boys and men leaving for France, after their brief
home leave. It always makes me want to howl that their father fought
like mine did, in the last War thinking they'd finished it all, and now
their children are left to start the whole terrible business again! I'm
sorry I ranted off like this, and I know, or I hope, you won't take it personally. As I said, I value every American friend I have more than I can
say. And it's the biggest ambition of my life to come out there, though
how is a different matter. I used to say I'd love to marry an American,
but then, until the War's over they probably won't show their faces near
poor old England, so I'll have to wait until the Wars over, and if it goes
on for ten years, Golly! I'll be too old to know what I do want. We are
meeting lots of Canadians over here, but then Canada is nearly as cold
as England, and it's really only the climate I want to get away from.
However, maybe I shall get round to visiting you in Kansas City via
Montreal or something. You never know what the War will do to a gal.

It is lovely and cold to-day, and my feet are frozen and most of our
Pipes at home have been refusing to work, so we have to practically bale
out the Sink every time we throw water into it. Also Heaven has seen
fit to send me a nice cough, and an Influenza cold that simply will not
budge, so what I think of the winter isn't printable.

I am now going to ask you to do me a favour and it really is a favour.
I'm anxious to get a hold of a copy of "PICTURE PLAY" dated February, *1936* Long time back isn't it? Well, I found out where I had to send
for it—i.e. "Picture Play" Circulation Dept, 79/89th. Seventh Avenue,
New York City (that is, of course if they have a copy in stock) so I was
all ready to send for it. But I now find out that International Money
Orders are not now available (I suppose they're stopping the money
going out of the country) so I'm stumped. I can't send them one of our
famous sixpences—it wouldn't be any good to 'em anyway, and there's
no way I can get an American coin, without practically getting hold of
President Roosevelt himself, so I was wondering if you'd write them
and try to get it for me. It won't cost much, about 15 cents, I think,
though I don't know if they charge much extra for Back numbers. But
if you could write them for me and ask if it s available and send it over
I should be very grateful. You see, they're not sending American Movie
Magazines over here now, and do I miss 'em? But if a private individual
sends one over here, all you have to do is wrap it up and address it to
me and mark it "American Film Magazine. No value" and your address,

it'll probably come through without the Censor touching it. I hope so anyway. I was very fond of my Movie Magazines. I don't half call Hitler some names for cutting off my supplies.

However, despite the Black-out the Cinemas and Theatres here are still packed nightly. Seems like the people want to enjoy themselves whatever happens. I don't go up the west End to the Theatre so much now because it s a bit of a job getting home and if there *is* an Air Raid I don't want to be too far from home, but I still go to the Pictures two and three times weekly. I don't know where I should be without my visits to this "Flicks" As you know, the British Film Industry is practically at a Stand-still now, but we are turning out a couple of Propaganda Films and where we are working in the First Aid Post in the Gaumont British Studios, they are making several comedies and a Picture called "Gestapo" with Margaret Lockwood and Rex Harrison.[10] We often go up and see the scenes being "shot".

I saw "Rulers of the Seas" last week and thought it marvellous. Also, quick succession—"Juarez" "The Women" "Gullivers Travels" and "Disputed Passage".[11] Talking of the latter, I was amazed to find that an actor whom I had never seen much of before was better than any young man I've seen for years. I think you've probably heard of him. Names John Howard, and I believe he's been frittering about in the "Bulldog Drummond" parts. Anyway, he was remarkably good in this. He even made up for Dorothy Lamour who was too awful to be believed. Of course, it s like me to like someone when I've probably missed practically every picture he's made. I've always held the opinion, shared by most English detective "fans" that Bulldog Drummond should be

---

10. *Gestapo,* also titled *Night Train to Munich* (1940; U.S), was American made, even though it was filmed in England.

11. *Rulers of the Sea* (1939; U.S.), starring Douglas Fairbanks Jr. and Margaret Lockwood, is the story of the first steamship voyage across the Atlantic. *Juarez* (1939; U.S.), the story of Emperor Maximilian and his wife, Carlota, in Mexico, stars Paul Muni, Bette Davis, Brian Aherne, and Claude Rains. *The Women* (1939; U.S.) is a marital comedy with Norma Shearer and Joan Crawford. *Gulliver's Travels* (1939; U.S.), one of the great animated features of its time, was made as a response to Disney's *Snow White.* The drama-romance *Disputed Passage* (1939; U.S.) stars Akim Tamiroff, Dorothy Lamour, and John Howard and is set during the Japanese bombing of China. Tamiroff, a Russian-born American who studied method acting under Constantin Stanislavsky in Moscow, was one of the greatest character actors of the 1930s, appearing in more than 150 film and television projects.

played by an Englishman, complete with the appropriate accent, and I suppose we're inclined to be prejudiced against an American playing the part. We shall have to see! Me, I think that Ronald Colman was one of the best Drummonds, though Ralph Richardson who's played it on the stage and films in England was very good too. Anyway, quite seriously you should see "Disputed Passage". Apart from Lamour, there is Akim Tamiroff, who is great as a Surgeon. I liked the film immensely though most of our critics said it was too gloomy for War time audiences and the Air Raid sequences were a little too realistic. When I thought of what we might be getting any time now, perhaps I didn't feel so good either!

I seem to have ranted on and on in this letter. I'm sorry if I've bored you too much and I certainly hope to hear from you soon, U Boats or no U. Boats!

Love,

P.S. Of course this took much longer than 10 minutes to type, and this time I'm certain the censor will start carving it about! I'm enclosing a clipping from one of our papers that might interest you!

B.


c/o. G.W.R.Goods Depot,
SOUTH LAMBETH
London. S.W.8. England
[March 7, 1940]

Dear Helen,

We seem to be writing each other in twos and threes, I received a letter from you about a fortnight ago, just about two weeks after I posted you a reply to your Christmas Card! Anyway, I want to thank you for sending me the "Readers Digest" also for the clippings. And I want to send you a couple of things that may interest you. I'm sending one of our leading Humorous Books "London Opinion". It s very funny and it gives you an idea of how we poor, bruised and battered Britishers can still retain our sense of humour despite the fact that we're always smashing ourselves up to help someone out of a tough spot. The latest bit of chivalry on our part is some idea of sending troops and ammunition to Finland. As if we haven't got enough to fight with Germany, we have to tackle Russia as well. Me, I don't think there'll be any of us left by the time this War is over. I shall probably end up in Finland myself, as a Nurse or something. Our trouble now is how to get help through to Finland, anyway. Sweden and Norway have turned a nice, deep, yellow and refused help of any sort, so if our troops march through there, we're busting up their neutrality. We can't go through German occupied Poland, and we can't get through Rumania, because they're scared stiff too, so we've either got to break a few international Laws (which Britain, being too polite for words, wouldn't think of doing) or do the proper thing and start telling the neutral what we think of 'em, which is what we should have done all along.[12]

I'm sending you a picture from one of our papers too, of a father saying good-bye to his wife and baby. It s one of the loveliest things I ever saw and it s typical of the scenes that you can see on Victoria station any morning when the B.E.F. go back to the Front. Thousands of 'em. Poor devils. It makes me sick to look at them, and think that a million British boys died in the last bust-up, just so their kids could grow up and do the same thing. And then they expect the British and Germans to like each other! I think I'll detest the Huns as long as I live.

I hear the clipper isn't going via Bermuda any more so as to dodge the Contraband control. British people feel very resentful of the American attitude over the affair. Especially as they've found thousands of packages for Germany amongst the stuff sent from America. They say America is trying to make Britain's task even more difficult than it is. Me, I don't care at all—because if the Censorship people aren't at Bermuda my Magazines will come through without being tampered with! As you will see, this is going to be some letter. Parts of it written, parts of it scribbled, and other parts typed, still I hope you'll be able to make it out. I won't be able to type for long as my Boss comes back from lunch in about 20 minutes and I have to get down to work again.

I haven't seen "G.W.T.W" for the simple reason that it hasn't come here yet, but it s having a premiere in three different London cinemas in the middle of April, and it s not being shown anywhere for a year

12. By February 1940 France and England had decided to send 100,000 men and some planes to Finland by way of Norway and Sweden. As Finland struggled against strengthening Russian forces, her neighbors refused to allow their neutrality to be violated by France and England. By March 12, Russia and Finland had signed a peace settlement (Malcolm Thomson, *Churchill: His Life and Times, 1874–1965* [London: Odham Books, 1965], 289).

at prices under 3s. 6d. each, that s nearly a dollar, and that means that the poorer people of Britain won't see it for some time. Most of them can't afford that price, and even if they could manage it they think it s too much, and so do I. Some of the London Cinemas charge terrific prices, and I nearly always try to wait until the films come out to the suburbs when you can get a good seat for as little as a shilling—25 cents to you. I love the flicks and couldn't manage without them, and I go so much that if I'm paying for myself I can't afford more than that price. Of course, when I am being taken it isn't so bad but even then my conscience pricks me at the thought of it costing so much. Now, of course, most of the boy friends are at the Front, or training in England, so it s the Suburbs and the cheaper seats for me. On Sundays in most Cinemas they show older films, and I've been chasing the "Bulldog Drummond" series around,—to date I have managed to see about five. I think I told you that I never went to see the "Drummond" films because I liked Sappers Books about the Amateur Detective so much and was disgusted at the thought of an American playing the title part. Now, of course, I have to go out of my way to see 'em. That s what's known as the Biter Bit.

I'd really love to come to America, and maybe when this darned War is over, if it ever is, and if there s anything left of my poor England when everyone is finished with her, I'm coming if I have to pawn everything in the house. I was rather worried about whether English people are allowed to stay in the States very long. The alien laws are very lax here. Anyone can come in and stop, and no-one seems to bother them. The Irish come over here and take the jobs of the British boys who are called up and because they're citizens of Eire and therefore supposedly neutral (how I hate that hypocritical, meaningless, word) they can stay and not be conscripted at all. However, they're bringing a new Law in now which says they must go back to Eire unless they are willing to accept the responsibilities as well as the pleasures of British citizenship. There s loads and loads of British subjects particularly in Hollywood, who did plenty of Union Jack waving, until they found that it might be necessary to fight for it!

Thanks for the article on "Disputed Passage" and the other clippings, and I'll be ever so grateful if you'll send me some Film Books. I do miss them so much. I'd like that February 1936, "Picture Play" if you can get it and I think it will reach me safely if you address it to the

Office, that is to me, c/o Great Western Railway Goods Depot, South Lambeth Station, Battersea Park Rd. London, S.W.8. Things are very unsettled at home,—Mother having lost her job in January—and we never know where we're going to land up next, but things will always reach me at the Office. We're living in Hammersmith at the moment, but Mother may be going to take a Housekeeping job and if she does, I shall take a flat with a girl friend, probably somewhere in North London. I wish things would get settled, or I could win a Sweepstake or something. Everything seems so precarious with the War on and the prices of things are terrific. We're just recovering from the Altmark business.[13] I don't know still how we managed to flout the Norwegian authorities and go in and take what was ours. We're usually too polite and law-abiding for words, and as for breaking a few Laws of Warfare, well! it just isn't done. Still, I think it s just about the best thing we've done since the darned War started—my private sentiments being to hell with Norway. If they can't keep their neutrality better than that, they deserve all they're going to get. The trouble with most of these European neutrals is they're scared stiff of Germany, because they know that they can offend England and always get away with it, but if they start getting tough with Germany then Heaven help 'em.

I'm determined to have a shot at coming to America after this War's over—that is, of course, if I can save up enough money. Things are getting so darned expensive over here and now there s some talk of compulsory saving.[14] They ought to give us enough salary to live on before they start stopping anything out of it. Anyway, I have a pal in New York who has kindly offered me a home if I ever can get to the States, so who knows—you and I may meet, after all. Just cross your fingers, and hope!

I hope you got my last letter safely. Were you able to get that Magazine for me? I'm sorry I had to ask you to do it, but as I've explained before, there s no possible way we can get money out of the country, and Woe is me—the Shops who used to get American film magazines can't

13. The *Altmark,* a supply ship for the *Graf Spee,* was captured by HMS *Cossack* in Norwegian waters and found to hold some three hundred British prisoners, who were then returned home (ibid., 286).

14. Compulsory saving was an attempt to keep people from spending their money on goods whose prices had not yet been established by government control.

get them now as the American Boats don't come to England any more. I think I'll head a deputation to Parliament about it! Anyway, I used to read "Picture Play" a lot, in 1936. I particularly wanted the February one. Most of the Shops here that sold American film mags used to get back numbers of 1936, 1937, and 8. Now they're so hard up they're getting numbers from way back in 1932. That s a bit too early for me. I'd hardly left School then.

I won't write any more now. You're probably bored stiff with what I have knocked out already, and you'll be thinking I write too much tripe anyway. Please write to me soon, and thanks for the Clippings and everything.

Love,<br>Betty

P.S. Go on writing to the Office. It's safer. Until we get really settled.

c/o. G.W.R.<br>SOUTH LAMBETH. S.W.8<br>April 10 [1940]

Dear Helen,

Am tearing off a few measly paragraphs in a terrific hurry as I want to send you a few clippings and I don't get much time to type unless my Boss is at dinner. Most of my work nowadays consists of writing and 'phoning. I have now been promoted to what is termed an "essential unit" and have been given a nice Badge to denote that I am doing my bit for my country by wearing myself out on the Railway. We are terribly busy, as usual, and what with the work and the worry, I don't feel so good.

Well! as you probably know by now, the Maniac has started prowling again and it's hard to tell what country he's going to walk into next. The news greeted me as I got up yesterday morning and turned on the Wireless at 7.am. I went in and told my mother, but we didn't quite believe it as it hadn't then been confirmed. Later on in work we got the papers and all read 'em and started cracking jokes about it won't be long now—"Have you brought your Gas Mask" "Do you know the German National Anthem" and so on. He's occupied Denmark and Norway, and Holland, or Belgium or even England may be next, but what is to be will be, I suppose. I'm not a prayer spouting person, but I'm going to say a little prayer for England and everyone in it now, every night, for this I think is the start of the big Spring offensive, and this is where our poor British boys start to get mowed down again just like they did in the last mess. Of course, we are going to defend Norway, although most British people felt rather bitter against the Norwegians who have been anything but pro-British during the past weeks. We would have helped Denmark too, had they asked for it, just as we struggled to help Finland, and couldn't because the neutrals refused to let us through. The neutrals have been digging their own graves these past months, and Chamberlain and Churchill have told them so on many, many occasions. Hitler has to be wary of the Balkans because Turkey stands there, and the minute Germany makes a move the Turks will fight, as only the Turks know how. I wouldn't mind betting though that he'll have a shot at occupying Rumania for her Oil, and Sweden for Her Iron Ore. We can help Sweden, but to get to Rumania we should have to cross neutral territory again and England simply will not break International rules and do that. Gosh! how I look forward to the time when Britain will be able to stop being the World's Policemen and concentrate on her own affairs. We have a Wonderful country and a wonderful Empire in which there is still so much to accomplish, and everytime prosperity seems to be looming ahead for us, we are dragged in to help some country out of a mess. Anyway, I'm learning up a couple of lines in German of the "Horst Wessel" song just in case, though no-one has ever conquered England yet and I don't think anyone ever will. The British are not a fighting race, but let anyone set foot on their soil and they go raving mad—so if you hear of me having a hand to hand battle with one of those lousy Huns in the middle of Whitehall don't be too surprised. And would you believe it there are still folks in this country who say "Love the German people!" I shall hate the German people as long as I live.

News has just filtered through to our Office that Norway has made terms with Germany. The stupid idiots! They prefer to have their country occupied than fight for a few hours for if all indications are right Allied help is already on the way. My God, if England and France were as lily livered as some of the European nations Heaven knows what the World would come to. My hat is reverently off to the Poles and the Finns. They did make some sort of a fight for it. What *can* the Allies do when the Neutrals are acting like a Hutchful of Scared Rabbits—we're trying to rid Europe of Hitler and Europe is thwarting us at every turn. But you pick up your paper and read from some foreign correspondent that the Allies are blamed for this, and the Allies are blamed for that. They should have done so and so, and they shouldn't have done this, that and the other. It s a pity the nations who aren't up to their necks fighting this War, don't keep their criticism to themselves.

I hear President Roosevelt got up at three a.m. and went to Washington, and that he, and the American people are worrying over Iceland.[15] Goodness me, Helen, the whole of Europe may be massacred tomorrow and the Americans are worrying about Iceland! I think every American should say a little prayer of thanks to his maker for having been born three thousand miles away from Germany, and in a country that is not expected to continually make the World a fit place for heroes to live in.

My brother is giving us all fits at the moment. He boils with wrath every time Hitler commits yet another dirty deed and threatens to join up in the Infantry. He is in a "reserved occupation" now, being a Railway Clerk, and cannot join up without permission from the Railway Company. Of course if they raise the reserved age to 30—he'll come under the Conscription Bill. He's 29, and all his friends are in France or on Home Defence. Most of my boy friends are either in the Army or waiting their calling up papers. My mother is broken hearted at the thought of Jack going. He's always been her favourite, I think, being an only son, and having lost my father through the last War it's awful to think that the same thing may happen to Jack. I wish to goodness he'd try to get out of it but he's the wrong type. My father was exactly the same. He tried three Recruiting Offices in 1914 before they finally accepted him and then the Chief Clerk in his Office got him out because he was a valuable man, but he got in again, and went to France in '15. He died when I was a baby and I don't remember him at all, though Jack has some fleeting memories of him. We've only got one photograph of him and that's in Soldier's Uniform. He looks pretty nice. I think he and I might have got along very well together.

15. On July 7, 1941, the United States reached an agreement with Iceland to protect the island in exchange for being able to base naval and air forces there.

I'm still determined to try to come to America when this War's over. That friend of mine in N.Y. says that she's sure I could get a job as a Telephone Operator, where my "English accent" wouldn't be handicap, which is very, very generous, but not the sort of thing I'd like to do for long. My mother glares at me every time I mention it, and the people in the Office, and my friends, particularly the females are shocked to death when I say that I'd like to marry an American. The very thought of it makes them look at me as though I'm an alien already. Me—the most patriotic gal on the face of the Earth!! Anyway, I haven't got an overwhelming English accent—personally, I'd call it neutral. Though to be honest, I could never have the remotest possible chance of being mistaken for an American. A Yankee accent is one of the few dialects that defeat me absolutely. I can manage to utter a lot of your wisecracks but the tone in which I say 'em is about as American as Westminster Abbey. Also, I *cannot* chew gum, and therefore could not classify myself as an American if I lived there the rest of my life. I have heard it said that all good Americans chew gum. Me, I always want to swallow the stuff.

To get the lighter things, I'm going to the first night at the Old Vic next week to see Gielgud in "King Lear". He took over the part of Mac-Heath in "Beggars Opera" from Michael Redgrave last week, and he was awfully good. MacHeath is a singing role, and to do John justice, I never thought he could warble a note! I can tell, you—he really surprised me! "Gone with the Wind" is opening next week at three West End Cinemas but I don't think I'll bother to go yet. I see from a Film Mag sent me last week that there's a new film out with Wally Beery, John Howard and Dolores Del Rio called "Man from Dakota", about the Civil War, and they gave a very brief outline of the story. It seems vaguely familiar to me, and I'm wondering if it's adapted from a story in the Cosmopolitan Magazine called "Arouse and Beware".[16] I only read about two or three chapters because I picked up a couple of spare issues of "Cosmopolitan" in Woolworths of all places, but it was a darned good story. If you see any reviews of it, will you send 'em over to me. I'm sure it must be the same story.

16. *The Man from Dakota* (1940; U.S.) was also known as *Arouse and Beware* in Britain.

Saw "Mr Smith Goes to Washington" last week and thought it fine, though the Senate and Congress etc, baffled me a bit.[17] They had a preface to the film over here explaining to British audiences how the American Parliament worked. I think it must be somewhere on the lines of ours. We have a majority party and an Opposition. At the moment the National Party which are really Conservatives—though not the old blue-blooded Torys—are the Majority and the Socialists the Opposition. We also have Liberals, Independent Liberals, and even the Independence Labour Party which is another name for Communists, though they are so scarce you can hardly see 'em. Every town in Britain has a Member of Parliament, so you can imagine what a crowd there must be when Parliament sits in full. I think the British system of Government is the finest in the world, but of course, being so darned red, white and blue, I'm probably hopelessly prejudiced. All our Colonies have their own forms of Government—in fact they're entirely independent of us—though they are all loyal to the Crown. They realise that being part of an Empire is our strength, and as most of them are of British blood they feel a bit sentimental to the little country that is "the mother of Nations". I remember knowing a little American girl when I was younger and she used to tell me off very smartly because we were such a small spot on the map. "We're a Continent" she said, sticking her small nose very high in the air. I was too young to give her a suitable retort, but when I got older and red "Little Lord Fauntleroy" I kept thinking of how I could have replied "And we're an Empire" sticking my nose even higher. My wit wasn't as quick, or as scathing when I was very little. I was always a very patriotic child and nearly always the one called upon to stand up, complete with large hair ribbon, on Empire Day and recite to the assembled school of Infants, some true blue poem like "What can I do for you England, my England" or "This Royal Throne of Kings, etc, etc". Gosh! what a brat I must have been! I used to be picked out to draw on the Blackboard on Empire Day (Believe it or not, I used to be able to sketch at one time) and I always used to attempt a large figure of Britannia squatting peacefully on her shield and surrounded by several hideous looking Union Jacks in red, white

17. Starring Jean Arthur, James Stewart, and Claude Rains, *Mr. Smith Goes to Washington* (1939; U.S.) is a highly acclaimed drama and comedy about a naive man appointed to the U.S. Senate.

and blue chalks. Empire Day was some celebration then. Now having reached the dignified age of twenty and a couple of years, I'm not even asked to sing even one little piece.

FLASH—Have just seen the evening paper and learn that the Norwegians are still putting up a half hearted fight, and that we've sunk the Blucher and the Karlsruhe in a big Naval Battle. Also, and here's the sad part. The Huns have sunk our H.M.S. Hunter. Still, I suppose we can't get away with everything, always. I wonder how many boys went down with her!

I hope you're keeping well, and that we'll still be able to write each other regularly. Everything you write seems to get here quite O.K. as I told you in my last letter. This one isn't very interesting, but I'll try to be a bit more entertaining in the next. We all rather feel that we're living on the "Eat Drink and be Merry for tomorrow you get blown up" principle. So if you don't hear from me for a long time, you can start writing nasty epistles to Hitler and tell him what you think of him. And add a couple of paragraphs for me while you're at it.

Love,<br>Betty

c/o. G.W.R. Goods Depot<br>SOUTH LAMBETH. S.W.8<br>England.<br>May 8th, 1940.

Dear Helen,

Was so very pleased to hear from you again. Your letter reached me in three weeks which isn't so bad considering. Last week I had a letter sent Air Mail by a friend of mine in New Jersey (she often does that) and it cost her 3/6d. that's about 80 odd cents in your currency, to send and took 16 days to get here. Talk about swift, speedy, transit. I suppose the Clipper took about two days and the other fourteen was spent in the crawling across Europe! I've told her now not to waste money on Air mail, because although it guarantees safe delivery, it's not really very much quicker.

Am typing this at a furious speed while my Boss is at dinner. I have to be very careful, because he seems to have a personal grudge against me, and watches me like a member of the Gestapo. He glares at my boy friends when they come and talk to me and tells me off if I have private telephone calls. He watches the time I come in, the time I go home, and when I'm out of the Office for a few minutes he enquires where I've gone. He's such a positive swine that I swear if I ever get any money and leave this Railway I shall take hours to tell him what I think of him. I used to think there was only one person in the World I loathed beyond reason and that was Hitler. I have now bracketed this blighter with him. He's just about the only person bar Adolf, that I'd really like to murder! He only takes a quarter of an hour for his dinner and then comes back snooping around to see what I'm doing, and if he caught me writing to you, he'd make no end of trouble. The old pig!

We had a breath of good old Kansas in the Office this morning. There was a Case of something on hand without labels in one of the Warehouses, and I and my colleagues went up to inspect it. When we opened up the case, we found a Bottle of what we thought was "Egg Flip" a kind of Tonic Wine, but it had an American label on it saying the makers of "Furbo" of "Kansas", and saying the stuff was "Butter flavouring" for Cakes and things. We'd never heard of it before and the smell nearly knocked us back. Have you ever had anything like that? Everyone rushed around in circles and invited everyone else up to "taste the Yankee Butter. Just in from Kansas!" Have just stopped typing in order to put a match to the fire. It's a bit chilly this morning, though we actually had some sunny days last week. I'm going down to Monmouthshire for Whitsun so I hope the weather will be kind. I've bought myself a new pair of American style shoes (straight from Hollywood the Salesman told me. The whoppers they tell!!) They are very pretty, but not a bit serviceable, and have practically no toe, so, if the rain comes down in torrents, Heaven protect me! Mum says she's sure they don't have any rain in America otherwise they couldn't go out in shoes like that. Over here, you can practically wear your goloshes [*sic*] all through the summer and no-one will stare at you if you carried an Umbrella through the whole 365 days of the year. And if you go out in the middle of July without a Coat, it's quite probable that you'll freeze to death before you go home. I have been wearing short sleeves for the past two weeks, and although my arms have occasionally come out in goose-pimples, and my teeth have chattered gracefully more than once, I have endured all without complaint, and be darned if I'm going back in long sleeves. Let the British climate do what it may!

Everyone is on this morning about the Government Debate yester-day. Most all of us think that Chamberlain will be forced to resign. I am a great supporter of Chamberlain, because he has always been a peace-loving man. If Neville had had his way England wouldn't be involved in a War of any sort, and I'm with him all along the line.[18] Still now that we are in War, and into it right up to our necks, we must have a man who will pursue the rotten business right to the end. Hitler hates England because he knows that she stands as a sort of Silent Sentinel in Europe, and the only obstacle to his dreams of expansion. How any-one in the World could say that Britain is fighting a selfish War beats me. What in God's name *can* we gain by it? All this affair in Norway! After our men have stood without a trench to shelter them, under a rain of shell fire and bombs and endured untold hardships, we read the headlines of the New York papers "British run away from Norway". "Run away!" Could anything be more damned unfair, unjust, and all the rest of it. Is it any wonder that the British people get fed up with this American criticism. Honestly, Helen, we *don't* resent your not coming in. We haven't asked America to come in. But you can't blame us for taking a "They shout the loudest, who do the least" angle on the whole business. I know nothing of the last War, but my mother lived through it and my father died through it. The British *were* grateful for Ameri-can help, but what was so intolerable were the Americans (and there were plenty of them, Helen) who came over and sneered at our boys and told them "We've come over to win the War for you!". You were in it from 1917, and we had been fighting and struggling and dying since 1914. For every one man you lost, we must have lost more than 10. There's hardly a man or woman living in Britain today who didn't lose someone in the War. There'll be millions killed in the Mess and it's up to the Government to see that they're not slaughtered uselessly. What these American Newspapers fail to realise is that each British Tommy and French Poilu[19] is an individual. They way they talk about

18. Chamberlain and the Conservatives held a majority in the House of Commons of almost 120 seats. However, the government's inability to secure peace with Germany or carry out successful military operations in Norway led more people to understand just how unprepared the country was for war, and the evacuation of Dunkirk drastically reduced the government's credibility (Winston S. Churchill, *The Second World War, Volume II: Their Finest Hour* [Boston: Houghton Mifflin, 1949], 10).

19. Man of mettle.

them and the methods of Warfare they suggest completely disregard that fact. They say "Britain should take the risk and attack at such and such a place" but they can sit back comfortably in their Chairs with the knowledge that every American mother's son is quite snug and safe, and that while Britain is "taking the risk" thousands of British lives are going to be cheerfully thrown on the Ash-heap, just as though they're a herd of Cattle. I am *not* anti-American. I never was. It's the ambition of my life to visit America and my best friends are there. But I do say that if they want to stay out of this War, let them stay out of it, and for God's sake maintain a decent silence about what is or isn't being done. All this howling for blood—British and French blood—is getting on everyone's nerves. And if they stay out of the War—and no-one in England blames 'em for it, although they haven't much faith in their motives—they must stay out of the Peace too. The Americans had a lot to say in the last Peace, and it wasn't any too successful. This time there must be some terms in that Peace that will put the clamp on Germany for good and all. There can be no safety for Europe while Germany is allowed to exist as a Nation. We are sick and fed up with Germany. As a race they're aggressive and bullying, they have no decent law, no heart and no sense of justice. In short I hate the sight of 'em. They've been the sore place in Europe for centuries. I've always said I want to marry an American and live away from here, not because I don't love England, but because I don't see the sense of marrying and having children, when the only future I can offer them is a German Bayonet and six feet of earth on some darned foreign Battlefield. Because if we let Germany rise again, there'll be another War, and yet another, for generations to come. Give the Huns a leader and they'll trample on anything in their path. Every-one laughs at me over my ambition to marry an American. "Why an American" they ask? And I always tell them it's because the Americans can stay out of any War and still keep their prestige. And another important reason is that I think America would be a swell place to live in. To most of my acquaintances I'm known as pro-American and am ragged unmercifully because of it. it seems rather strange that you should think the other way around!

About those War Debts, it's just as well to say that we *did* go on paying you for a long time, even though we weren't paid a sou of what was owed us by the various Nations. Most of our gold is going to America now to pay for Aeroplanes, so you see Helen, the States aren't doing anything for the Allies without being paid for it. You know, if Germany had the money and the transport you'd be selling her Aircraft too. You'd have to, to keep your neutrality.

The whole trouble with the British through this and through any other War is that they re too darned soft-hearted for their own good. They abide by International laws when every one else is breaking 'em right and left. The smaller neutrals know this. They know that Britain is a marvellous Enemy compared to Germany, so they cringe and crawl at Hitler's throne and let him do just what he likes (Witness that dreadful Altmark incident!) We should tell the smaller neutrals just what we intend doing if they start any of the "helping Germany" tricks and start a bit of invading ourselves. Then we may get somewhere. And, b[r]inging up painful subjects again. Do you know that America has been smashing the British blockade to smithereens so now where are we?

Anyway, it's all just a dreadful jumble to me. I rely on the old British saying "Thank God, we've got a Navy!" And what a Navy! There's no braver man in the World than the British sailor; They've got a tradition and by Heaven they live up to it! The Battles in Narvik and around the Coast have proved that whatever else has changed in the World the Boys of the Bulldog breed are still the same. I suppose you'll think I'm just a Flag-waver. I'm not really. Britain's got her faults, but Cowardice certainly isn't one of 'em. We may lose this War, and there s just a possibility that Adolf will have a smack at invading England, but we'll come with our heads "bloody but unbowed". The old Twirp's got a tough task when he starts subduing the British. Me, I've made up my mind to spit in his eye!

I don't mind *you* criticizing us Honey! God knows you have enough to put up with from me. I honestly don't know why you keep on being so nice to me? When I think of how much I talk and how marvellous you are to me, I get thoroughly ashamed of myself. I really think someone should come and sock me in the Jaw. Still, I hope you know how sincerely I appreciate everything you do, and I only wish there was something I could do for you in return. My goodness! *how* I wish I could come to America! I know two fellows who have been to America, (they work in the Office) and we all sit down forlornly when we feel at our worst and talk about what we'd do if we had enoough money to start at New York and travel right over every state. Nick would settle down in Phoenix N.J. where he has a girl friend, and me I'd go straight to California. You can tell your pal from Chicago that I am lost in envy. Fancy going to live in California for a whole year! I have a friend in N.J. (the one I mentioned the beginning of this letter) and one of her boy friends who has something to do with the New Jersey Board of Education is quite certain after seeing my Photograph that I am his "dream girl"! My goodness, I wish he lived in California! I might be tempted to do something about it!

Thanks so much for those movie clippings and everything you sent me. After reading the article by young Mr Howard on "The Girl I'd Marry" I've decided that I'm absolutely cut out for the job, if I sort of took myself in hand. I really think you ought to do a pal a favour Helen, and write and tell him to cease his search, because you know someone who'd suit him exactly, except that she's some six thousand and a couple more miles away. Alas and Lackaday, the Fates are definitely agin' me. I'm afraid I shall definitely have to stow away in an Oil Tanker!

I haven't received "Picture Play" yet, but it's grand of you to send for it for me. And I've nearly fallen over myself with excitement over those stockings. You see the blinking old Government is going to ration us shortly on Silk stockings—sort of cut down the Shop's supplies—and it'll be lovely to get a pair all the way from America. I don't think the duty will be too much, but whatever it is, I'll pay it. I'm like you, I have a long foot and I take a "10". Also I have a long leg and if I get the larger size they're longer. If you do send them, perhaps you'd better send them to my house—that's No. 43, The Grove, Hammersmith, London. W.S. because then Mother'll be able to pay the duty if I'm not in. Go on addressing your letters and Clippings to the Office though. It's really much safer. We've moved about so much lately, I'm absolutely sick of it. Mum is waiting to be called for a job on the Red Cross Civil Nursing Reserve but Employment for women isn't so plentiful. And prices are going higher and higher so you have to make the money last so much more. Due to the hard winter and the War we've been eating the weirdest things for Greenstuffs. Turnip tops and Parsnip tops and God knows what. Last week Mum paid 6d. a pound (10 cents to you) for a funny looking plant that looks like half a flower, half herb, smelt like a weed and tasted like nothing on earth. Even the Greengrocer didn't know what it was. The Butter ration will probably be chopped again shortly also the Sugar ration, though the latter doesn't worry me at all, not half as much as my precious Film Books.

They're trying to get "G.W.T.W." banned here, because it's so dear. I do think Selznick could act like a gentleman over it. After all he's already made enormous profits in the States and theres no question of not getting his money back. It's had rave reviews over here and everyone wants to see it. That film "Man from Dakota" definitely seems to be connected with the story I read only it was called "Arouse and Beware" and it was in the Saturday Evening Post not the Cosmopolitan! Author is a bloke called Cantor. No relation to Eddie I should imagine!

Saw a fine British film last night called "For Freedom" All about the Battle of the River Plate, and the beyootiful end of the brave "Graf Spee" also the Altmark Rescue. You know when they yelled out "Any English" down there" and when the answer came Yes! out went the shout "Well! the Navy's here". Whoopee! You haven't seen it I s'pose? Also, did you ever get to see "The Lion has Wings". Ralph Richardson was in it. he's in the Fleet Air Arm now, and David Niven is in an Infantry Regiment. Poor devil![20]

I hope you had a grand time in Chicago. You lucky thing! Is it really the wild kind of City we always believed it to be? One of the girls in my Mother's shop went to live in Cleveland, Ohio, and married a boy from there, and she says that's a beautiful City. I wish I had some relations in America, but I don't even possess a thirty-second cousin twice removed who lives out of England. Although my mother's people used to be very proud of the fact that a man named "Pendleton"—that's Mum's maiden name—went over to America on the "Mayflower". He did, honestly. and he's supposed to be a relative of ours. Gosh! I wish we could find out what happened to him!!

I'll close now and give you a well-earned rest. You're probably tired of reading all this bilge. Once again, thanks for everything and do let me hear from you soon. Give my regards to your friends who enquire

---

20. *For Freedom* (1940; UK), about the sinking of the *Graf Spee*, depicts events leading up to the war, Chamberlain's efforts to avoid conflict, and the sinking of British ocean liners but is not a heavy-handed propaganda film. *The Lion Has Wings* (1940; UK), starring Merle Oberon and Ralph Richardson, celebrates the British Air Force at the beginning of World War II. Completed soon after the outbreak of the war, it was credited with proving the morale-building and propaganda value of movies to the war effort, allowing the British film industry to remain active. In World War I the cinemas had not been kept open.

after me, and tell them that I am still going out without my Gas Mask, in strict defiance of Government orders!

Love,
Betty

c/o. G.W.R.
SOUTH LAMBETH. S.W.8
[May 30, 1940]

Dear Helen,

Received your Card from Chicago yesterday. Do hope you had a wonderful time and didn't mind coming back too much. Also that you liked Olivier and Leigh, also that when you write your friend who has gone to live in California tell her that I am pink, green and yellow with envy. You just *wait* until I win my Crossword puzzle!

Have decided not to be too gloomy, although things look about as black as Ink and there doesn't seem to be much civilization left. I heard about the invasion of Holland and Belgium on our 7 oclock news, and from then on we've been calmly waiting for the worst. Actually his occupation of Holland has brought him very near his goal,—which is, I believe, Air bombardment of Britain and the killing off of as many Britishers as he can—and the surrender of the Dutch Army came as a nasty shock, but it makes me rather proud to feel that while the Germans have been walking in everywhere, and killing and butchering all nations and peoples, it took the boys of the B.E.F. to hurl them back in Belgium. I don't think the Belgians will give in as easily because Allied aid can be more effective in that country, and the R.A.F. are there, as always, to batter down the Huns as much as possible. They've got to the stage now where they hate the Germans with a kind of poisonous venom and they'll do anything and everything they can to them. And that's the way it should be! There never will be any feelings of goodwill and friendship towards Germany in this country ever again. We've had enough! All this silly business about our quarrel not being with the German people has gone down the Drain, where it should be. My brother went to try to join the Parashooters, which is our new Defence Corps to stop a Parachute invasion, and he said there were hundreds of men of all ages, ready to risk their lives to shoot German people. All they intend to do is shoot without mercy, which is the only way. They are going to train men on most of our big stations now, to use their Guns, and if any of Hitler's little Germans try anything in England they'll get a nice, warm welcome. His Air War, of course, is unavoidable, but as I've said before the British people never panic. We know it will come and we're prepared for it. And for the first bomb that falls on London the RAF have sworn to drop two on Berlin. If one Britisher has to die, it seems almost a comforting thought that two Germans will pass out at the same time. I am now taking my Gas Mask with me like a good girl, because it'll be my own darned fault if we have a Gas raid and I'm without it. Some 5000 Americans left England to-day on the advice of the American Embassy and I understand they're leaving Italy in droves. There's nothing like a War scare to drive 'em all back home!

All our Whitsun holidays were cancelled, so I didn't get down to Monmouthshire after all. It was awful! I'd got myself nice, new clothes, and I'd been looking forward to a few days off for ages, and then the King signed a Royal Proclamation washing out the Whitsun holiday, and did we curse! Being Government workers of course, we had to come to work, while most of the private firms and Shops gave their employees the time off, as arranged. That's what you get for working for the Government. Still it roused the population a bit, because Britain has, as usual, been very complacent about the whole affair, and calmly gone on thinking "We've always won every War in our history so why should we worry?". Now they realise that every effort counts, and they're prepared to go on making more and more sacrifices for the Victory which we must get. Because if the Allies don't win this War then every hope for a decent, and honest civilization in the World has gone. I know this that before Germany conquers England she'll have to kill every man, woman and child in it. We're the free-est nation of peoples on God's earth, and our country has been ours from way back in the mists of time. The thought of it belonging to anyone else is unthinkable— particularly to the Huns whom we hate so much! I am sending you some of the pictures from our papers of the poor refugees in Belgium trying to escape. They make me shudder to look at them. The German Air Force machine-gun them as they are going down the Roads. Women and babies and even Cattle. It's all the same to them. God! what a nation. 100,000 killed in the Air Raids on Rotterdam—and that's what he's aiming to do to the towns of Britain. Churchill spoke last night on the Radio and said that in a few days we can expect an attack on this Island. I suppose that means bombing, bombing and more bombing, and then an attempted invasion by Parachute troops. I'm only scared they'll smash up some of our lovely Buildings, like the Abbey and St. Pauls. Although dear Adolf hopes to be crowned King of Britain in Westminster Abbey. Yeah? over everybody's dead body he will! It's obvious from what Churchill said that everyone of us will be called in to fight, girls and all, if there s an attempt on Britain. So wish me luck, I shall die happy! Anyway, I'm warning everyone around me that if the Fritzes do get here, I am hopping it to your country, and quick! The desire of my young life is *still* to see California and I'll get to Los Angeles or bust! I'll probably bust! We heard Roosevelt speaking from Washington last week. Heard him quite clearly, too, except for a couple of crackles. We generally have an American Commentary from New York on Saturdays by a guy called Raymond Gram Swing, but this week for some mysterious reason they cut him out. I believe someone was giving a lecture on Air Raid precautions or something. We haven't even got an Air Raid Shelter in our garden, so I'll have to go down somebody's Basement. We're getting all the sleep we can now, because we'll probably be up half the night before long. If you don't hear from me for more than six weeks, honey, you'd better start addressing a protest to the German Government! My poor mother is worried to death because my brother will be called up shortly. He's made a vow with himself. I hate to even hear him mention it. He says England's his country, and if England is worth living in it's worth dying for! I don't know what to think. Our men have died for England for centuries, but I hate the thought of anyone belonging to me getting slaughtered. My poor father had to go and die because he thought he was saving his son from the Huns, and now, here we go again! I'm getting now I hate to read the papers of a morning, and listening to the Early News Bulletin is like slapping yourself in the face! Before the News we used to get a programme of Bing Crosby records just to cheer us up but now they've decided that Bing's a bit too frivolous, and they've inserted a nice, religious talk called "Thought for to-day. Lift up your Hearts" wherein the preacher proceeds to tell you to "Prepare to Meet your God!" or something equally bright and sunny. Still, we have the "Keep fit" exercises at 7 am. You know, "bend, stretch, and bend again" to keep my waistline! With my mother yelling from the Bedroom, "Turn that damned Wireless down, you'll wake the so and so House!" the funny thing is that after we've all gone to work the programmes become too light and airy for words, presumably because we can't listen to 'em.

Now I must tell you something funny. You'll probably think it's about time after the two preceding pages of gloom—you know that "Picture Play" you sent for. Well! what do you think? The Circulation Department skipped 10 years and sent me the February, *1926* number. Blimey, I was hardly out of petticoats, then. So, I made up my stubborn mind that you'd been put to enough trouble already so I sent it back to the "Picture Play" and told them that they'd made a little error of 10 years, and asked them to send the correct one. I am now crossing my fingers and hoping. Some of the Stars in the Book were a little weird to say the least of it. But it was ever so interesting to read and see how the Industry has progressed.

*5.0 pm.*

We've just been having a wow of a time for the past hour. Have all decided, with brilliant forethought, to learn German and can now count up to ten and also get as far as Wednesday in the days of the week. We have been simply choking ourselves with laughter at some of the weird sentences we've been producing!! We now have a smashing vocabulary consisting of "Nein. Ya. Mein Kampf. Lebensraum. Ersatz. Blitzkrieg. Wilhelmstrasse. Fuhrer. Verboten. Sauerkraut. Berchtesgarten" and a perfectly marvellous phrase given to me by an Austrian servant gal "Schmutzigg ald Swinehund" which she assures me means "Dirty old dog". And who am I to contradict her? I can also spit out "Achtung" and "Got in Himmel" with a gloriously guttural accent. However, if a German asks me to do something I don't want to I shall tell him in plain American "Go, fly a Kite!" Hitler doesn't like the Americans, I hear. But comfort yourself, honey, the old Twirp don't like us either. They do say though that the Hun boys like Blondes. In that case, yours truly is going to follow the fashion and dye herself brunette!

My boss and another girl are just discussing the marvellous holiday they had in Germany last year. He spent four days at Berchtesgarten, and he didn't even chuck a stone at Adolf's window! There's a patriot for you.

Have not seen many good shows lately. "Rebecca" that you liked so much is coming to the Odeon in town next week. That was the play that Gielgud was gong to appear in but he decided to go to the Old Vic instead and Owen Nares is playing Max de Winter, and making a passable job of it.[21] "I haven't seen "Gone with the Wind" yet and still can't make myself pay the money for it. All my boy friends are in the Army and most leave has been stopped and its orful for a gal to have to pay all that dough herself. My girl friend saw it last week and she said it was wonderful—in fact everyone is raving about it who has seen it. I saw "Of Mice and Men" last week, also "The Roaring Twenties" which was a bit too American for British consumption, and another thing called "Brother Rat and a Baby" which didn't even raise a laugh. Durbin is on in "It's a Date" and "The Shop Around the Corner" is due next week.[22] The film "The Man from Dakota" is, as I prophesied "Arouse and Beware" and they're showing it here under that title. I saw a couple of revivals last week. A flick called "The Bowery" with Beery and George Raft, (How I *detest* that sleek, slimy, second Valentino!) and two films of John Howard's. "Grand Jury Secrets" which was all about "Ham" short wave Radio fanatics, and a gruesome affair called "Penitentiary" which I'd seen before and in which I think Walter Connolly over-acted worse than anyone I've ever seen, and Jean Parker was so cloyingly sweet she made me want to tear my hair.[23] She's another of my pet abominations. The others are George Brent, John Boles, Henry Fonda, Claudette Colbert,[24] Dorothy Lamour, and that Ersatz He-man, Clark Gable.— he of the protruding Ears—also, as an afterthought, his daffy Mrs. The

21. *Rebecca* (1940; U.S.) stars Laurence Olivier, Joan Fontaine, and Judith Anderson. The thriller, directed by Alfred Hitchcock, is set in an English mansion haunted by a widower's first wife. Owen Nares (d. 1943), active from 1914 to 1940, was not in the film version.

22. Based on John Steinbeck's novel, *Of Mice and Men* (1939; U.S.) stars Burgess Meredith and Lon Chaney Jr. *The Roaring Twenties* (1939; U.S.), a gangster film, stars James Cagney and Humphrey Bogart. The comedy *Brother Rat and a Baby* (1940; U.S.) stars Priscilla Lane, Wayne Morris, and Eddie Albert, with Jane Wyman and Ronald Reagan (who was credited with giving the best performance). The comedy/romance *It's a Date* (1940; U.S.) also stars Walter Pidgeon, and the romance *The Shop around the Corner* (1940; U.S.) stars James Stewart.

23. *The Bowery* (1933; U.S.) stars Wallace Beery, George Raft, Jackie Cooper, and Fay Wray. *Grand Jury Secrets* (1939; U.S.). *Penitentiary* (1938; U.S.).

24. Colbert became one of the biggest stars as a result of *It Happened One Night* with Clark Gable.

Luscious Lombard.[25] However, next to Hitler, Goering Goebbels, Von Ribbentrop and my Boss, I think it would be George Raft[26] that I'd like to wipe off the face of the Earth!

I didn't intend to gabble on so much, but I seem to forget all about it. I hope to hear from you very soon. If Italy comes into the War I suppose our mail will have to come via Portugal. I'd wish Roosevelt hadn't banned American ships from British waters. The letters would come so much quicker if they could come via Plymouth or Southampton, instead of travelling across Europe. Still, it maybe by the time you next write there won't be any Europe for it to come across. What a comforting thought!

Bye for now, Helen and don't forget to write to your friend in California and tell her that I think she's the luckiest dame ever! And tell me, if I ever get to Kansas, am I very *far* away from the Wild West? I seem to think that you can hop a train at New York and get to San Francisco a few hours later. I need educating!

Love,
Betty

Have just read the latest outburst of your Colonel Lindbergh. We'll never forgive that man for accepting our hospitality then stabbing us in the back. If he ever comes to England again he'll be lynched!!! Hes an ardent Fascist, isn't he?

25. Carole Lombard, a comedic star and the wife of Clark Gable, was the highest-paid star in the movies during the 1930s.

26. U.S. actor known for playing gangster roles who was reputedly a gangster himself.

# III

## "France Has Surrendered and We Are All on Our Ownsomes"

On June 10, 1940, Italy entered the war on the side of Germany. France surrendered, and Philippe Pétain, hero of the battle of Verdun in World War I, headed the French government located at Vichy in unoccupied France. Paris and the French Atlantic ports were incorporated into the Third Reich. The United States provided war matériel to Britain under the "Lend-Lease Agreement" with British ships transporting the goods.

Butter, sugar, meat began to be rationed. The "blackout" began as well, as citizens were required to carry and use gas masks. William Joyce, "Lord Haw-Haw," in his broadcasts from Germany sought to sow defeatism among the British people.

In August the bombing of London began again. In exchange for forty "over-aged" destroyers, the United States gained the use of British naval bases in the Atlantic area. Starting in September 1940 the air raids on London increased to at least five each night. The noise and the destruction prevented restorative sleep, and Betty's health deteriorated.

Wendell Willkie, FDR's Republican opponent in the 1940 election, visited England to see firsthand the effects of the bombing and the British response. "Give us the tools and we will finish the job," Churchill broadcast.

c/o. G.W.R. South Lambeth.
LONDON. S.W.8. England.
[June 19, 1940]

Dear Helen,

Have to take a chance on your getting this at all. As you know Italy declared War yesterday[1] and that means that your Liners won't be calling on Mussolini no mo', so God knows how the mail will travel. A friend of mine in New Jersey informed me that her last letter came by British Liner, though I didn't know that any one of them were crossing the Atlantic with anything. Also if this does go by a British Liner the odds are that the Italians or the Huns will sink the damn thing and bang goes my letter to a watery grave. Only ray of hope is that Portugal, God bless her, is still neutral and maybe the Yankee Liners will be allowed to call there, I hope so! Your "refugee" ships are coming to Eire, but they don't carry any mail.

I was saying yesterday that I wish to goodness I had a very young baby and then the Government might evacuate me to Canada![2] Only difficulty being of a course, that at the moment I am not in a position to acquire a very young baby, not being that sort of a girl, so it seems I shall have to stay here and be blown to bits, or alternatively pinch somebody else's baby. I certainly don't feel like taking the plunge into a War marriage, and the responsibilities appertaining thereto. When I marry, I want a husband with his life in front of him, and if I have any children ever, I want them to have some sort of a future to look forward to. No kid of mine is going to grow up to fight the Germans. I'd rather not have any at all. I'm not what you could call a "baby-lover", in

1. On June 10, 1940, Roosevelt said in his radio broadcast that "the hand that held the dagger has stuck it into the back of its neighbor."
2. By July 14, 1940, the Children's Overseas Reception Board listed more than 200,000 offers from Canadians and Americans to take British children. By September, the Board had sent about 2,600 children to Canada. More than 5,000 children settled in the United States, most under private arrangements (Calder, *People's War*, 129).

any case, though like everyone else I'd probably be mad about my own. My mother gets perturbed because she is not yet a grandmother—my brother having been married five years—and me, as usual, undecided about the whole thing. My mothers younger sister has been a grandmother these seven years. She was one of the youngest grandmothers in the town I think. She's about forty-five'ish now. Mum is forty-eight. She used to look years younger than that but this War is getting her down to such an extent that she's getting a fine crop of grey hairs and wrinkles. My brother will be called up in August, and neither she nor I can bear to think about it. Whatever we'll do if anything happens to him, I don't know. Particularly my mother. He's absolutely the eyes of her head, and he's been idolised and spoiled all his life. Mum swears that she'll go crazy if he gets killed, and I'm nearly going crazy worrying about her, and him. I've got boy friends in the Army, and I should hate anything to go wrong with any of them, but it would just about knock the stuffing out of me if anything happened to Jack. We've quarrelled and scrapped from the time we were kids, but we've always thought the world of each other, and anyway, we're all that Mum's got. Jack remembers my father coming home on leave in the last War—I was a mere babe of course, so he's not even a memory to me, and poor Daddy's main hope was that he was going to save Jack from all of it. My fathers brothers didn't go and fight—they stayed home and prospered, and now their kids are going to be able to do the same thing, because they're all older than us, and in "reserved" occupations. Whatever bad luck there's been has always descended on poor Mum's head, and it looks to me as though we're going to go through it all over again. I may sound pessimistic, but I'm quite certain in my mind about it. Even Jack's got some idea that he won't come back. He's always saying it, and joking about it. He's been made to join the Army and seems quite philosophical about it, now that his time is coming, while my mother's gone completely to pieces and I'm so scared I don't know what to say next. All I wish is that I could pack up my family and take them to an Island about 10,000 miles away, where no-one could touch us, and we could all be together. Heaven only knows that's not much to ask of life, but it doesn't seem that we're going to get it. I keep telling Mum that I wish we could have all emigrated to America or something years and years ago—although if I know Jack the silly blighter would have come back and fought anyway. He's full of this "doing his bit for England" complex, I suppose I wouldn't have him otherwise being such a patriotic Briton myself, but I'd rather he could live for England than die for it!

We had bad news yesterday, the little girl who used to live with us and was married last October, has just lost her husband. He was a fine boy, only 22, and had everything to live for. He was in one of the Regiments wiped out in the Defence of Calais—you know the boys that were ordered by the Germans to surrender, and refused and fought on until they were all wiped out. Four thousand went into Calais and thirty came out, and our poor Leslie wasn't in the thirty. His pal who went with him has gone too, and he's only been married a month or two. We lost thirty thousand in Belgium and would have lost many, many more unless the Navy, Army and Air Force had all rallied round and evacuated our poor Tommies from Dunkirk.[3] I saw some of them after they arrived home, dirty, tired without hardly a sole to their feet and still trying to smile and look cheerful. Some of the sights they've seen must haunt them at nights I should think. The Huns have been machine-gunning women and babies, and running tanks over the children. They had to wait on the Beaches at Dunkirk in the middle of a hail of bombs and shells and Bullets and they did it without turning a hair. They came home in Paddle Steamers, destroyers, fishing smacks—anything and everything available, and they brought with them Dogs, and Cats saved from the wreckage of the homes. What fools Englishmen are over animals! (I'm a good example—I cry for weeks over stories of dying Dogs and tortured cats) The irony of it is that all the poor animals had to be shot because of the Quarantine regulations.

Our office boy lost his father when the ship he was sailing in from Dunkirk was bombed by an incendiary bomb, caught fire and sank in ten minutes. Jim's Dad was burned nearly to a Cinder. They were volunteering to get the boys out in anything that would float. I've seen pictures of the evacuation of Dunkirk on the Newsreels and I'm not emotional, but when I watched it I howled like a baby! I can't bear to watch the pictures of those poor kids—the flower of British youth—going to their deaths without a tremor. And I always feel if anyone ever

3. It seemed after Belgian defenses collapsed that only about one-fifth of the 250,000 British troops could escape, but German armor, under Hitler's orders, halted on May 24 and did not start to roll until May 27. Belgium surrendered on May 27—the same day evacuation began. By June 4 when the rear guard was withdrawn 338,236 had been evacuated; 225,000 were British (ibid., 124–27).

says the British Tommies aren't the bravest and toughest race imaginable, they must be crazy.

Four of my brothers pals—boys I grew up with and have known
all my life—are missing. They were fine people, and I can't believe it
yet. Our nice, quiet World that we grew up in seems to be slipping
from under our feet and the Lord only knows what's in store for us
now that Italy has come in. Their chief aim seems to be to bring Britain to her knees. Why, in heaven's name? What has poor Britain ever
done that she should be the subject of hatred and envy, and the rest
of it. We've always tried to be a decent influence in the World and
we've poured our men into Battle to fight for freedom from way back
in the mists of time. The average Britisher is a quiet, conscientious
chap who loves his home, and his kids and his garden and his country.
He's not a bit aggressive or dominating and he's only ever asked to live
at peace with everyone, and yet we always seem to be thrust into War,
just when we're picking up the threads of progress again. After this
War, where will we be financially? You know Helen, that we're paying
the United States enormous sums of gold for every Plane that we get.
You should be the wealthiest country in the World shortly, if this "Cash
and Carry" lasts much longer. With all the money that you're getting
selling War Supplies, what the heck are we going to use when all this
is over. That's the one grumble I've got about the American idea. Your
papers say you are helping the Allies. Most every Britisher is asking
one question—*how* is America helping the Allies? You're only in the
position of Shopkeeper—you give us nothing that we don't pay for,
and even the Guns and Bullets of the last War had to be settled for in
good, hard, Cash. So where does the help come in? Even if you offered
us your Air Force, that would mean another sizeable lump of Gold—in
fact, I doubt whether we'll be able to afford to keep paying you like we
are, and you know that under your present law, if Hitler and Musso
turned up with their Cash, you'd have to sell your Planes to them too.
And probably would. You know, Helen, I don't mean anything personal.
You're a grand person to me, and always have been, and as individuals
I sing the American's praises all over the place—but I still don't understand what exactly you're doing to help us so much. I stayed up last
night till half past midnight to listen to Roosevelt's speech. He says the
Americans are disgusted with Italy, and the Americans sympathise with
the Allies and so on and so forth. Disgust and sympathy are all very

well, but they're not very helpful. The resources of the United States, as far as Machines are concerned, are to be made available to us—But all at a price! £80,000 for one Bomber, Helen. Just think what poor Britain and France are forking out for the dozens they buy, at 400,000 dollars a throw. That's why the majority of the British think of Uncle Sam as Uncle Shylock. Not one Britisher in ten thinks that American will come into this War. They're absolutely under no false illusions whatever. And as for dragging America into the War, we haven't even sent Propaganda to the States like the Germans have, we've always referred to you in the most glowing terms in all our Newspapers, though to be quite frank Helen the 'man-in-the-street' still thinks that America will continue to sit on the fence, and make money out of this War, despite the fact that it's as much her Battle as ours. I've got a bet with a young man in the Office (off to join H.M. Navy in a week or so). He says America *will* enter the War, I've bet him two shillings that they *won't*. He thinks I'm crazy and I think he's nuts. But we're still the best of pals. He's one of the boys that rushes in every morning and says "have you had your American mail?"

Feel very tired to-day, as I didn't have much sleep last night. What with waiting up to hear Franklyn D. and then my mother waking me up in the early morning, 4 a.m. to be exact, swearing she heard an Air Raid siren, I don't feel so good. The Planes flying over the House are very nerve-wracking, and we live close to a Railway and the screech of the trains is pretty deceptive. We haven't got an Air Raid Shelter, which makes me a bit nervous, especially now when the Italians are threatening to turn London into a shambles, but I suppose Kismet is Kismet, and if I'm picked out to be one of the thousands of poor civilians who're going to die, there's nothing much I can do about it. I hope they don't used these damned blister Gases.[4] They're horrible, particularly the Mustard Gas variety. Burns through your clothes and your skin. Oh. blimey, what a life!

I'm off to see "Cavalcade" again to-night. Feel like a darned good cry, and every time I think of Diana Wynyard's toast "Let's Drink to the

---

4. The poison gases that so many feared were never used in the Blitz. The government, however, took elaborate precautions in the event they were used, including issuing millions of gas masks.

England we love, etc" I feel like bawling, so maybe the floodgates will really break loose when I see it again.[5] What they want to revive it for is beyond me. The Great War for Civilisation isn't going to be a patch on this Mess-up. I'm going to see that Wally Beery film "Arouse and Beware" on Sunday—that's all about the Civil War, and we've really had enough blood and thunder, but me, I still like John Howard so I shall have to go and see it. I saw Gielgud in "The Tempest" last week and he's still very wonderful. Wonder how long it will be before he gets called up into the European Stew-pot? You'll probably notice I don't talk so much about the Theatre lately. That s because there really isn't much doing in the British Theatre now, and I don't go hardly at all. At one time the thought of giving up the Theatre would have killed me, but now, apart from seeing John, of course (I'm like Mrs. Micawber, I shall never, never desert Mr Gielgud) I don't go to the Theatre, but stick obstinately to the Cinema. I am now probably the worst "movie" fan in the Kingdom. Most of us in our Office are. My colleague has a large photo of David Niven gazing steadily at her from above her Typewriter (poor guy, he *was* somewhere in Norway, but Heaven knows where he is now) and I have John Gielgud hanging to my Paper Shelf, and a large picture of the aforementioned Mr. Howard in a very affectionate attitude with Dolores Del Rio. The lads here call it "Betty's inspiration"! My little typist told me last week that she's going to get out her Yacht and take me to California one day, so you can't say that she hasn't got the kindest thoughts!

I'd better close now, as it s getting late, and you're probably sick of this gloomy epistle anyway. I'll be ever so much more cheerful next time, that is of course, providing I'm alive at all. Gosh! there I go again!

Write to me soon, because my famous "American mail" is the one thing I really look forward to.

Love,

*June 19th.*

Have been a week posting this letter and now look what's happened! France has surrendered and we're all on our ownsomes, and Heaven

5. *Cavalcade* (1933; UK), based on a Noël Coward play about English life from 1899 to 1933, stars Diana Wynyard, a leading lady on British stage and in British and American films from the 1930s to the 1960s.

help us! We can now look forward to some mass bombings and a nice, little invasion in a week or so, or maybe even a day or so. Don't know if you've heard Churchill's speech at all, they've mostly been broadcast to the States. The one he made last night told us what was what in plain terms without trimmings. In fact, we're up against it, in a big way. This, I suppose, is where we all come in and fight for poor old Mother England. Well! I never thought I'd live to see the day when Germany would whack the hide off France, but seems like they've done, just that, though they've used the most appalling methods ever known to mankind to do it. They've killed women and children by the hundred and Hospital Ships mean precisely nothing to them. We've all received our order in case of invasion and we've been told that we must not move under any circumstances, as refugees along the roads hamper the movements of the Soldiers and are a target for Nazi Airmen. We had a raid on our East Coast last night, and 11 people were killed when a row of Houses was bombed. I expect we'll be getting it hot and strong in London, a City which he threatens to completely devastate. Adolf's aim is to kill as many British women and children as he can, "then" sez he, "the accursed British race will die out". "There is only one thing we want to do to the English" sez this little bundle of sunshine, "and that is destroy them. Destroy them by any means and any methods". Oh! boy, how that man does love us. Well! the thought of dying makes me shudder, and I suppose we're all nearer to it than we have ever been in our lives, but there's one consolation. If Britain survives this, she will be even greater than she was before. We may go down in history as the Saviours of mankind, but after this, please God! no more military alliances! No more rushing to help other nations. Just you look at how the other nations rushed to help us!! We're going to have to try the Isolation principle, for ourselves and our Empire, and to hell with prestige and criticism.

I received the 1936 "Picture Play" last week. It was the one I wanted, and thank you Helen, very much. Also thank you for the clippings. I love receiving them. I do hope that they won't blockade my American mail, because it's all I have to look forward to. A friend of mine in New Jersey, (I've told you about her before) wrote to me Air Mail last week. She has a man friend who is a Politician (A Republican whatever that is) He is very rich and has taken some sort of a fancy to me. He wants to pay for me to come over to the States and keeps asking Grace to send me the money. She won't accept it, and rightly too. She now says that if I can get over she's going to fix things herself. So although things look pretty hopeless for ever getting out of the country now, maybe if the War doesn't last more than a couple of years I will be coming over, and then by hook or by crook I shall come down and see you if I have to walk, or do what you Yankees call "hitch-hike". If miracles do happen and I do come over, I should be staying in the East. I can live with Gwen in New York, or Grace in New Jersey. Grace rather wants to marry me off, I think, to one or the other of several eligible Americans, all of whom seem to have a fancy for English wives, but that would take me months to consider. I'm not a bit struck on getting married for years yet, and if I did marry an American I should lose my British nationality, and that s a big step to take. Also I'd have to leave me mother, whereas if I come over and get a job, and be completely independent, I might be able to have her over. That is, if she'd come, of course. I'm always telling her that one day, I shall land in California if it's the last thing I do. Anyway, it's useless to do any planning at all now, because I can't leave the county, and God knows, we may all be dead before we can go anywhere!! Aren't I a nice, cheerful little so and so?

I hope you don't read this letter to any of your friends. Sounds awful to me. Keep on writing me, because even if the darned Huns starve us into submission (quoting A. Hitler Esq) they aren't going to interfere with my American mail if I can help it!

Love,
Betty

c/o. G.W.R. SOUTH LAMBETH.
S.W.8
England.
July 10th. 1940.

Dear Helen,

Was so glad to hear from you. Your letter and the Stockings arrived this morning, having been something like a month and two days en route. My goodness, how I sigh for the days when the old "Queen Mary" used to chug to and fro and bring me my American letters in a week! Nowadays I suppose we should consider ourselves lucky to get anything at all, and I have yet to find out how they *do* arrive here—whether it s by British or American Boat. Your letters arrived two days after the latest American "refugee" steamer arrived in Galway, so maybe they came over on that. Anyway, whichever way they came thank you so much for the stockings. They're lovely, and have caused quite a minor sensation here. Anything new in the wearing apparel line will cause a flutter among the female staff, especially now we are being told to wear our clothes till they drop off us, and with the prospect of stockings being rationed. The Paper this morning says that anything and everything will be taxed shortly, including cosmetics and all that we wear, eat, look at, smell and touch. Blimey! talk about Merrie England!

Well! since I last wrote you all sorts of things have happened. France has gone Fascist and we are left, as usual, to carry on the Battle for the smaller nations on our own.[6] Where are all our bright and beautiful allies, now? Talk about Gone with the Wind! The surrender of France, though it came as a body blow, was not entirely unexpected. I believe most of us knew all along, that the final battles would be fought on the soil of Britain, though the feeling of venom towards the Petain Government can never be described. They have given into the hands of Germany the deadliest weapons of Warfare to be used against us, their Air Force, their Factories, everything. Last week we had to step in and take part of the French Fleet, and it was a very unpleasant thing to have to do.[7] Everyone hated it, most of all the British sailors who had such a short while before been fighting by the side of the French "matelots", but it had to be done, and done it was. The French Fleet in German or Italian hands would have been terrible for England, and we must think of ourselves now, for a change. We have done too much fighting and dying for others. In all our long history we have been involved in War after War because of those two devils—British principles and British

6. On June 16, Paul Reynaud, the French premier, resigned and was succeeded by Philippe Pétain. On June 22, an armistice was signed. The new government established itself at Vichy in central France (Calder, *People's War,* 128).

7. Article 8 of the armistice agreement explicitly stated that the German government had no intention of using the French fleet in the war. But Churchill did not believe those assurances and ordered units of the fleet to be rendered harmless. After the French refused to meet British demands to scuttle the fleet, on July 3 the British opened fire on the stationery French ships at Mers-el-Kébir near Oran in Algeria. Twelve hundred and ninety-two French officers and men were killed (Charles Williams, *Pétain: How the Hero of France Became a Convicted Traitor and Changed the Course of History* [London: Little, Brown, 2005]).

prestige. After this terrible business is over, and we win, please God
we will have no more military alliances with any nation, small or large.
Surely this must be the War to end Wars? It will have to be everyone's
task to rebuild our country and make her great again. Wherever I may
be, if I'm left alive, I shall always love my England and admire my
own Race, not because they are more superlative than any other, but
because they can keep their heads and remain calm even though their
very existence is threatened, and they stand to lose everything in their
lives that is dear to them and even life itself. I know no-one here who
is showing the slightest sign of panic—they lend their money to the
Nation to help pay for the War—they pay their taxes with a characteristic British grouse but they pay them just the same—they work all day
in Factories, in Offices and in the Front Lines, and they come home
and work all even and often through the night in the Civil Defence
Services. Everyone goes about his business with a queer sort of faith
that everything will come out right and that Justice will triumph, and I
can only hope they won't be disappointed. Whatever faults the British
may have, Cowardice certainly isn't one of 'em, and whatever Hitler
may do to England, he'll never stamp out what she has stood for all
these years. Somewhere, in some part of the Globe he'll find the old
Union Jack flying like Blazes and telling him to get to Hell and they
hope he'll like it. Its funny but the Patriotism we thought was dead
has been revived this War in no small manner. Everyone lived in the
"tight little Isle" and took for granted what was offered, but now when
invasion is coming nearer and nearer the old love of country is coming
back. I know I'd rather die than see one of Hitler's Huns set foot on an
inch of English soil, but in my heart of hearts I know that if they do
it, we shall probably bear it with the same imperturbability that we've
gone through other things. Perhaps I shouldn't say "we" because I know
nothing of the last War, and this is the first great crisis I've had to face.
When this War started I was like most of the young people,—too optimistic for my own good, and imbued with a blind faith in the French
Army and the British Navy—but now when everything has gone so
wrong, I can see that this is the turning point in our history, and we
either sink or swim. London will never be surrendered as Paris was, so
if there s a gigantic Battle for London as there may be, I hope I can
take some part in it. I can imagine nothing sweeter than killing off a
couple of Germans before breakfast! I never thought I could loathe a

nation so much! I could kill a million of 'em and not suffer a twinge of conscience. And at one time in my young life, I couldn't swat a fly without faintly worrying whether he had a wife and family!

London has been remarkably free from Air Raids for the past nine months but it is extremely doubtful whether this state of affairs will continue.[8] The usual rumours fly around that Hitler won't bomb London because he wants to make a triumphal entry here and he wants to keep it intact. As far as I can see the only Blankety Blank entry he's going to make is on a Hearse, if we've got anything to do with it. I went down to my Home town last week end and had a terrible time of it. We were up all Saturday night watching the searchlights and listening to the Gunfire and then up all Sunday night when the Sirens sounded three times. The German Planes come over every night about 12.30, and when I go down home I sleep with my young cousin Eileen, and somehow or other she can tell the difference between the German Engines and the British. Saturday night was bad enough, because we couldn't stay in bed with the Planes practically over the house, but Sunday I was tired out and about 12.30 Eileen said, "Here's Jerry!" suddenly, sitting bolt upright in bed. I told her not to be daft, and to go to sleep, but she couldn't and she suddenly heard a terrific "boom" and said quite quietly "That s a bomb!" I knew it was then, and she clambered out of bed and there was another terrific detonation somewhere that nearly shook the House. So yours truly, crawled out of bed grumbling as usual, and as I put my one foot out the Sirens started to wail and I just had time to put a coat on over my "nightie" and my shoes, and as I was dressed first I dashed into my Auntie's room and picked up the Baby, Geoffrey, he's 18 months old, and chased down the stairs with Geoff s brother Ken, who's 5, at my heels. Poor Kennie had one shoe on and one off, and as I chased out of the House down the Road to the Air Raid shelter with Geoff in my arms, Ken grabbed the back of my Coat and clung on to my legs and I couldn't budge an inch. He wasn't scared, only excited and he kept saying "Betty, is it the Germans again??" and I bent down and said to him "Don't be frightened, Ken, they're only a

8. The official British account dates the beginning of the "Battle of Britain" at July 10, 1940. On August 2, the German Luftwaffe was ordered to destroy the RAF. By September 1940 systematic bombing, several raids a day, had begun. The battle pitted unarmed civilians against incendiary devices and explosives and firemen, wardens, nurses, doctors, and rescue workers against an enemy they could not touch.

couple of damned Germans". Afterwards, I thought, "I'm sure I've heard that somewhere before" And I suddenly realised and chuckled "Blimey, it was Scarlett O'Hara!" Only she said they were only a passel a damned Yankees! You should have seen us in that Air Raid Shelter though. The baby had on a miniature Tin Helmet (bought from Woolworths for sixpence) and Eileen and I had the Curlers in our hair and sat cheerfully playing a Mouth Organ. A little girl about five sat on my lap and sang "Jesus loves me, Yes I know" at the top of her voice and then finished off by rendering "Roll Out the Barrel" and some old chappie and I attempted to whistle "Pack up your troubles" but my whistle was always lousy, anyway. When the "All Clear" sounded it was 2 am. so we went back to bed for about fifteen minutes and then the darned Huns came back again, and we all had to turn out again, and this time we crawled down under the Stairs and got ourselves all covered with white Plaster. We were down there about half an hour, went back to bed again and the Sirens sounded again about ten minutes later. This time I said "To hell with the Germans" and stayed in bed, but it was impossible to rest with all the guns sounding around you, and the knowledge that Jerry's up there in the sky only too willing and ready to pop you off if he gets a chance. I had to travel back to London Monday morning, and it took four and a half hours and I'd had no sleep for two nights so you can imagine what I was like in work that afternoon. You'd die laughing at my Auntie though. When she goes to bed at night she puts Ken to sleep with his clothes on and ties their labels on all their clothes (We have labels and discs for identification) and she has a large Paper Carrier she takes down the Shelter with her. In it, honey, are her Marriage Certificate, her Insurance Policy, the kids Birth Certificates, a bottle of milk, a packet of Wadding, two cups, her knitting and God knows what. We nearly split ourselves laughing over the Marriage Certificate. By the way to straighten the Family tree out. my Auntie is mamma's sister. She has two children Eileen (two years younger than me, and Charlie who's 28) Charlie is married and Ken and Geoff are his two kiddies, and they all live in the same House. When I was running down to the Shelter with Geoff and Ken, the Planes were right overhead, and I could see them dropping Flares. And my sister' in-law had a worse experience last week. She was on one of our staff trains going to work and the Train was bombed. They had to jump out of the Train and run and hide in the Woods. Muriel had a first class view of the Swastikas on the Planes, and the bomb dropped about a hundred yards away from 'em. I daren't tell you where it was because the Censor won't pass it, if I do. Muriel is working on the Railway for the duration, and she's working with the evacuated staff down in the country. So much for the safety of evacuation! It is useless for us to evacuate from London. Our livelihood is here and we couldn't live without the weekly pay-packet in the event of an invasion. Streams of refugees along roads are a beautiful target for the Nazi Airmen and thousands of civilians were killed in this way in France. Also it isn't clear yet whether the invasion *will* come wholly from the East. If De Valera persists in being so blind and stubborn it s more than likely Germany will invade Ireland and use that as a base for attacking the West of Britain, which is now considered safer than the East. I was born and reared in the West Country till I came to London just over four and a half years ago, and they never saw anything of Aerial Warfare in the last War. Now they are getting it hot and strong just like the rest of us. If it wasn't for the fact that Ireland is such a menace to our own security, I'm all for letting the Irish stew in their own juice. They're the most ungrateful lot of rabble on earth, and their beastly I.R.A. has caused untold havoc and loss of life here. The Ulster people are still fiercely loyal to the British and are willing to co-operate with the Southerners only if they will declare their allegiance to the cause of Britain. "Dev" still lives in a beautiful Paradise of wishful thinking—i.e. "We can preserve our neutrality". I've heard that statement somewhere before. No country in the world can be neutral to-day. They're either -pro German, or pro-British. The pro-Germans are mostly those Nations who want to grab a bit of something belonging to someone else, or those countries who are scared out of their wits. And talking of grabbing, our papers often print rumours that America has her eyes on this or that British Island, and denounce it furiously as German propaganda. Quite seriously, German "prop" has driven a wedge between France and Britain, and may succeed with the British and the Americans. The British feel that the American are doing all the talking and nothing else, and your Statesmen don't help things by standing up and uttering sweet little platitudes like "put American guns in British boys hands, to save them being put into the Americans" and "Britain is America's first line of Defence", and that jovial laddie who implored us to surrender Britain and take our Fleet over to Canada to help the New World out of the mess. I don't think

that many Britishers think that America will come into this War. They
know the good, hard, facts and they know that we're entirely on our
own feet as far as the fighting is concerned. The general opinion is what s
to happen when we run out of money and the Americans won't send
us any more Planes? Personally speaking I think it s disgusting that
with all the unemployed in this country something couldn't have been
done to keep the millions here, and employ British labour for it. That s
not being nasty, Helen, it s just sensible. I can tell you though, that I
defend America right and left, to everyone. There s so much about the
country and the people that I admire, and I always adhere to the principle that the place is so vast, and so scattered, and filled with people of
so many different nationalities, that it s a wonder to me that all sorts of
internal dissension don't break out. You have millions of Germans and
Italians, too. What a mighty fifth column! I do so want to see your
country Helen. You made me feel tired and fed up describing all those
lovely places, and I was stuck in the middle of a country that is likely to
be at War for months and months, where we're worked off our feet, and
where we aren't even likely to get any holidays. And then I say to myself
that those thoughts are all wrong, because I've been glad enough to take
what Britain has had to offer me, and now when she's in trouble it isn't
for me to grumble. I wish when I'd seen your country I could bring you
here and show you mine! I know you'd love England. I'd like to show
you all round my lovely London for a start, and then then take you
down to the West Country, to Cornwall and the Devon and Somerset,
and through Wales and the Garden of England, Warwick and Stratford
on Avon, that s the most beautiful place. Even if Shakespeare hadn't
been born there it would be quite the loveliest small-town I have ever
seen. And the Lake District is wonderful, too. I've seen quite a bit of
Britain, because working on the Railway I can travel very cheaply. But
what is a terrific journey to us would seem nothing to you. I once spent
a day travelling, from one end of Britain to the other. I went from
Cornwall, to Scotland, and I thought it must have been the longest
journey ever undertaken by anyone, anywhere! Anyhow, to get back to
the States, one day by hook or by crook, I am going to see California.
How I don't know, but see it I will. You can tell the young man who's
been there for a few summers, that it isn't fair that he should have been
there all those many times, and me not once!

No that wasn't broccoli I ate ducky, we often eat that, or at least we did in Peace-time. This vegetable, if it was a vegetable, was absolutely unlike it. But such a pretty smell! We are luckier now, as it s Summer. We are having quite a few Garden Peas, and the good old Beans are always handy. I suppose Limas are what we call Kidney Beans. I've never heard of Calivos and have only tasted Melon once in my life.

I told 'em in work about the Butter flavouring. It was definitely marked "Kansas". They must be kidding us. And by the way, when we say "Yankees" we mean all Americans everywhere. Over there you seem to think the Yankees are different people. We've been seeing a lot of Civil War films lately and though we're not quite sure whose fighting for who, and why, they interest me a lot. I always liked Civil War stories, but we never learned any American history in School so I didn't get a chance to learn much about it. We had enough to do tackling British history. Think how lucky the average American kid is compared to the British. He's only got about 250 years of history to learn, and we poor devils had something like 2000, with an unbroken line of Kings for 1000 years! I used to wish sometimes that the Ancient Britons had been wiped off the face of the earth, when I was in School.

I saw "Arouse and Beware" and like it very much. I'd certainly love to read the Book, but it doesn't seem to have been published over here. I asked them in the Library, but they say McKinley Kantor wasn't listed in their Authors so that was that. I only read a couple of chapters of it, and that was some time ago. I'm sorry you don't like John Howard, but then tastes differ, honey. As you know I can't abide Laurence Olivier so there you are! Actually, I don't think Howard is so good looking now as he was when he was very, very young, (he's now reached the advanced age of 26, I believe) and I saw him in "Lost Horizon" and a couple of other things including a flicking with the weird title of "Valiant is the World for Carrie".[9] Although I distinctly remember kicking up hell when I saw "Lost Horizon" because they'd put an American in the part of George Conway. I don't know if you've read Hilton's Novel but the Conway brothers were definitely most British, and with Ronald Colman's perfect accent just right for the part, to give him a younger

---

9. In *Lost Horizon* (1937; U.S.), a plane crash strands a group in Shangri-La. *Valiant Is the World for Carrie* (1936; U.S.) is the story of a mother's love and sacrifice.

brother with the most Yankee twang I ever heard seemed like sacrilege to me. In fact when I spoke of John Howard in that film I called him "the pretty one with the awful voice". I still keep my opinion about the awful voice. I've seen the young man as "Bulldog Drummond"—my beautiful Bulldog, only in the Book he wasn't Beautiful—and his accent gives me the willies. In "Arouse and Beware" he even calls a Dog a "Dawg" and when he asks the girl if she feels better, he leaves out the t's altogether and says something like "berrer". I can't make it out at all. Still, I suppose you understand it. You and my friend and my mother all seem to agree. They always say that I like the "pretty boys". I think it s most unjustified myself, but there you are, there s nowt I can do about it.

Talking of Olivier. Listen Helen, the British Government haven't *made* anyone come home. The little squirts know that, that s why they're sitting so safe and snug while the rest of their countrymen are fighting like blazes. Olivier and his girl friend haven't budged an inch off American soil and aren't likely to. The last I heard of 'em they were flying to Montreal to get a house for his family who were skipping in to Canada. The majority of the "fan" public over here are disgusted at the number of our gallant film heros who are doing their bit 5000 miles away. We don't ask them to come and fight especially—I should be the last to urge any man to go into the Front Line—but when the cowardly little so and sos shrink from coming home, even to make Propaganda films, there s very little to be said for them. Most of our big Producers like Korda, and Saville and Herbert Wilcox and a dozen and more others did a bunk as soon as War started and there s been hundreds thrown out of work through it. I wrote something to one of our two National Film Journals a month or so ago, and W.H. Mooring the leading British journalist in Hollywood saw it and wrote me a charming letter (four pages of it) trying to explain things. I am going to write back to him soon. But you don't need to worry about Olivier and Leigh or any of the rest of 'em. They're quite safe where they are. Richard Greene is supposed to be coming back, and the British Consul advised a few of the younger ones to return, but I don't think many of 'em will. After all this is a fight for Britain and one Britisher or any Britisher should not be allowed to sit back and let the rest of his compatriots do his fighting for him. When this War's over, and things pick up again, they'll all come crawling back. And I suppose we'll be silly enough to do the old "Come home, all is forgiven" act. There was a suggestion in Parliament not long ago that they deprive those people who had deliberately run away, to avoid Military service, of their British nationality. I believe they were referring to several Poets like Alec Waugh and Christopher Isherwood, but it could cover a lot of territory. I should worry. I think they're all a lot of worms, anyway.

That film "Twenty-one days" was made in '36 and shelved till now, I never saw it, though I like Leslie Banks. "Mortal Storm" hasn't reached here yet.[10] Lots of films are held up, and will be delayed a long time, I imagine, due to the difficulties of transport. I wish they'd revive some of the films made in the last four years. There s heaps of them I haven't seen, that I'd like to see now. I never saw "Young Mr Lincoln" either. We had several films about Lincoln, and really they didn't go over well here, because they came right in the middle of all the War there is, and we aren't very familiar with Lincoln at all. I know he made some speech at Gettysburg, though when I ask people about it, no one seems to know it. I think I heard in "Ruggles of Red Gap" something about Government by the People, for the People, not perishing from the Earth: That s as far as I go. I also know that Abe had a beard and was bumped off in a Theatre, by a chappie called Booth, or something. Come to think of it, I believe I saw Walter Huston as Lincoln, in a film ages ago.[11]

Yes! I get the "Picture Play" or have done for the past four months, and thank you so much. They said that you subscribed for six months. It s awfully kind of you; I wish there was something I could do in return. I saw the pictures of John Howard, too, and whatever I saw about his awful accent, he seems to be quite a clever bloke. Speaking for myself, I couldn't sharpen a pencil properly, much less make furniture!

I'm sorry I've got to write on two sides of the paper but we have to exercise the strictest economy in Paper, now. When we get letters here, we have to turn the Envelope inside out, and re-stick it, and use it again. My young typist has stuck dozens of new labels on old addresses.

---

10. The drama *Twenty-one Days* (1940; UK) stars Olivier and Vivien Leigh. *The Mortal Storm* (1940; U.S.), the story of a family living quietly in the German Alps until caught up in the turmoil of the Nazis rise to power, stars James Stewart.

11. The Oscar-nominated farce *Ruggles of Red Gap* (1935; U.S.) stars Boland, Zasu Pitts, and Charles Laughton as an English valet who, brought to American West, must assimilate. *Abraham Lincoln* (1930; U.S.), directed by D. W. Griffith, stars Walter Huston as Lincoln.

She says she's "licking and sticking for Victory". A new Order comes into force on Aug. 5th. banning our Iced[?] Pastries, Eclairs, Cream Buns, and anything with Sugar Icing on it. They're also experimenting with a new diet in which we'll get less Meat and more Potatoes and Vegetables. Maybe after all this, I shall emerge with a really sylph-like figure and get transported to Hollywood.

That Phoenix I told you about is in New York State. This friend of mine said the Post Office Clerk in San Antonio Texas, didn't know it either and he had to turn it up in a Book. Nick is naturally most anxious to get out to the States, but unfortunately he's made himself thoroughly unpopular here by keeping on about it all the time. He's sure I'm his only pal on the station and frequently comes in and says "What about you and me clearing off to Yankeeland as MR and Mrs Preston??" He's a funny little man, and it s a good job he doesn't see the way I laugh at him sometimes.

About my using slang, you should hear my relatives grumble at me for it. My mother gets furious, over what she calls my "Americanisms", and says that it s soon enough for me to talk like Americans when I get there, if I ever do. I don't really speak American at all, though; I only use an occasional slang term, picked up from the Films. Why I can't even imitate an American properly!

Perhaps if Cleveland is full of foreigners they'd let me go there! The girl Mum worked with thinks it s a marvellous place. She was Jewish. Pittsburgh is where all the Steel Mills are, isn't it? My friend from New Jersey seems to think that N.J. is the most beautiful State in the Union, especially her lovely Jersey City, and if I come out there it looks as though that s where I'll have to settle. Gwen, in New York, used to live in Rochester, but she's always had a hankering to go out West and go to Los Angeles. We'd probably have to hitch-hike, as far as I can see. Anyway, though it s such a long way from New Jersey to Kansas City, I might be able to get down to see you if I can once get past the Statue of Liberty without her noticing me!

The evacuation to Canada seems to be off temporarily, anyway. The Government can't spare the Warships to convoy the kiddies and they're afraid to send them over unescorted. You know how the Germans would love to kill off a couple of thousand British children. Most of the rich ones have got their kids out, though and there s a lot of bad feeling about it. The system in England is going to be vastly changed after the War, methinks. I'm no Communist, but I'm more and more Socialistic every day. If you see anything in the Paper or Movie Books that might interest me, you'll send it won't you? And Please keep on writing, even if it s only a couple of lines a week. If invasion comes, I'll go on writing to you somehow, and in any case it'll be weeks before they get at London. We're ready for them, the swines!

I won't write any more now. It s Saturday, and I have to go shopping and to the Hairdressers, and a dozen other things. Don't forget, I'm relying on you to keep writing whatever happens,

Love,<br>Betty

P.S. You say it s comparatively cool at 88 degrees. To-day is July 13th. and it s so cold we've had to wear Woollen Coats. June was a lovely month, but I don't suppose the temperature went over 80. That s real hot to us!

c/o. G.W.Rly<br>SOUTH LAMBETH. S.W.8.<br>England.<br>[August 9, 1940]

Dear Helen,

Just a short letter this time to tell you that we're still alive and kicking despite the horrible whoppers told by Doctor Goebbels in your Newspapers. I understand the gentleman says that London is in Ashes and that Big Ben actually struck thirteen, he was that scared! Well, London's a heck of a big place to be laid in Ashes, and as for the dignified big Bernard striking a stroke more than he oughter, such a thing has never been known in British history and certainly isn't likely to start now. London and Londoners remain comparatively calm and unruffled, despite the fact that Goering's boy friends have been playing Boomps-a-Daisy with the good old English earth. Yesterday we knocked down 140 German Planes and lost 16 ourselves—the day before that it was even better, the Nazi Pilots are biting the dust in good large, mouthfuls—so don't think we're beaten yet—we've got plenty of tricks up our sleeves yet, before Hitler installs himself at Buckingham Palace, which believe it or not, he thinks he's going to do, though at the moment, he isn't quite sure how.

London had its first Warning for months last Thursday evening at 7 p.m. I had just come from the West End and put a bag of Plums on the table, when the Sirens started. The next day was even funnier. The boss goes to Dinner at 12.30 and we were all sitting round talking. I was supposed to go on the Telephone Switchboard for half an hour, to relieve the regular Operator, and I happened to mention that if the "Red" warning came through, I should just have to sit at that Board, surrounded by Bombs. My young tracer, Ian, started to roar with laughter, and I said to him "You'll regret that one of these days, my lad" when his face changed suddenly, and he gulped something about Sirens, and slid out of the door in about half a second. I turned round to see where he'd gone, and then I heard 'em. Whereupon we all trooped down the Shelter and stayed there for a hour, singing, and doing our own version of the Lambeth Walk and the Rhumba. The "All Clear" went about an hour later, and we went back to work. The next warning was worse, though. It came at 5.15 pm. and I was standing with my friend right on the end of the Platform waiting for our train, when the Sirens went. We ran right down the length of the Platform into the Booking Hall, but as there was no protection there at all, we ran back up the stairs, got into the train, and went to Victoria. That station has a huge Glass Roof so we couldn't stay there. We decided to take a Train and get home. The "All Clear siren" was going just as I got in the House. Sunday the blighters came over twice, once at 1.30, when I was in the middle of cooking the pastry, and again at half-past five, when I was laying the tea. My Apple tart was completely ruined! The pastry had to be left so long, it was as heavy as lead. I don't mind what Hitler does but I object when he starts mucking about with my pastry. Actually Friday they smashed up a bit of Croydon. Lots of our girls here live in and around Croydon, and had a first class view of the Aerial Battles, with the big Black German planes dashing across the skies and our Hurricanes and Spitfires chasing on their tails. My typist, here, was out on Mitcham Common when the Alarm went Sunday and lay down under a Hedge on her tummy, crawling out after ten minutes beautifully covered with brambles, and chunks of mud. The swines have been Machinegunning the streets, unfortunately, and that accounts for a large number of Civilian Casualties. It's that which worries my mother, more than anything. She's scared I'll be caught out on the street, and get a basinful of Deutschland bullets.

I see you're going to get bases on some of our Islands, in return for some old Destroyers.[12] There's one thing about you Yankees, no-one can deny. You're experts at striking a bargain, and at picking the right time to do it. Another time if we hadn't been in such a mess, I don't think you'd have got those Islands so easily! Anyhow, there's one thing—you're getting your "lebensraum" bloodlessly! That's more than some folks can say.

I have written you twice in the past few weeks. I do hope you got them alright. Actually, I'm sending you this short note because I want you to have some snaps. You'll probably recognise me—I'm the one with the curls. And don't please believe everything you read on old Goebbels' propaganda sheets. We've still got our chins up and we're still the Rulers of the Seas, *and* the Air. In fact, the worse news of the War to me is that there's going to be a shortage of cosmetics and perfume—and I *adore* perfume. I'm not going to worry until the Germans achieve the impossible, and walk into London, and if they do that I'm going to bump myself off. I know I'm perfectly safe in saying that, because they won't get within a hundred miles of the place.

Cheerio for the present, and write soon.

Love,
Betty

P.S. Thanks for the clippings and if you see any reviews of "Date with Destiny" will you send them to me? I'm going to Cornwall on Friday for a week and will send you a Postcard from there.

---

12. In May 1940, the British government asked to borrow or lease some forty or fifty U.S. "over-age" destroyers to help its navy protect trade routes and defend its coasts against invasion. An exchange of letters on September 2 formalized the deal: fifty destroyers plus rifles, flying boats, and other matériel in exchange for bases in British possessions such as Trinidad, Jamaica, Bermuda, and the Bahamas (Langer and Gleason, *Challenge to Isolation*, chap. 22).

c/o. G.W.R SOUTH LAMBETH
S.W.8. England.
[August 24, 1940]

Dear Helen,

Received your letter last week and am going to make a determined effort to answer it to-day. The Censors are asking us not to write so much to friends overseas as they are overworked, poor devils. What they can ever find in my letters that might be of information to the Enemy is beyond me. Just as though I could unearth some secret code, and hide it in the tripe I write! However, for their information, if they happen to be reading this, I am anti-everything the British Government tell me to be. Which seems to be all that is required.

Well! I'm getting another letter away and hoping that it will cross the Atlantic safely, though how it ever does is a marvel, what with Musso and Adolf's submarines, lurking hopefully on the Ocean bed waiting to bust up anything and everything with a British look about it. Whatever happens, even if this long threatened invasion comes off, I shall try and write a couple of lines, so you'll be able to show it to your friends and call it "Despatches direct from the Battle Front". I shall probably write in a Tin Hat and my Gas Mask on, which may somewhat damp my usual high spirits, but write I will, and Hitler and all his perishing Nazis shan't stop me. That's the Bulldog British coming out. If all reports are correct the Germans are training invasion troops on the Norwegian, Dutch and Belgian coasts and are also rigging up extremely long range guns on the Coast of Northern France to bombard us.[13] I always thought, somehow, that that would be the method they'd use, that and waves of bombing planes. They can bombard London from Northern France, so it looks as we'll be having a nice time shortly. I hope they'll give us fair warning, anyway. It will be most upsetting if the fireworks start while we're eating our lunch and the Roast Beef and Yorks gets all mixed up with large lumps of shrapnel and a couple of stray bullets. Apparently Adolf is very upset because we wouldn't accept his Peace proposals[14]—the man has *such* a kind heart, and all he has

13. Hitler, on July 16, in his "Directive No. 16," said he was beginning preparations for, and if necessary would carry out, an invasion of England.

14. After France fell, Hitler delivered a public speech on July 19, 1940, in which he assumed that he had defeated Britain as well. He offered to accept Britain's control over the Empire if Britain accepted German control of the Continent. In a speech the same

ever asked from anyone is all Europe, half of America and peace!—and he says that he's going to blast us out of existence once and for all. Poor old Britain. All she is is a spot on the map, and yet she gives Germany such a terrible tummy-ache. At one time they said Hitler's greatest ambition was to have an alliance with England,—he thought Germany and England together would have conquered the world—but now he wants to be the first to bring the apparently invincible Old Lady to her Knees. Someone should refer him to Shakespeare's little piece about "This England never did nor never shall, lie at the proud foot of a conqueror". In any case, Hitler says that Shakespeare was such a genius, he probably had some German in him somewhere. God forbid! Fancy *anyone* being unlucky enough to have German blood in 'em.

I certainly wish you had done something to Old Man Petain when you had the chance. It seems awful that France is now virtually our enemy, although to be quite candid, I never was in favour of the "Entente Cordiale" business. I think we've been far too much the ally of France and when people dare to say that we let France down, they don't think of what France did to us. Churchill never guaranteed enormous numbers of men to France. Why did they want them? They were supposed to be the finest and best equipped army in the world, and what happens to them. They fight for a few weeks, and then flop. The men we sent to France acquitted themselves nobly and well, but they were surrounded by treachery. Leopold, curse him, led them smack into a trap in Belgium. Holland was riddled with Fifth Columnists. The French, accidentally or deliberately, failed to blow up the Bridges over the Meuse and the Germans poured into Northern France and surrounded our men there, and it was only through the heroic actions of the R.A.F. that the Bridges were eventually destroyed. Then the French surrendered Paris without a struggle and gave up the fight without even advising the British High Command in time for them to get our boys out safely. Allies you call them. I've got some other names, and they're certainly not pretty. That's what I feel so mad about, Helen. It s always left to Britain to fight for the freedom of the world, and for Democracy

---

day to the Reichstag, Hitler urged the British people to listen to reason and accept his offer. Winston Churchill had said on July 14 that Great Britain would stop at nothing to defeat the Nazis, and in fact the British people were utterly unimpressed by Hitler's "peace offer" (see Langer and Gleason, *Challenge to Isolation*, 652, 654–55).

in general, and we gain nothing by it. We've policemanned the world for centuries, and the world doesn't thank us. Of course, we understand the American idea of not sending their boys to die, but did the Americans think of that way back at the time of Munich? They cared little or nothing for the lives of the British boys, when they urged the British Government to declare War on Germany, and do you remember the bitter, horrible and sarcastic things they said when Chamberlain tried to get us out of it. They said that we'd let democracy down. Our prestige was supposed to have sunk to a new low level in the States. That's what *we* get when we try to save our boys lives. I notice the Americans aren't so keen on getting involved themselves, though. I wonder what they'd have done if they'd been in our position at Munich? It's hard for us to reconcile American democracy with the way they're acting now, Helen. They've let all the free countries of Europe die without raising a finger to save them, and it's my belief they'll do the same thing with Britain, and Britain is just about the world's last hope, at the moment. I know that your country is making great preparations to defend itself against aggression, but if we had followed the same principle and refused to declare War on Germany until they actually attacked us, who can say what would have happened? I think a lot of the bad feeling here has been caused by your Press and by this "Cash and Carry" principle. I know from your point of view, it's probably right, but you have no idea how mercenary it sounds, coming from a country that is supposed to be a fellow democracy. And the Press have yelled for blood so much that it got on people's nerves. Our Papers used to answer back in their "refined" British manner, but now they have completely silenced any criticism of America, and are being diplomatically silent. You needn't worry what the British press are saying. They refer to everyone and everything American in glowing terms and throw in Hitler's face the "aid" America is giving Britain, though I'm quite certain it doesn't bother Adolf one little bit. With Italy, Fascist Spain, Japan and a terrified Rumania behind him, he should worry—to say nothing of his being pals with that old enigma, Russia. To counterbalance that, we haven't an influential pal in the world who'll be ready to step in and help us, except a very hesitant Turkey, and an America, with a slightly pro-British East, a still Isolationist Middle West, and a "what-the-heck's-it-all-about" West. Despite the fact that I loathe Communism like poison, I wish we had wooed Russia a bit more. It's rather funny, though, to see how we have to go in to aid other nations, and then when we're in trouble, see how many nations come to aid us. Gosh! I wonder if the British are learning their lesson at last, that helping the other fellow out of a jam sometimes gets you into a worse one yourself!

I hope like you that we will be able to take a ruthless line in dealing with the Germans. The "military objective" angle is all right if both sides do it that way, but the Germans never were great believers in fair play, and their Raids here have proved that military objectives are certainly not what they're after, unless their bombing is so atrocious they don't know what they're hitting. Women and babies are their pets, I think. Little suburban Houses, and Cottages, and even a School here and there, for good measure. Of course, what we're getting now, is probably chickenfeed to what they will send over when the British blitzkrieg really gets going, but let 'em come. We can take it, and dish it out, if and when the occasion arises. If Germany finishes us, there won't be much of Germany or the Germans left to do any triumphal marching. And Hitler will have to wear plenty of Bullet proof waistcoats, if he starts riding down Whitehall. Anyway, I've thought of a swell place to hang him. Right on top of Nelsons Column. It's right in the centre of London, and there's loads of Pigeons circling round and round, and you know what Pigeons are. He said once that the British people would probably hang old Churchill there, when they found out what an old so and so he was. Golly, I can just picture old Winston hanging anywhere—probably dying with that Bulldog look on his face, as usual. I think Winston's a funny old bird anyway. He really reminds me of a tough old Bulldog, though Heaven help us if anyone puts him in a Peacetime Cabinet. That bloke would fight his own grandmother, if he got the chance.

Seems funny when you say about America being uninterested in Europe in the last War. I don't remember anything about it at all, of course, and I suppose we didn't know much about you then, either. Nowadays every Britisher knows American life from the films, and American slang is used a lot here—though without the "through the nose" business. It's amazing how the pictures have educated us, really. Even when I was growing up I always pictured an American as a man in plus-fours with horn rimmed "specs" and smoking a big Cigar. And the American accent was practically an unknown quality to most of us, until the "talkies" came. The first one I saw was called "The Dummy" and I didn't understand a word they said.[15] I mentioned the fact to my mother and she said "Of course, you can't understand them. They're talking American!". Up to that time I only had a vague idea that my beloved movies were made thousands of miles away. I believe I told you how terribly upset I was when I found that my childhood "crush", Buster Brown, and his Mary Jane were American children. I used to haunt the Cinemas when they had a Buster Brown comedy on, and when I discovered that the kiddies in "Our Gang" were American too, I never felt the same, even though I wasn't quite sure how far away that was.[16] I horrified my Geography mistress when I was eight by asking her to point out Hollywood to me on the Map of the United States, having looked vainly through the index of the Atlas and found no mention of that magic place. It gave me great satisfaction that the Teacher had never even heard of Hollywood, and it wasn't until some time afterwards that I found the place was in California and a sort of suburb of Los Angeles. We did a chapter on California in Geography, and read all about its climate and its fruit Orchards and Orange Groves, and that started me off about it, I suppose. Ever since then I've been determined to go to California before I die; that climate sounds perfect to me. Here, I'm so miserable and sick in the winter, I feel that life isn't worth living. And the prospect of a black-out winter, with frequent Air-raids frankly appals me. Not 'cause I'm scared of the raids but because it's going to be so darned cold getting out of a warm bed and hiking down to the Cellar!

The people in my native part of my country are getting Raids much worse than we are, at the moment. My friend wants to go home for the holidays—mine are due to start on August 24th—but I don't see the sense of spending half your days and nights in an Air Raid Shelter. I should love to go to my little village in Cornwall where I spent several happy holidays in Peace-time, but the fare is a bit expensive for my friend, and her mother is still living in my hometown, and she has to go and see her. It's funny, but right at the back of house is the Recreation ground where Frances and I used to fish for tadpoles—we called 'em "Tiddlers"—when we were kids, and the Germans dropped a bomb on

---

15. Probably the 1929 U.S. melodrama starring Ruth Chatterton and Fredric March.

16. The Buster Brown comedy shorts made in the late 1920s were based on the cartoon created by Richard F. Outcault. The *Our Gang* films, a series of silent comedic shorts directed by Hal Roach, evolved into the popular TV series *The Little Rascals*.

it. Frances' mother thought that London was so dangerous and begged her to come home and live when War broke out yet they're getting more than we are, now. Frances went home right at the outbreak of War, and it's a good job she did because she was terribly ill with speticemia and nearly died. Even now the Doctors are non-committal about her future chances.

Lots of the folks here are a bit waxy over the War Debts question. They say if any more countries had continued paying you, you would have had a worse crash on Wall St. in '29, than you had, because you were practically drowning in your own gold, then. After the last War America had practically a monopoly of every country's money, and after this one you'll have a large proportion of it. How long we'll be able to keep paying you in gold, I'm not quite sure, and what *we're* going to use for money after all of it, is past my understanding. Also, we went on paying America huge sums for years and years until every country decided to wipe out War Debts, altogether, and it's just as well to add that millions and millions of pounds were owed to us by different people and we didn't get a cent of it back. Yet there are still Senators and Congressmen who stand up in Washington and suggest that this or that British Island be ceded to America in payment of the debts of the *last* War. And there are others who admit that Britain is America's first line of defence, but insist that we pay, and pay well and truly, for the privilege. Still, while we still have the money, our Government will go on paying you, so there's nothing I can say or do, will make the slightest difference. We are grateful that American ships may be sent to take British children to the States, although the law is framed so that children of all nations may go, and you may receive thousands of darling little Huns to look after as well. If you do ever get near a German child, give it a good, hard, walloping with a hair-brush from me, will you, honey? I've no patience or pity for anything German and I'd like to see the German brats treated like the poor little French, Belgian and Dutch babies were—shot, and blown up and mangled by Tanks, the same things that they'll do to our kiddies if they get a chance.

I got your envelopes of clippings and thought they were so interesting. If you get any pictures, or articles in your periodicals about anything or everything British, will you send it to me? I like to hear American opinion of us. The Corn on the Cob looks very funny, I somehow don't think I should like it. My mother had a shot at eating one once, but she got in a terrible mess, and felt most self-conscious. She started off by trying to eat it with a knife and fork and eventually gave it up as a bad job. I don't like any cereals but Sago Pudding. We have packets and packets of Corn Flakes and Porridge in the Cupboard but I never touch the stuff. We don't eat Corn here, though the breakfast-foods are much the same as America. You seem to drink a lot more Fruit juice than we do, and also the funniest salads. I saw one in a Book made of Oranges and Onions. And Prunes stuffed with Cheese. Seems like there s a lot I'll have to learn when I get to America!

My mother is still worried stiff about Jack. He'll be called up this month probably, and he'll either have to stay here in the Defence Forces, or go to the East, when Mussolini is having a go at invading our African colonies.[17] Jack's very upset because all his boy pals, that he has known from childhood, are missing in France. Six of his friends went out, and only one came back, and he feels terrible about it. I'm just as bad in a way, because they were the boys I grew up with, and all my "growing-up" memories are concerned with them. They used to be such a happy crowd, with their football and cricket and innumerable girl friends—it s awful to think of them all gone. Muriel, my brother's wife, has her young brother training to be a Pilot in the Air Force, a suicidal job if there ever was one, and lots of the lads from the Office are going one by one, into the R.A.F. the Navy, and the Army. It's an awful business, this War, and it's so dreadful to think that these boys fathers had to go through all of it, only 25 years ago. Most of them went off with my father. Poor old Daddy. It s a good job he isn't alive to see the mess the World is in.

Well, to get to lighter things—yes, I liked "Man from Dakota" very much, (it was called "Arouse and Beware" here) I'm very keen on Beery, and thought Del Rio was quite good, and very beautiful. I'm looking forward to "Date with Destiny" though I can't stand Ellen Drew, and I wish John Howard would carve off that moustache. "Our Town" hasn't arrived here yet, but it undoubtedly will be shown and I shall go and see Martha Scott, when it comes. "Northwest Passage" hasn't hit London

---

17. In September 1939, Parliament passed the National Service Act under which all men between eighteen and forty-one were liable for conscription. In the third quarter of 1940, 460,000 men aged twenty to twenty-five were "called up" (Calder, *People's War,* 59, 138).

yet either. "Lillian Russell" arrives next week, and I'm going to see it because I like Alice Faye, and am very keen on Don Ameche! I saw him in "Swanee River" last week and thought he was very good, indeed. "The Sea Hawk" has just had its premiere here and is hailed as an excellent piece of propaganda, though Errol Flynn isn't very well liked in England after his dirty, rotten trick of turning American, supposedly to avoid paying British Income tax.[18] I wish they could ban all the little rotter's films in the British Empire and hit him in the place he likes least, his pocket. Honestly Helen, the British actors in Hollywood are giving the folks at home acute attacks of nausea. People like Richard Greene making reams of publicity going to Canada "to join up" and deliberately choosing a Regiment that wasn't recruiting, and asking for a commission, and having naturally been told there were no vacancies for Officers this little Beauty goes brightly back to Hollywood, amid more reams of publicity, and says that as the British Army don't require him he'll continue his film career. Oh, my goodness, what a prize bunch of Garden Lilies we've got out there gracing the Silver Screen and performing gallantly behind the footlights. People who made their name, fame and money in England—lots of foreigners like Alex Korda and the rest, who became naturalised, but as soon as there was a sign of trouble—whoosh! they were off to Hollywood as fast as their cowardly legs could carry 'em.[19] As for your precious Olivier, I've just read an article in "Picture Play" which for sheer bilge would take some beating. All Mr Olivier has done to date, is a lot of talking and I believe, he's taken a trip to Canada to find a house for his family. The worst case is that of Gracie Fields, "our Gracie", who was idolised here

18. Scott, considered a highly talented actress, was nominated for an Academy Award for her role in *Our Town* (1940; U.S.), the Thornton Wilder classic about small-town life in New England. *Northwest Passage* (1940; U.S.), a fictional treatment of the French and Indian War, stars Spencer Tracy. *Lillian Russell* (1940; U.S.), a biography of the musical star, features Alice Faye, Don Ameche, and Henry Fonda. One commentator has dubbed this "the dullest biographical film ever made." Faye was one of the biggest Hollywood stars of the late 1930s and 1940s. In *Swanee River* (1939; U.S.) Don Ameche plays the role of Stephen Foster. In *The Sea Hawk* (1940; U.S.) Errol Flynn plays a pirate.

19. Korda came to England from Hungary and became a major force in the British film industry during the 1930s. He was criticized for spending most of the war years in the United States but apparently was serving as a courier for Winston Churchill during that time.

and who unfortunately married a wop of an Italian, a Fascist too, called Monti Cianchi,—we don't mind having Gracie back because she's ours no matter what she's done, but America is welcome to Master Monty,[20] also to the beautiful Mr. Flynn and the equally beautiful "Dimples" Greene. I saw "Rebecca" last week, and thought it a trifle gloomy—but I liked Joan Fontaine, and Olivier was as good as he could ever be, to my prejudiced way of thinking.

I know I must sound ignorant to your cousin, saying I don't know what a Republican is—but to comfort her tell her that 99 and two thirds percent of the British Public don't know what a Republican is, and some of the British public are very intelligent beings. Honestly, though—we know that theres a Democratic and Republican party in America, but we don't know what the difference is, or what their policies are, naturally. I bet your cousin doesn't know the difference between Conservative, Liberal and Socialist, but *I* do, so there you are. I used to be a rabid conservative, but now I'm not so sure of my ground. The Socialists are certainly getting things done here, and are out to stop this "money buys everything" business, and I'm all for it. The people here are apt to think that Roosevelt is slightly pro-British, and from what they've read of Wilkie [*sic*] he's more than slightly isolationist, so although they have no direct interest in the proceedings, the majority vaguely hope that Roosevelt will win. Wendell Wilkie comes from Ohio, or something doesn't he? They seem to breed Republican candidates for the Presidency. I had a Newspaper from that friend in New York with a whole page in it about a man called Cox,[21] from Cleveland, who was the Republican Candidate in the twenties, and even after reading it still don't know what a Republican officially represents. I shall have to read all about it someday. Maybe I can even come down and see you and argue it out with that cousin of yours. I do hope so, anyway.

20. Fields's move to America during the war put an end to her successful film career. Mario Bianchi married Fields in 1940 and went with her to Hollywood to escape internment in England during the war; they remained married until his death in 1950. Also known as Montague Banks and William Montague, Bianchi was a screen and stage actor as well as a producer and film director.

21. Betty is probably referring to Ohio governor James M. Cox, the Democratic candidate for president in 1920 against Republican Warren Harding, also an Ohio governor. It was unusual for the candidates of both parties to be from the same state. Hence Betty's confusion.

I shall have to close now, darling, as it's getting late and everyone who passes my Desk keeps asking me what I'm doing working so late. The Balloon Barrage is going up outside, and that *sometimes* means there's German planes about somewhere over the Coast. Please write as often as you can, just to cheer me up.

Best love,<br>Betty

c/o. G.W.Rly<br>SOUTH LAMBETH. S.W.8.<br>England.<br>[September 16, 1940]

Dear Helen,

Am writing this under difficulties and I don't even know whether it will be a long letter, how long it will take to type it and whether the Raid warnings will start before I've finished even a page of it. At the moment, honey, I don't even know whether I'll be alive to write all of it. I have had the most nightmarish time of my young and blameless life these past two weeks, and this morning I feel like something that wants to crawl in a hole and die.[22] Still, I can manage a smile, as ever, and my sense of humour isn't entirely gone, though it's worn a bit thin at the edges.

I have just come back from my holidays—if one could call it that—as a rest it was a complete flop, and as an antidote from War nerves it was worse. I went down to my village in Cornwall, and the journey took us thirteen hours—due to a Nazi Airman dropping a couple of salvos of bombs on the Line and the train had to be stopped and held for four hours while the Railway staffs picked them up—they were unexploded ones—and got them out of harms way. We arrived in Cornwall tired and hungry—but the weather was beautiful, and things looked peaceful and the food was grand and somehow, although when we sat on the Beach we could hear the sound of Air Battles off Falmouth the usually isolated stretches of Beach were peopled with watchful Soldiers, and

---

22. Night bombing of British cities began on a large scale on September 7, but it was preceded in August by a systematic attempt to destroy the British air defense called the Fighter Command (Calder, *People's War*, 161–62).

child evacuees; the War seemed far away and we could almost imagine ourselves back in our old, peaceful England. I hated to leave, but I had promised to go home to Newport to see my grand-mother so we left Penzance on the night train which was due in London at 7 in the morning. The Germans decided to bomb that train for some reason or other,—we hadn't got half an hour on our journey before the train lights went out, and we could hear the throb of the German Engines and the Rattle of the Bullets as he swooped and dived over the train. The Driver ran us into a Siding to try and avoid him, but he still followed and although his aim was faulty—his bombs fell about 300 yards from us on each side of the track—it was a most appalling five hours. We sat there, unable to switch on a light, listening to the screams of the bombs dropping and watching the Searchlights play over the sky, trying to pick him up. I had brought a tiny kitten with me from Cornwall, and I held him on my lap and talked to him as though he could understand, telling him not to be frightened, and so on and so forth. I christened him "Jerry" a most unpatriotic name for a 100 per cent British kitten—but I thought it was appropriate for an animal who emerged unharmed from a couple of German Air Raids. I prayed for the dawn to come so the Plane would go and we could get the train across the Bridge, and past Plymouth. When we eventually arrived at Plymouth the "All Clear" siren was sounding. It was five in the morning, and the blessed Dawn was breaking and although we were eight hours from London, I felt as though I'd died and been born again! We got to London at two in the afternoon, and I got into the House in time to hear the Air Raid warning again, but I was so tired I got to bed and slept,—a thing I never do, in an air Raid.

Well! the next day I went down to Newport, and naturally things were pretty hectic there. The Sirens go during the day, often when you are out shopping, and every night about nine oclock—over they come and the Lights start, and the Guns boom and the Citizens don't bat an eyelid, so accustomed are they to this sort of thing. My friend and I walked home on two evenings with the Planes directly above us, with our knees a trifle shaky, and our complexions a little paler than usual, but without a scratch, I'm thankful to say. I think my Fairy Godmother was watching over me, or something, for the shrapnel was falling from the Guns, and the Searchlights were making the sky as light as day. One night as we sat playing Cards, trying our darndest to forget that a bloke called Hitler ever existed, we heard a shrill whistling sound and a terrific crash which shook the house and knocked all the windows out, and sent us flying under the stairs, after my pal had collected her Ham sandwich off the table in case we all starved! We found out afterwards that a screaming bomb had fallen in the next street and taken the roof off a house and smashed up a garden—and all the owner of the House seemed to worry about was his Prize Chrysanthemums. "They were coming on fine" he declared mournfully. "Might have won a couple of prizes this year. And they got my Tomato plants, too!" You have no idea how much the average Britisher thinks of his garden!

*1.30 pm.*

Just interrupted, as I thought, by the wail of the Sirens, "Tootles" I call it, though the usual term is "Warbling Winnie" and Mr. Churchill calls it "the Banshees". Anyway, we had to run to the Shelters as quickly as possible—my colleague rushed down from the Staff Dining Club with his plate of Sultana Pudding, declaring that no blankety blank German was going to do him out of his grub.[23] Apparently there has been some sort of Air Battle up above us, though we won't know that until the Air Ministry reports come out. We have had an appalling time for the past three nights—the raids have started at eight in the evening and finished at six am. and we haven't had more than six hours sleep since last Saturday. It's a wonder to me that any of us are alive at all, so horrible and senseless has been the slaughter inflicted by the Germans.[24] They have bombed indiscriminately—hospitals, Maternity homes, Blocks of Flats Workers cottages, anything and everything in sight. The havoc is awful—particularly in the East End where they are only working people. They have bombed streets where there is not a Military objective within miles—it's been awful. Nurses have been trapped under tons of masonry, babies have been killed by the score,

23. The bombing of London that began on September 7 continued for fifty-seven days. Many Londoners rarely left the shelters. Trenches were available for one-half million people. Also available were one and a half million steel Anderson Shelters. Each one looked like a clamshell buried about four feet in the ground and could hold one average family. Public shelters were built aboveground. About four percent of the people used the underground subway stations, or "Tube" (ibid., 181, 188).

24. During the first two months of the raids, 12,696 people died. During the course of the war, 12,222 tons of bombs were dropped on London, killing 29,890 people (Louis L. Snyder, *The War: A Concise History, 1939–1945* [New York: Simon and Schuster, 1960], 118.)

surely if there is any justice in the World, or a God in the sky, these German swine will pay for what they've done. I have spent three nights in a cold, draughty Cellar with the House shaking from the explosion of bombs and Gunfire. On Saturday night, Mother and Jack had gone out and I stayed in. At nine oclock the sirens went, and Mum dashed home and when they got to the door two screaming bombs dropped practically on either side of them. My mother yelled for me to get into the Shelter and I dashed down the stairs, and we'd hardly got in there before another bomb dropped with a thud that nearly shook our dinners out of us. We sat there all night, until about 4 am. (we'd been listening for seven hours to falling bombs and Anti-Aircraft fire and shells exploding) there was a dull thud, and our windows at the back of the house splintered and cracked. Jack ran out to see if it was us that had been hit, but by some miracle Incendiary bombs had fallen two houses away, and on a garage opposite and set the place ablaze. We went up to see what we could do then, before the Firemen arrived when they did get there, they got it under control in ten minutes. But if Saturday night was awful, Sunday was a nightmare. The raid lasted ten hours and often during the night, my mother grabbed me round the neck and we both thought our last hour had really arrived. Every time a bomb dropped it sounded as though it was in our back garden! Mum was a bundle of nerves, because I had gone out to the Pictures and was in there when the Sirens went. The Manager came on to the stage and said that if any of us were going we'd better go quietly and at once. They opened the doors to let them out and wallop, a bomb fell a couple of streets away, the guns blazed at the Planes, and the noise nearly deafened us. When I eventually got out I spent the worst hour of my life trying to get home. I had to run through the streets to get a Bus with the Planes overhead and wondering every minute whether a lump of shrapnel would slice off a limb or two, or put me out of my misery altogether. I waited half an hour for a Bus and when it eventually came, we had to crawl along without lights. There was a huge red glare in the sky from a big fire, Bombs were thudding in all districts and the Driver wasn't keen on going on, but we implored him so frantically that he eventually did it. He was a brave chap that Driver, if there ever was one. He took his own life—and ours in his hand—and came through smiling. When I got to Hammersmith, they were having a smack at some Shops and Houses there and it seemed like hours before I could run home. Poor Mother was nearly in hysterics wondering where I was. Her Hospital had been bombed, and another Hospital near them had got it so badly they'd moved all the patients and she'd been dressing casualties all day. Two of them had got their legs filled with shrapnel outside Victoria station—the very place where I'd gone to the Cinema. We got no sleep that night, and last night the sirens went at nine p.m. and I crawled upstairs for an hours snooze at 6.30. a.m. I had to be up again at 7.30. because it takes much longer to get to work through the damage they've done to the Railway Lines. It's pitiful to go along some of the streets near here and see what they've done to the homes of working people, who have struggled all their lives to keep their few possessions together. It's just Mass murder against people who have nothing to fight back with. Still, it's this or surrender, and surrender is a word not included in the British dictionary. Even through all this ghastly wreckage the Cockney can still laugh and grin and bear it. They know what Hitler threatens to do, and they're prepared for it. Germany has some nation to tackle when he gets to grips with the British. The civilians, the Policemen, Firemen, Nurses, everyone has been magnificent, and there has probably been more heroism in this City in the past three days than has ever been known before. Paris gave in after one Air Raid, and Paris was France to the average Frenchman. London will never be given away like Paris was and even if London was laid in ashes, the rest of the country would fight like blazes—but as it is, it is on the Londoner the burden is falling, and it is a blessing that they can stand so much without cracking. I don't mind admitting that I've said my prayers on many an occasion during the past three days—I've sat in the Dug-out and muttered "Lord, don't let it hit me"—but we've laughed afterwards at many of the things we've said and done. On Saturday night, when the screaming bomb fell, my sister-in-law threw her arms round my brothers neck and shouted "Jack, darling, this is the end!" and crossed herself like a true Catholic, though she hasn't been to Church in years. Poor old Jack's baffled expression tickled me pink, tragic as the whole thing was. And on the Bus coming home on the Sunday, every time a bomb fell the Conductor took off his Cap, scratched his head and said "Cor blimey, what a whopper!". It amazes me that the Cockney humour can still stand up to it.

*Thursday.*

As I prophesied, this letter is taking me days to type. The raid last night lasted 9 ½ hours, and I had exactly 1 hours sleep. Heigh-ho, I think I'm learning to do without any rest, though my Schoolgirl complexion is suffering a little. Last night our Anti-Aircraft Gunners [had] a smack at the raiders and the noise of the Guns shook the House—but it was sweet music to me. I felt as though they were taking care of us, somehow. If someone asked me the finest feeling in the world right now, I should say to hear the "All Clear" and come out into the fresh air and know that you're still, alive. Everynight when the Office bids adieu to each other they say "Au Revoir and Good Luck" because none of us know when we're going to get a pretty basinful. Several of the people in this station are minus their homes, and camping out in other peoples. Well! we'e still got ours, praise be, so maybe I should be grateful.

The people round me are now swatting flies by the dozen and pretending they're Nazis. Ain't life grand.

All our Cinemas are shutting from now on at 9 oclock but I do hope I shall be able to get there sometimes. I haven't been this week because mother is terrified if I'm out when the Sirens go but they can't take away my pictures from me. Thanks for sending me the story of "Date with Destiny".[25] And don't forget anytime you have a spare film mag to send it over. I look forward to my American mail more than ever now and it still seems to be able to get through, God knows how. Churchill spoke last night and seemed to be awaiting invasion at any time now but I'll keep writing as long as I can and you must keep writing to me. We're well prepared, we've a marvellous Air Force, a wonderful Navy and Army, plenty of food, and the will to win, so whatever happens if we ever go down, the German War Machine will be so battered about it won't have time to touch you at all—which seems to be what some of your Isolationist Senators think—and hope! At the moment I don't

---

25. This title is difficult to identify but could be *The Mad Doctor*, which was released in the United States in February 1941 and titled *A Date with Destiny* in Britain. The film was based on the true story of an Austrian World War I veteran and serial killer who took the identity card of a dead soldier. He traveled to New York and worked as a janitor. He was identified by a police detective as he emerged from a subway but escaped and years later died in his bed in 1959. It is possible this circulated as a story in a 1940 movie magazine that Helen sent Betty. The movie starred Basil Rathbone, Ellen Drew, and John Howard.

give a damn—though if I could only get about six hours consecutive sleep, I'd be able to face those blasted Huns feeling a lot stronger. As I feel now, I wouldn't be much good to anybody and the "typist helper" is so worn out she just can't lick and stick for victory until she gets a good night's sleep—we're all that stiff through sitting in draughty shelters.

No! I didn't mind at all about the letter in "Kansas City Star". If any of my letters are any good to them I'll feel honoured to have them use them. I'm two years younger than they say I am and they've said Jack is in the Army instead of waiting for call-up, but I don't care what they say. If it'll help my England I'd write and say anything.

I received the last issue of Picture Play last week—at least I should say I *nearly* received it. The wrapper arrived, minus contents. I was very mad because I was anxious to read it. I like "Picture Play" very much. Another American Screen Mag I'm keen on is "Motion Picture", and I like the Books with the stories in. "Movie Stories" And "Screen Romances". In fact I like 'em all, especially now that we can't get any.

I received the stockings in perfect condition and have worn them off and on for *six* weeks without laddering. They must be far better than silk. I didn't have to pay any duty on them at all—one pair is taken as a "gift" I should imagine—it's only on large consignments that there is any duty. Thank you so much for sending them, and I certainly hope "Nylon" will come on the market here soon.

*Saturday.*

We had three raids yesterday, and have just come up from the "all clear" from this morning's packet. Last night I had 1 hours sleep in the Coal Cellar. Whoopee! what an existence. They bombed my mothers Hospital yesterday, and burned out the Children's Ward. The Germans love bombing Hospitals and they have been machine-gunning the Civilians in the London streets—just for fun. Our poor typist had a narrow escape running to work yesterday. A bomb dropped fifty yards from her—over at the back of a house, and she was momentarily blinded and choked with Dust, before she got pushed into a Shelter. She came into work looking a wreck!

I shall have to write the rest of this, as it's impossible to type it. You get so far and the sirens go, and whoosh! down to the shelter you have to dash. Trying to finish this between raids. We had seven yesterday and last night I slept on the Stone floor of a Shelter under the garage near us—at least if you could call it sleep. Try it yourself—Lie on the floor of the Cellar without a coverlet or pillow, or anything, and then get someone to fire about a thousand guns above you. We've had 3 raids so far, and in the first one we had hardly got into the Cellar before "plop" down came a couple of bombs! I'm getting used to it now, but oh dear, my poor London! The girl in our house is the coolest customer, though She washes and curls her hair with the bombs literally falling around her, and doesn t give a damn!

Saddest sight for me is the mothers putting their babies to sleep on the floor underneath Benches in Shelters, and sitting watching them until the Dawn breaks What a heritage! Let's hope their future will be a bit brighter for them, anyway, if God spares them, or any of us for that matter. Still, I suppose the tide will turn for us, sometime and the only thing to do is to grin and bear it. I can still grin but I feel terribly tired and my mother is breaking up badly. She'll get better, though, as time goes on. It's us or England, and England is pretty important to all of us. I wish we could do more, but all we can do is sit and and wait and curse those blasted swines, the Germans. If I could annihilate every one of them, I'd be doing the world a service.

I must close now, as we have to prepare for our all night sojourn in the Cellar!!! Who cares anyway?

Do write soon.

Love, Betty

c/o. G.W.R
SOUTH LAMBETH. S.W.8.
England.
[October 16, 1940]

Dear Helen,

Just a comparatively short letter written in the Air Raid Shelter, where we now work all day, not emerging into the blessed light of day until it is time to go home, when we dash like blazes to avoid the next Warning—We have been down here since 11 am. and the Raid started five minutes after—it is now 1 oclock and no sign of the "All Clear". The little gal who was licking and sticking for victory is now knitting furiously to keep her nerves from being completely shattered. She has what she calls a "Shelter cold", a complaint which has affected me for the past 4 weeks. I have had 2 colds in that time and am expecting 20 more before the end of the winter—if I ever see the end of the winter. I no longer suffer from Housemaids Knee but have developed instead "Shelter back" due to lying flat on my back on the cold stone Platform of an Underground Railway. When we think the nights are going to be particularly bad we go down the Tube—not that every night isn't as bad as the next one—but sometimes when the rain falls and the wind blows they only hang around for eight hours instead of the usual ten or eleven.[26] Then we are able to get to work before the next one, which usually commence about 9 am. or thereabouts. After that we get five and six raids a day and are getting a bit fed-up with the while damned business. The one I envy most is the boy in our Office who is going on holiday next week to Scotland and will probably—if he has any sense at all—stop there. Unfortunately he has a crush on the typist who licks and sticks and thinks he will stay for her sweet sake, although she has no time for him at all, as she only gets half an hour between her dinner and the Air raid warning to wash her hair and do a bit of ironing. So the course of true love is running very rough indeed and he says he is finished with dames for good and all. At seventeen he should be able to make a prediction like that, and the typist who licks and sticks is not so worried as she should be, because as I tell her often there will be such a shortage of blokes after the War is over that she may have to keep him on a Chain. She is a blonde, like me, but has a very nasty disposition—not like me. However, I think she is softening a little and may say "Yes" any time now.

We are having a horrible time and I do not feel the girl I was at all. I haven't slept in a bed for four and half weeks and it looks so inviting that I am composing poetry to it. The day raids are getting awful now, particularly on cloudy days when we never know from one minute to another whether that minute is going to be our last minute as the Germans have a most nasty habit of diving out of the clouds and dropping a couple of Molotov Breadbaskets. Also when we have to walk through the Gun barrage it may look very pretty, but large lumps of Shrapnel

26. By October 1940, London was being bombed heavily and repeatedly (sometimes five raids a day). When raids lasted for ten or eleven hours, many Londoners went to the "Tube" for shelter. By the end of September some 177,000 people were sleeping in some seventy-nine stations of the underground shelter system (Calder, *People's War,* 211–12.) Although Calder states that the Tubes were warm and dry, Betty's comments belie that.

fall around you and if it s *too* large, it s just too bad. I had a terrible experience last week when they bombed Central London during the rush hour, and I was walking down the street wondering whether to go on or stay put. Suddenly I heard an awful "swish" and someone yelled "Lie Flat"—so down I went with about a dozen others and down came the bomb and covered us with dust, even though it was round the corner. Gosh! I nearly had my breakfast shaken out of me. The night raids are the most terrifying through. You just sit and listen to the Guns booming and the bombs dropping and you wonder how long you're going to live this time. What an existence! We are all taking up knitting here—even my friend Peggy who was never very domestic anyway, but is now finishing off a masterpiece of a Pullover for her Spouse. I have suffered with her during the making of it, but have now got to the stage when I am trying to make myself a jumper so shall expect her to suffer with me. Things must be pretty bad for me to take up knitting!! I cannot go to the pictures which is shattering me completely, but I would rather be shattered than bombed and Hitler's boy friends have a liking for Churches, Pubs, Hospitals, and Cinemas. The last Cinema I went to is now a neat pile of ashes, which upsets me very much. I have lost the roses from my cheeks, a couple of pounds in weight, and though I have no grey hairs, I have symptoms of a Crowsfoot appearing round my right eye. Peggy, however, has two or three grey hairs, of which she is very proud. All this is known as suffering for our country—and from what Mr Churchill said last night, it looks as if we shall just have to suffer and suffer for many moons to come. Heigh-ho, do you know anyone who wants a couple of nice English wives, one blonde, one brunette, and now both able to knit. The typist who licks and sticks has decided to stick to her Guns come what may, though I think she may weaken after a couple more Shelter colds.

To get back to serious things—most of the people here feel very strongly that we should do to Berlin what they are doin to us, but as our Government has the last word there is very little we can do. Churchill's speech last night sounded very gloomy, and it s appalling for us to think of going through this ghastly ordeal for three years or more, but if the alternative is surrender to Germany, I think most of us would rather go on for a lifetime if necessary. They say "Britons never shall be Slaves" and that s what we would be if there was anything of the Vichy business done here. The morale of the people seems to be standing up remarkably well, and there has been no panic and no hysteria, even though this is supposed to be the worst bombing ever known in the World's history. Anyone in the world who is anti-British now, should come over and see what the British people are enduring without a murmur, and I don't think they'd be anti-British for long. The trouble is that we are fighting with the usual "Kid-Glove" method, and are afraid to be merciless because the world might think it "un-British". We *must* bomb German women and children if we are to win this War—and it s going to take our Government a lifetime to see it.

I hope your country will take as firm a line with Japan as you urged us to do at Munich. America called us enough names over our "appeasement" policy, and it is to be hoped that she will not let her "phoney" neutrality lead her into the same mistakes. We are to re-open the Burma Road now and that means trouble with the little Yellow men, and if Japan comes in, Spain will try to get Gibraltar and we shall be fighting practically everybody. With no-one to help us. My poor old England—Why does she always have to get in such a mess through helping people out.

We have just finished our dinner. Food is pretty plentiful—except for a slight shortage of chocolate (candy to you) but clothes are not so good.[27] We have to pay double the price for stockings that are half as good. Peggy bought a pair last night, which politely laddered right down this morning and she paid five bob for 'em (a dollar and a quarter to you). Needless to say she is hoppin' mad. The stockings you sent me are marvellous. I have had them for two months and they have not laddered yet, and have saved me several shillings buying new pairs. (Calamity has just occurred We have broken one of our dinner plates and it is the day before pay day—we shall have to put something in hock to pay for it). There are now lumps of cabbage stalk and gravy where there used to be a clean floor. Things are going from bad to worse! Treacle is what you call molasses. We have it in Tarts and Puddings, and also make toffee out of it, and Buns. Billboards are hoardings,[28] where they

27. Although rationing of food, clothing, and coal had become increasingly severe and extensive, in June the first application of "points rationing" was applied. Meat rationing began on March 11, with each person being entitled to one shilling ten pence worth of meat per week (ibid., 275, 282).

28. That is, *hoardings* is the British term for "billboards"—typically board fences around construction sites where notices and advertisements were pasted.

advertise different things. Our Corn is wheat. We don't have canned corn or anything like you do and don't eat so many cereals. Corn on the Cob would just be baked maize to us.

I received the last of the six issues of "Picture Play" this month. I would rather have "Picture Play" than "Glamour" regularly, though "Glamour" is certainly a smashing Magazine. One of the outfits in it particularly took my eye, and if I can wangle round the Post Office to let me export some dough, I would like to send for it. Some of the Patterns are marvellous.

I can't write any more now as I have to clean my face with one of those new fangled Dewy affairs, and then put my face back on again. I am afraid to go up and wash for fear the "Spotters" will whistle that the planes are right above me and I shall be caught with a naked face and a shiny nose. I cannot even have a bath unless I can run the water on the last note of the last "All Clear" and be out and dressed on the first note of the next warning. As you will note, we have just had another accident as the spring of the Typist who licks and sticks Typewriter broke suddenly and I have to finish this on Peggy's Machine, so I can't say much because she has forbidden me to write more than one paragraph for fear I will break her spring too.

I will write you again if I am still alive—next week. Say a prayer for me every night because I shall certainly need it.

Best love,<br>Betty.

All the Clippings and Mags got through allright and I was ever so grateful. The only thing we can do from 6.30 pm. in the evening is read or knit, and there isn't much to read nowadays.

I should love to hear from Sara if she'd like to write me. I still have a longing for California and anything about the place interests me. I shan't be able to write very long letters to her yet, with conditions as they are, but I'll do my best. To-day is Monday—and I feel too tired for words, but I suppose it'll wear off later in the week. We get used to going without sleep and I don't believe I'd know what to do with a Bed if I had one!

B.

Helen,

Have just received your other letter and am typing a few lines in reply. The "All Clear" is sounding now as I write this after our fourth raid this morning. The first at 8.15. when I was on my way to work, and after deciding foolishly to walk through it I had to get into someone's House because the Jerries dropped a couple of whoppers a few streets away from me, and the Guns were pounding like blazes. The second was about half an hour later. The third about 11 oclock and the fourth midday. Last night was the worst night ever since the "blitz" descended on London five weeks ago. Bombs dropped all night long. And on the usual places, Houses, Hospitals, Churches, Blocks of Flats (they're still digging them out of one Luxury Block) and on Public Houses. Where we live the district is sprinkled with Time bombs, which are exploded by the Royal Engineers (a courageous regiment if there ever was one) and it s nothing to be standing washing yourself and nearly be blown off your feet by one exploding suddenly in someone's garden. Cloudy days are a nightmare to us all, though. We can't get to work because there are constant warnings, and when we walk through it there s the danger of indiscriminate dive bombing and machine-gunning. So many people have been killed here walking out trying to do a bit of shopping. The Germans always go for the crowded streets, and the more babies they can bump off, the better. Whatever happens Helen, if I ever live through this War, I could never, never bring my self to look at a German without wanting to tear him to pieces. I've seen too much. And we British are not normally a bitter race, and we don't bear malice to ward anyone. Perhaps we should do a great deal better if we did.

Jack was called up last week. He is an Observer and Wireless Operator in the R.A.F. He will go with the big Bombers over Germany, and I hope and pray, come back safely, though my mother is nearly demented about it. Her nerves have got very bad these past few weeks, through worry about Jack and me. Him going in the R.A.F. and me working in such a "Hell Fire Corner" so to speak. Our station is still there but we've had bombs of all shapes and sizes dropped round us, and I suppose we shall get the same as the other before long. In the winter when the raids start at four oclock (it gets dark at that time) something will have to be done to get us beds in our Shelter at work, so if they get the station then, I shall definitely not be writing you anymore! Mother has been offered a transfer to Oxford, and I could probably go with her, but

I love my London, and can't bear the thought of leaving her when she's in so much trouble. However, if Mum gets very bad I shall have to see what can be done. I should go on writing to the Office if I were you because it stands a much better chance of lasting a while longer than the house does.

Shall have to finish now, as the warning is off again and I must collect my work to do in the Shelter. I am going up to the Underground station ("Tubes" we call them) to try to get a nights sleep to-night. I shall get about three hours rest at least, and that, honey, is not to be sneezed at in these hard times. Gosh! you should *see* the lovely purple circles under my eyes!

Love,
Betty

P.S. Am hopping mad because we couldn't have any dinner to-day. The dirty tikes bombed the Gasometer and there wasn't any Gas, and therefore it naturally follows—no dinner either. I'm writing that bloke Hitler to tell him that he can do what he likes to the military objectives, but when he starts interfering with my grub, then I get annoyed. Now I shall have to exist all day on a sandwich and a cup of milk! It s enough to drive a girl to drink!


GREAT WESTERN RAILWAY

GOODS DEPARTMENT,
SOUTH LAMBETH STATION
LONDON, S.W.8.
[November 15, 1940]

Dear Helen,

As promised, I am sending you a short letter every so often to let you know that I've escaped the Bombs so far, but only just. In the past fortnight, I have been machine gunned twice, have missed a large chunk of shrapnel by about an inch and a half, and have laid down flat on umpteen wet, muddy pavements. I have also managed to distinguish between the "swish" of a whistling bomb and the "swoosh" of one of our own anti-aircraft shells, as they shot into the sky, ready, we hope, to burst in that portion of a German airman where it would do the most damage. When we got home yesterday morning,—having spent a most comfortable night in an Underground station, parked in front of the Litter Bin (Ash-Can to you)—our sitting room was filled with broken glass and lumps of tree-trunk, and we didn t have a window in the whole of the Family mansion. My mother sat down and wept at the sad sight of her best carpet. The bombs fell four doors from us and knocked down a couple of houses. It's a grand life if you don't weaken!

It's a rotten day to-day, wet and misty—the sort of day the Luftwafte loves. When they can dive out of the clouds and bump off a couple of hundred harmless devils, who wouldn't hurt a fly. It's Saturday and I'm going to risk a trip to the pictures. So incidentally, is the typist who "licks and sticks", who has at last realised the worth of her Scotch boy friend that I told you about in my last letter, and is going to hold hands with him for three hours this afternoon, come what! She doesn't care now whether she's bombed, out, blown out, or blasted out, and complains that she can't sleep on a quiet night because she has no swishes and swooshes to lull her to sleep. I think we're all getting as accustomed to this business as we ever will. We work in London's No. 1. Danger area, and every day and night they have a pot at us—it's nothing to work knowing you are surrounded by pretty little Time Bombs, and we're quite used to the terrific noise they make when they explode, sometimes quite unexpectedly, in the middle of the day. We work to a "spotting" system here, which means that we take no notice of the sirens—just go on working until the man on the roof whistles that the Planes are overhead, and then we do a scuttling act down to the Shelter. Sometimes he isn't quick enough, though, and we're chasing across the yard while the bombs are dropping. We're never down the dug-out longer than five minutes, and our knitting is suffering disastrously in consequence. I only did about two lines yesterday, because the Planes were not directly over our district!

*Tuesday.*

As I prophesied this will be finished in snatches. I came into work early this morning to do a little more. I have avoided an Air raid so far, but it is a vile day windy and cloudy so I suppose "Wailing Winnie" will be starting her dirge any moment now. Last night was quiet for a change, the "Raiders passed" being sounded at 9 oclock but that was because it was running a high gale, and the rain was coming down in torrents. We had a miraculous escape two nights ago. The bombs that knocked out all our windows and hurled lumps of tree trunk into the sitting room, fell 4 rooms from us, and horror of horrors a murder was committed there the same night. Talk about excitement! Anyway, we're lucky only to have parted with our windows. Some of the bombs that fall demolish five and six houses at a time.

Our Air Force had a fine day yesterday, and drew first blood against the Italians—commonly called the "Wops". Night before last we bombed Munich, just when dear, darling Adolf, was going to spit out some more smoke and fire, and as a "reprisal" the dirty swines came over yesterday, and bombed Civilians paying homage at the Cenotaph for Armistice day. Can you imagine anything more barbaric? I only wish that Hitler had been at Munich, and that one of the bombs had dropped right on that rotten neck of his. But he was probably miles away, complete with Bullet proof waistcoat and all the rest of his Tin underwear.

Mr Chamberlain died on Sunday, and I felt as I listened to the Announcer giving the News, that I had lost someone I know, personally. Chamberlain was a great man, and a great gentleman—and we shall not see his like again for many years. I was always a staunch supporter of his policy, because he wanted peace, and like me, he loved his country beyond everything. I never wanted War for England—I knew, and I think he did, that it will take this Island years to pull herself out of the dreadful mess that will be the result of all this slaughter. Neville may not have been a great War Minister—he did not have the ability to speak the colourful, and often bombastic, rhetoric that Churchill can, but I rated him higher than Churchill in everything. Churchill may be a Man O'War, but I am not one of his admirers, and I never have been. He hates the Germans that's one thing I like him for, and he's ruthless, which is what we need. If I had my way in forming a Cabinet I'd throw out all the milk and water "Old School tie" enthusiasts, and religious cranks like Bishop Halifax,[29] and get down to some good, heavy *and*

---

29. A devout Anglo-Catholic, Halifax succeeded Anthony Eden in 1938 as foreign secretary. In the House of Lords, he was one of the "appeasers" of Hitler, yet he was Chamberlain's preferred successor as prime minister rather than Churchill. On May 7, 1940, the House of Commons began a six-day debate on the fall of Norway. The Labour Party agreed to serve in a War Cabinet headed by Churchill. Chamberlain resigned, and on May 13 Churchill addressed the House as prime minister. In December, Halifax was named ambassador to Washington (Calder, *People's War*, 93–101).

indiscriminate bombing. None of this "If you can't find a military objective, bring your bombs back" business.

I had a shocking time trying to get to work this morning. The station I usually get off at has been bombed right down to a pile of ruins—rumour hath it that 37 were killed in it—and I had to go a tortuous, in and out, way by 'Bus. My poor old London—I only pray that she may rise again and look something as lovely as she used to look! It breaks my heart to see all her history battered about like this, by people who are only modern savages. May God forgive them for all they're doing, and if he can't find it in his heart to do that, may they be punished as heavily as possible. And may God forgive me if I ever speak or look at anything German after this business is over, or an Italian for that matter—for they're every bit as dirty as the Huns.

Do thank your Aunt for all the kind things she says—and for the lovely handkerchief. She sounds a lovely lady. I think you'll have to include me in the "Bundles for Britain" business soon. I shall have to get me some new clothes, and God knows from where. Silk stockings are banned from next month—a coat with Fur on costs about six weeks salary and in any case, you haven't got time to buy 'em, even if you had the money. I can't get into a shop in time to buy a tin of Cold Cream. I've been trying for three days, but either the damn place is shut, or there's a Raid on and I have to hurry home in case my mother goes hysterical. She goes completely to pieces if I'm out in a raid, and as I'm more often in one than out of one, you can imagine the state she's in. I do wish she'd go away. I've been trying to persuade her to go back home to Monmouthshire, but she won't go without me, and I don't want to leave London. She's a great worry to me, because she's a bit jittery, and half blind in the Blackout, and I could tear along the streets pretty quickly if she wasn't trailing behind.

*Thursday.*

Here we are again! I hope you don't mind this silly way of writing a letter, but it's the only possible method. The licking and sticking typist has just come in (complete with boy friend) so I shan't have much time. Two envelopes of clippings of a magazine from you are on the desk by me, and I was so pleased to get them. I love hearing from you—in fact it gives me something to come to work for. I only hope when this affair is over, I shall be able to meet you and thank you in person for all you've done for me.

We gave the Wops a terrific Naval beating yesterday and I suppose Musso will feel like throttling the lot of us. There's something rotten in the air though concerning this trip of Molotovs to Berlin. If Russia comes in against us, Heaven knows what we shall do. The British people can put up with a hell of a lot, God knows—if it means freedom and honour for Britain—but after all, we've a terrific struggle already with Russia on top of it.

I see Roosevelt got re-elected—which is what most of the people here seemed to want. Our papers are under the impression that the Axis wanted Willkie,—he's supposed to be of German descent, and anxious to keep America out at all costs, and so on—and naturally anything the Axis wants is poison to the average Britisher. We didn't really under-stand a great deal about the American election however, I really though Willkie would make it—he seemed to have most of the Press behind him, from what I could judge. American papers are so vastly different from ours, however. The British Newspaper is terribly conservative, and prints very little in the way of scandal, or sensationalism. The nearest approach we have to one of the N.Y. papers is our "Daily Mirror"—but it's a bit of a rag, and most people only buy it because of its convenient size, and the fact you can read it in the train on your way to work without blacking your neighbour's eye.

My Boss had just asked me if you can send us some Pins!!! The Pin situation in our Office is getting pretty desperate, and we've been borrowing from each other for weeks. Of all the things to ask me to send for, he couldn't have picked anything sillier!

I won't write any more now, Helen, but will try and send you a couple of lines again next week. I hope you can make this out—it's typed badly, and the both sides of the paper business annoys me intensely, but it has to be!

Bye for now, and do write soon.

Love,
Betty

c/o. G.W.R
SOUTH LAMBETH. S.W.8.
[December 21, 1940]

Dear Helen,

First of all I must apologize for the shocking paper I'm typing this on, but it's all I can find at the moment, as we have what is known as a paper shortage and we have to utilize whatever is lying around. You'll never kid me that things are as bad as that, but the Railway Companies want to save money and we must abide by what they say.

I was very pleased to hear from you last week but surprised that you haven't heard from me for six weeks. I must have written you at least two letters in that time. I have heard from you several times, and got some magazines and clippings, and I have answered faithfully each time. I hope you've heard by now.

This will have to be a very short letter as I do want it to get to you by Christmas, if possible. I got your Christmas card and the lovely hand-kerchief yesterday and I also had the lovely hankie from your Aunt. Do thank her for me and tell her, and all your other friends, how much I appreciate their kindness in even giving me a thought at all. Christmas for us will probably be a horrible affair—if I guess rightly we shall be well and truly "blitzed" on Christmas Eve, so that the Huns can kill off a couple of hundred British children who are waiting for Father Christmas—so I suppose we shall spend our time in the Shelter. And most of the things that make Christmas what it is will be missing from the Shops and the Table. Lord Woolton told us last week that all fruits are to be cut out from now on—Onions and Lemons have already vanished—Chocolate and sweets will be getting scarcer and scarcer, and what is Christmas without Fruit and Sweets and Nuts.[30] Most of the Poultry and stuff will be taken to feed the troops, and we shall be left with very little indeed. The Sugar ration goes up to 12 ounces and the Tea to four ounces for Christmas week only, but I don't drink Tea and never take Sugar so it doesn't affect me. The Butter ration remains at

30. Frederick Marquis, Baron Woolton, a former social worker in the slums and the head of a chain of department stores, was the minister of food in the Chamberlain government and remained in that position until 1945. This ministry, which in 1943 had 50,000 employees, not only determined the amount of rations but also conducted public relations campaigns to influence consumers' buying (ibid., 440–43).

two ounces, and the Meat ration is to be cut again. Someone told us at the beginning of this Bust-up that we had enough stocks of food to last us for three years. Someone must have been telling us awful whoppers! What upsets me most is that we're all rationed on Chocolate, I believe you call it Candy. That's about the only thing I'm sweet-toothy about. And what is most drastic of all is the coming ban on silk stockings, and the rationing of Cosmetics, of all things. Threepennorth a week—that's 5 cents. What a life!

*Monday.*

This will never get you by Xmas now—I simply didn't have a chance to write a line last week, we were that busy. And last night was one of the worst "blitz" nights we've ever had. I had about two hours sleep! Bombs were falling around like hailstones, and there were enormous fires. He's been smashing up the Provincial towns this past week, and only raiding London for about five or six hours, which is quite short compared to the 14 hours we had last night. We had our 400th Air Raid warning on Saturday, and on some days we've spent 18 hours out of the 24 under an "Alert". Three-quarters of the day being bombed! I went to the West End to the flicks last night, to see "Texas Rangers Ride Again",[31] I came out just as the Sirens were sounding which is just as well, because about half an hour later they dropped five bombs in that vicinity. I didn't see my brother yesterday either, which upset me very much. He joins the R.A.F. on Friday—Friday the 13th—could anything be worse? My mother is nearly frantic.

The War seems to go on never-endingly. I can't see what the finish will be or when it will come—if it ever does. Sometimes I could take every member of our Government and strangle them slowly, they do such insane things. They refuse to bomb Germany indiscriminately, although they know that it would lift the public morale here 100 percent if they did. Surely out of every six bombs our Pilots take over two could be spared to be dropped on a couple of Hospitals or Houses, or Schools. I thinks I'd give up half my salary if someone would drop a bomb on Cologne Cathedral, or some of Germany's precious monuments for what they did to our beautiful Coventry, and our equally lovely Bristol and more than ever, what they've done to my London. The people here

31. A Texas western (1940; U.S.) about cattle rustling starring John Howard and Ellen Drew.

are full of optimism, cheerful, and braver than anyone, but they can't go on like this for ever, unless they know that the Germans are taking the same medicine. And why in heck they don't bomb Rome to fragments is beyond me. I suppose it's because the Pope happens to take up a bit of space there. The last thing I heard about the Pope he was blessing some Italian Officers "for fighting for their dear fatherland!" I had my photo taken in the Shelter last night and it will probably go in one of the Papers. If it does I'll send you a copy, although you probably won't be able to see much of me as I pushed my head under the Clothes when I saw the Flashlight! God, I looked terrible!

I had a magazine from one of your friends, who I don't know at all. She was staying at a Hotel in Kansas City. Unfortunately I have mislaid the Envelope and don't know her name, but I'm very grateful to her for it. The Magazines and clippings and everything seem to be arriving here alright, despite the terrific losses in Merchant shipping. I wish someone would offer me a free seat in the Yankee Clipper. What a dream!

We are all still knitting frantically here. I have started another jumper, Peggy has made umpteen different articles, but our Hazel is still in the middle of the last Jumper but one. Her Ian may be joining the Air Force shortly, so she'll have to settle down and make him some nice, woolly gloves, or something. They've got past the hand-holding stage now, and things are looking pretty serious!! She says if there's any trouble I'll have to take the blame, because I started it all! Always the fairy godmother, that's me. I have a terrible cold coming and a sore throat and don't feel a bit like going home and spending another night underground in the Shelter, but if I don't I may not be in a fit state to do anything. There's heaps of ways I'd rather die than be smashed to bits by a Bomb. My goodness, what a life this is!

I won't write any more now, as all this is pretty rambling anyway. I'll write you again after Christmas, always providing I last out till then.

Bye for now, and please write me often.

Love,
Betty

P.S. This won't reach you until well into the New Year, but I'd like to wish you everything that's good for 1941 . . . you and all the people there who've been so good and thoughtful to me.

P.S. I read this morning that David Niven has at last got a commission in the Army—after waiting four months for it. He's a Lieutenant in an Infantry Regiment, so if he comes out of this alive, he'll be lucky. The Infantry do most of the heavy fighting. Still, he did come home to do something, which is more than most of Hollywood's lily-livered British Colony did!

P.P.S. One of our girls has already decided to start knitting socks for him!

B.

*A postcard of Betty striking a Hollywood pose. On the back she wrote: "This is me looking darned untidy but a bit happier than I feel at present. Taken the week War was declared (Sept 1939) on what is now German territory i.e. Jersey (Channel Isles). The day we returned, War broke out!"*

150

# CHEERIO, OLD SON

*This clipping appears to have had iconic significance for Betty, who lost the father she never knew in World War I. In her letter of March 7, 1940, she wrote: "I'm sending you a picture from one of our papers too, of a father saying good-bye to his wife and baby. It s one of the loveliest things I ever saw and it s typical of the scenes that you can see on Victoria station any morning when the B.E.F. go back to the Front. Thousands of 'em. Poor devils. It makes me sick to look at them, and think that a million British boys died in the last bust-up, just so their kids could grow up and do the same thing."*

*Betty and her mother, Gladys. Betty wrote on the back of the snapshot: "This is Mum and me in our garden." Possibly taken in 1941.*

152

*Betty; her brother, Jack; and his wife, Muriel. On the back of the snapshot
is written: "This is me, my brother, and his wife taken at Richmond, just
before I went away to the San. I'd lost a stone and I look terrible."*

*One of the "dark men" Betty claimed to be devoted to. This is probably Ted,*
*the Grenadier guardsman who broke both ankles in paratrooper training.*
*The snapshot was taken in 1941. Betty wrote on the back, "This was taken*
*in the garden this summer about 2 days before I went into the Sanatorium.*
*The Bars look as though we're in jail or a mental home!"*

Sept 28, 1946

c/o. D. G. M. O. (Rates)
2, Irwell St
Liverpool. 2.

Dear Helen,

You will no doubt be surprised to know that I am writing this in bed, propped up with umpteen pillows, having really nearly kicked the bucket this time. I was taken ill about 3½ weeks ago, couldn't breathe, couldn't move, went a peculiar bluey-grey colour, & had a temperature of 104 or there abouts! The Doctors diagnosed Pleurisy & Pneumonia, & put me on ·M· E·B· Tablets, which, though they made me pretty sick, I'm sure saved my life. I was transferred to Hospital in the middle of it, & sent home because I was lying awake all night

In 1946, Betty wrote Helen from the hospital, writing by hand from her bed.

*Betty's open-toed white shoes are probably the ones Helen sent. Although they caused quite a stir for Betty and her mother, given the privations of the postwar austerity, they look suspiciously like the sort of shoes nurses wore at the time in the United States. The picture is dated 1947.*

*Betty and probably her husband, Bob Arnold, "the man with the corn colored hair." They were married in 1950. The picture was taken in 1949.*

there is so much I'd love to tell you if you are still alive — I am now 78 years old and still enjoying an old lady's life. I went to Europe four times, three times to England — I loved it so much — I am so sorry now that I didn't try to reach you.

Aug. 18, 1969.

Dear Billy:

yesterday I finished re reading all your letters to me. I had saved them all and I surely wish I had read them again long ago. I was filled with sorrow and guilt. I quit writing to you because I could not take any more of your criticism of the U.S.

Now after reading again of all you had been thru. I know I should have forgiven you anything. I am writing after 19 years without much hope of finding you to tell you that I am sorry.

Your letters to the Churchill memorial in Fulton, Mo. where he gave the "Iron Curtain" speech. They are so good they should be published.

I'm hoping that this letter may find its way to you — not likely after all this time — affectionately, Helen.

Miss Helen Bradley
5 West 68 St. Terrace
Kansas City, Mo. U.S.A. 64113

*Helen Bradley's returned letter to Betty Swallow, written August 18, 1969.*

*Helen Bradley, 1970.*

# IV

## February 1941–Early 1942

For Betty Swallow, this was the most difficult period of the war. Although potatoes and carrots were plentiful, rations of butter, eggs, and chocolate were further reduced. "I long," she wrote Helen in May, "for a nice juicy orange, an apple, or a banana." Betty in February became a volunteer "Fire Spotter" as German air raids on London intensified—a prelude for an expected invasion.

Wendell Willkie, the defeated Republican candidate in the 1940 presidential election, favorably impressed British officials, as well as citizens like Betty, during his fact-finding trip to England. But Willkie's fellow Americans Ambassador Joseph Kennedy, Senator Burton K. Wheeler, and Charles Lindbergh, "a potential fifth columnist," angered her for their isolationist positions. And Betty, as in the past, angrily objected to British bombers attacking only military targets while German bombers targeted British cities.

Not until August did Helen learn that her pen pal had been sent by her doctors to a sanatorium in East Anglia, outside London, where she tried to recover from pneumonia. After seven months of convalescing, Betty was back at work in December and thankfully acknowledged packages of candy, stockings, and cosmetics from the States.

Dear Helen

Received your letter two days ago and am going to make a determined effort to answer it. My boss is away with the flu and although I
am up to my neck in work, I think it is about time I had a bit of leisure.
Life is one long rush nowadays. Either you're running to get to work
before the Raids start, or you're running to get home. Last night was
quiet for a change, but the very stillness, kept me on the alert. I lay
awake half the night waiting for the ominous "boom-boom" that usually heralds the approach of Goering's Luftwaffte [*sic*], and the wail of
the sirens afterwards. It's a great life once you get used to it.

I can't understand why my letters have taken so long to reach you.
I have written fairly regularly, but probably a lot of correspondence is
resting on the bed of the Atlantic, along with a lot of our food and
other commodities. No as you see I am not dead yet. I've had some
narrow squeaks; it's a case of "Here today and gone tomorrow" with
most people. It's amazing how after you've had months of it, you accept
the whole thing quite calmly. When I sleep at night and the raids are
on, I never know whether I will wake up and see the morning and yet
the only thing I hope, is that I will be asleep and won't know anything
about it. I'm such a light sleeper and it is this lying awake and listening
to the guns and planes, and the whine of the bombs dropping that used
to get me down. I certainly don't want to die, but if it's written in the
fates that I have to I want to be unconscious at the time. Mother shud-
ders so badly when she hears the guns, that I sometimes go to shelter
with her, and when we do, we go down to the subway—the tube we call
it—where they have fitted up bunks for shelterers. But it is actually not
all that safe down there. If a bomb falls on the air shaft you'd be suf-
focated, and if it fell on the water main as it did in one South London
tube station, you'd be drowned like rats. It's all a gamble anyway. You
might as well stay in the house, and trust the Almighty to look after
you. I don't want to be crippled or maimed or anything. And I don't
want anything to happen to my mother or brother. I should hate to be
the one who got away. People over here are so brave, that anyone who
is afraid would have cause to be ashamed of himself. The Civilians are
joining up to be Fire Fighters, wardens nurses, anything to help. I'm
going to join a Fire Spotting party, to deal with the hundreds of incen-

diaries they drop in an attempt to set our City alight.[1] They burned our lovely 14th century Guildhall, and some of our loveliest churches in a raid about a month ago. Anything that's beautiful those Swine set out to destroy. God! How I hate them.

Most of us are digging in now awaiting invasion, which may take place any time now. I suppose it will mean more terror, and slaughter—more of the cruelty that belongs peculiarly to the Hun. But we're ready for him and he'll get a welcome he'll never forget. The only thing I dread is the fact that he's going to use poison gas and blister gasses. They're so horrible, Helen. The poor people will die like flies and mustard gas is dreadful to contemplate. To use poison gasses on civilians is probably the most ghastly crime of all time, but there it is, It's coming and we shall have to endure it as we've had to stick everything else. If my turn comes with the rest of 'em, I only hope I shan't lose my nerve.

I haven't had the stockings yet, and certainly wish they would come through. The position in England seems to be awful to me, but I never lived through the last war and mother says that in 1917 things were worse. It seems strange to me to see half empty shops, though we are far from starving, of course. It's often a bit of a problem shopping for a family. You get so little meat, eggs are scarce, fish is so expensive that it would break the bank to live on it. Bacon is rashioned [*sic*]. And the butter—Golly, Helen! If you ever get a spare bit of butter for heaven's sake remember your old pal and send it over. I hate margarine, even though the Government have produced some new fangled sort that is supposed to contain vitamins A and B. It tastes like nothing on earth to me. Another thing that bothers me is that we can't get any chocolate—Candy to you. Whether it's all gone to the army or cut down because of the sugar ration I don't know, but we certainly can't get it. There's a regular battle in the office when someone appears with a bit of chocolate to sell. But there—so many things are scarce now and if it's going to win this war I suppose we must pull in our belts even tighter before it's all over.

1. The first Fire Watchers Order was issued in September 1940, but it applied only to large factories, warehouses, and such. By New Year's Eve, all men between sixteen and sixty had to register as fire wardens. Women volunteered for this duty (Calder, *People's War*, 239).

Your Wendell Willkie has been over here the past week seeing for himself. He has made a very good impression here—people like a man with courage enough to come to a country that's having a bit of trouble, instead of passing opinion on it from a desk in Washington. I hear that he is going back in a day or so t[o] give evidence in this Lease and lend bill affair.[2] My opinion of American hel[p] is the same as ever. For what they have sold us we are grateful, but it is useless for American munition people to brag about the help they will be able to give Britain in 1943, or thereabouts. If Germany is to be stopped, we must get help now within the next few weeks. After all, Britain is fighting for all and if we go down America goes with us. In view of such facts, it seems appalling that isolationists Senators still stand up and bicker about what we are going to pay you for this, that and the other. It reminds me of some one fighting a bully outside America's ho[u]se and America obligingly coming to the door peeping out and charging for a stick to hit him with. It's that that has given Uncle Sam the Uncle Shylock label. We don't really doubt your sincerity or that you're trying to help but those damned isolationists leave a taste in the mouth that all the sugary declarations don't get rid of. While they keep asking to know what Britain's war aims are, they make me sick. Our war aim at the moment is to survive and to keep some sort of liberty living in a bit more healthy position to give them a couple more details. And if they want us to survive why the heck don't they do something, instead of talking so much. If all this sounds "sour grapes"ish to you. I'm sorry, Helen, but after all it's such a horrible business, this war and we must get it over as soon as possible, otherwise we wo'nt [*sic*] have our lives or any of our country left. Some of our cities have stood up to nights of bombing and it's amazing sometimes how little damage is visible as you walk through. When I come to work sometimes in the morning I pass through about five different suburbs, and although you sometimes have to pass enormous craters in the roads, and see houses that are only

2. The Lend-Lease Bill, passed into law in March 1941, gave Roosevelt the authority to supply anything Britain needed. For the moment the supply of arms under Lead-Lease was less important than were shipments of food such as powdered eggs, evaporated milk, bacon, beans, and lard. One-fifteenth of all food arriving in Britain in 1941 was the result of Lend-Lease (Calder, *People's War*, 266–67).

masses of rubble, it's not half as bad as it might have been. Of course, when invasion comes we shall have to endure a complete bombardment by land, sea and air and it will probably be twice as bad as the "blitz" nights of last September and October, and that will be pretty bad, believe me.

I have been going to the pictures lately, two and three times a week and defying the air raids, It is not very pleasant coming home with guns barking and the Jerries zooming about overhead, but it's better than sitting out in the black-out. Although I am very short sighted, I can see like a cat in the dark, but mother isn't so fortunate. She can't see a hand in front of her and when she comes out with me, it's torture trying to get her along—specially when there's a raid on. Mum has a bad habit of shuddering every time she hears a gun going. I'm so used to them now, they don't worry me at all, although some of our own unexploded shells have been doing as much damage as the bombs. One of the nurses in Mum's hospital had her foot sliced completely off by a fragment of anti-aircraft shell. A tin hat is the best protection for the skull, but we can't all manage to get them. The best of them naturally go to the Civil Defense services.

I loved to hear about the goodies you were cooking for Xmas. Our Christmas was very quiet, and subdued. I had a good time in the office on Xmas Eve when we all tried to forget there was a war on, and we had some sort of a "truce" on Xmas Eve and Xmas night—at least that's what the Huns said, though personally I think the only thing that stopped them coming over here was bad weather. But my brother was away, and everyone seemed to be separated. No! it wasn't a happy Christmas by any means but I hope you enjoyed yourself good and proper and ate one of those candied fruits or "cookies" or whatever you call 'em for me.

Your "pash" Olivier is back in England now with his wife. Leigh is going back to the States, I understand, but Larry is staying here to join up or do some shows for the forces. I am going to see Gielgud in "Dear Brutus" on Saturday. It's been put on for matinees only. The Theatre where I used to go to see him, the Queens, has been bombed right down to the ground. I hope John Howard was good with Ginger Rogers. He is very popular here, strangely enough—principally because of the "Drummond" films. But I can never imagine how they can say the British fans thought he was an Englishman.

The Book (For Whom The Bells Tolls [*sic*]) sounds good.[3] Too bad it is dirty. Honey! over in England we never even get a chance to read *anything* that's dirty. They take such marvelous care of our morals. You wouldn't believe. Personally I was never made that way. To put it mildly, words speak louder than actions for me. I don't mind *reading* a bit of dirt, but otherwise—no thanks! Although war time naturally tends to make morals slip right down the drain. All these lasses parting from their laddies and never knowing whether they're going to see them again. Still in our office we are all firm believers in the old adage "Virtue hath its own reward"! Only our Hazel says she's not quite sure that it is!

I was caught beautifully last night. I was listening intently to the Radio—There was a Scotch program on and I am balmy on Scots—they were playing my favorite, Skye Boat Song, I don't know whether you've ever heard it. Anyway, there was a sudden terrific clatter outside, and the guns opened up in all directions—the plane dived down, and there was a sound like the creaking of car gears, and wallop! down came a couple of beauties, that shook the windows and banged the doors, and scared the poor cat nearly out of his nine lives. This went on for about half an hour, with frequent thuds and booms. And then they suddenly decided to sound the warning and let the folks know there was a raid on. It's ever so funny! We've often had the most terrific explosions in the day with no warning at all. I'm going fire-spotting next week. Stalking about on a drafty roof, till 3 A.M. to help put out the incendiaries. What a job!

Have just heard that Wendell Wilkie [*sic*] is purely German descent. What a blow! And I was getting all ready to fall for him. He has gone back home now.

No I am not joking about the pins. They are terribly scarce here and we are having the devil's own time getting any. *Everything* seems to be rationed here, except breathing.

I received some mags from Miss Wheeler. I'm very grateful to her for them. Please thank her for them, and tell her how much everyone in the office here enjoyed them.

3. The novel by Ernest Hemingway dealt with the Spanish Civil War of the 1930s, in which Hemingway fought on the side of the Republic against General Franco, who was aided by Germany and Italy.

I must close now Helen, as Hazel wants her typewriter, and we are all having to get down to it in earnest. I forgot to tell you, as I started this letter three days back, the Old Man has now returned from his bout of 'flu looking more miserable than ever.

I hope you get this quicker than the last letter and write soon, won't you.

P.S. I got the clippings. They were ever so interesting.

Love,
Betty

GREAT WESTERN RAILWAY

GOODS DEPARTMENT,
SOUTH LAMBETH STATION
LONDON, S.W.8.
[March 6, 1941]

Dear Helen,

Have just had two letters from you within a week of each other but before that hadn't heard from you for some time. I wrote you about a fortnight ago but with the way the Boats are being sunk I doubt very much whether anything will be getting there. I was very pleased to hear from you, you can imagine. I am still getting papers and things from New York, U-Boats or no U-Boats. Lots of things have gone down, though, much to my despair. I've lost about six pairs of stockings, and stockings are as precious as gold now. The "Western Prince" went down off the Coast of Ireland, and on it were two nighties, stockings, Books and other miscellaneous Christmas gifts. I suppose if I could pay a visit to the bottom of the Ocean, I'd see some darned Mermaid garbed in my nightie, having her honeymoon! I don't care about the stockings being warm—and in any case those Nylon ones you sent me before were quite warm enough. I'd just like to look good, for a change. Still it s no use crying over spilt milk, but I could strangle that so and so Mermaid!

I'm so glad my letters give someone enjoyment. They aren't really well written now, because I have so little time to even write down proper English. Maybe if I'm still here in the Summer, when the longer evenings are back, I'll be able to spend more time at it. Nowadays, whatever correspondence I do has to be done in the Lunch hour. It gets dark too early to stay behind and do anything in the evening. The Sirens are getting a *bit* later though, that s one blessing. Sometimes they'll wail about 7.30, or 8, which gives you plenty of chance to go home. But I suppose with the advent of Spring, hell will be let loose again, and we shall have those 8 and 9 hour massacres, with the bombs whistling down one-a-minute. As it is, hundreds of poor, innocent women and kids, who never harmed a damned soul, are getting killed nightly. Every morning the Demolition Squads have to go and dig some poor, devil out of the ruins of his home. It s a beastly business, this War. All the homes that have taken their owners years to build are just so many military objectives to Hitler and that lousy nation of his. I wish they could all drop dead in their tracks—the whole rotten lot of 'em. At the moment, we are sitting tight awaiting the inevitable invasion, and the equally inevitable Poison Gas. Hitler *must* invade England or he's lost the War, he knows that, so to save his own skin, and to buoy up his people, he'll be bound to have a shot at it. Funny thing here is, that most people seem to welcome the idea. The British are a funny lot. They do very little cheering and yelling, but give 'em something to fight for and they'll go at it like demons, and there s nothing better in the world for them to fight for than their own country, their own homes and their own people. Hitler will find that the average Briton will never give in like the French and the Belgian and the rest of that hopeless European crew—to whom we should never been allied in the first place. There'll be much suffering, and slaughter before it's over and done with, but with the help of God, and the wind in our favour, as the poet said, we shall whack the living daylights out of him. Gas is certainly something to be dreaded though. If the Swines use the lethal gases, as they seem to be threatening to do, we shall all quietly cough our lungs up, unless our Gas Masks can withstand it, and if he uses Mustard Gas, that will penetrate through anything, and burn your skin off. Ye Gods! what a cheerful prospect for a gal of my tender years. If ever I come out of this alive, I shall never complain about anything again. I shall just pass a vote of thanks to my maker for getting me through all of it. As it is, I'm a lot thinner, and my nerves aren't so good as they used to be, but I'm still alive, and when I wake up in the morning, I never fail to marvel at it!

I told you about Xmas in one of the letters I wrote about six weeks ago. My brother joined the R.A.F. the week before. He came home on leave last week. He looks thin and tired—they have to work so hard, passing Examinations, and the like—but his enthusiasm is boundless. They're rather bitter now, these R.A.F. boys. They want to give the Huns a taste of what the Hun has given us, and please God, when we have the Machines, they will be allowed to do it. As it is, they must abide by the Rules, and find a military target and bomb that, and that only. Nothing indiscriminate or Un-christian like if you get the idea. I firmly believe that our Government will continue to play the gentlemen until we are absolutely on our last legs, and then they may decide to do something about. If they continue with these Milk and Water methods, the people may force them to alter their ways. The British people aren't so silly and soft hearted as they used to be. They've endured so much in the past six months, I doubt whether any other nation in the World could have lasted out under the strain. If anyone calls the British degenerate after this, they deserve to be hung, drawn and quartered.

The "Lease and Lend" Bill seems to be taking an unconscionable time to get passed, but as it seems to be hindered at every turn by a crowd of isolationist nit-wits, that s hardly to be wondered at. Lindbergh, I could cheerfully strangle. It beats me why you Americans make such an idol out of such a Rat. If ever there s a potential fifth columnist it s your little Flying boy. In England he would have been forgotten long ago. What has he done that s so marvellous for God's sake, except turn on a country that showed him nothing but kindness? He reminds me of that other super Rat-cum-Rabbit—our pal, Joseph Kennedy, for if he ever sets foot on English soil again I shall make it my personal business to pick the nearest thing handy and hurl it flat at him. Kennedy is supposedly American-Irish, which may explain it. While they're on about the Irish hating the English, I think the positions should be reversed and the English should start hating the Irish. If you saw some of the ungrateful, shanty, Irish scum that I come in contact with, who live in England and work here, enjoy her bounty, are exempt from the Conscription laws, and then stand on Soap boxes, and call the dreadful, cruel, English all the names they can think, up, you'd understand how I feel about them. As for their part in this War, the least said about it the better. I think Hitler is doing his damndest to cripple our West Coast ports so he can invade Ireland first and then make an attack from the West. Or, of course, he may start on Scotland—invading it from Norway. Theres one thing he's got something to meet when he encounters the Scots. Theyre a marvellous people, brave and tough, and whatever differences, they, too, have had with England in the past, they won't take advantage of a time like this to stab her in the back. They're British—the Scots. Thank God, we don't have to own the Irish or put them in that category. Give me England, Scotland, Wales and Northern Ireland, and you can take Da Valera's Eire and stick it on the Wall!

I'm sorry about the duty on food, but there, its only to be expected. Some things are very short here, its no good the Government saying otherwise. I've not tasted an Orange for three months, and an Onion for about six! Its hopeless trying to get enough Meat to satisfy your appetite—the Butter's just a scrape—cheese is non-existent, Eggs are like gold. Sweets—Candy, to you, are rationed so severely that a Bar of Chocolate tastes like Golden Nectar. Most of the prices here have jumped to a terrific level, and Shopkeepers are having a job to get enough goods to keep their Shops open all day. The Government have controlled the prices of essential commodities—Bread, Butter, Margarine—things like that, and they're experimenting with different vitamins, trying to put them into the plainer foods. They're imploring us to eat plenty of carrots, and Potatoes, for energy. Carrots make you see in the dark—a very necessary thing in this country of Black-outs. I sometimes go out at night into a well of blackness. It doesn't worry me because I can grope about in the dark, but I often look at it, and wonder whether my England will ever be the same again, and whether we shall ever see her all lit up as she used to be. Sometimes, when theres a raid on and the Searchlights are up and the Shells bursting like fireworks, it's a magnificent sight, but a dangerous one. A piece of shrapnel on your head, and its good-bye for ever, in other words. Still, we all have to take a chance at one time or the other.

I've been trying to get some information about that precious Larry of yours, but the clippings of their arrival here went with the paper to the Scrap paper dumps. I didn't think you'd be interested. I heard Leigh on the Radio last Sunday, doing something for the troops and L.O. is going to do a Show for the Air Force next week. Jack says he is joining the Air Force shortly as a Pilot, so his Commanding Officer told him. They seem very happy to be home, which is something in their favour.

That friend of mine in Jersey City wrote me last week, asking me to come out straight away. Apparently she has the money for my fare, and a good job for me, and she wants me to cable her so she can make all the necessary arrangements. Well! I'd like to, in a way, but it means leaving everyone here, and then I might not even get there due to the blasted U_Boats, and worse still, I don't think they'll give me an Exit permit. I'm going to see about it next week though, and will let you know what happens. I wish I wasn't quite so sentimental about England. I realise that theres greater opportunities in America, but I keep on thinking of the three thousand miles of Ocean between me and London. And theres my mother and everyone. Still, we shall see what the Passport Office have to say about it. I'm going to write them after I've finished this letter which may be tomorrow. I must go up and have some lunch now; otherwise there may not be any left by the time I get there.

*Friday*

Have just received your letter dated Jan.23rd.No.3. I don't remember how many letters I've written you in 1941. but I'll have to call this No.3. then I think it will be alright. I got the envelope of clippings from "Life" and am anxiously awaiting the Movie Mags. We do hope they get here, because we haven't a darned thing to read. I got a copy of "Life" and a copy of "Pic" from New York yesterday, but young Ian was going up to Glasgow to see his mother on the night train last night, and like the soft-hearted softie I am, I lent 'em to him to read on his 14-hour journey. I gave him strict instructions to bring 'em back with him, so I shall have to inwardly digest them later. Theres a fine article about Churchill in one of them. I'm no Churchill "fan" but the man does love his country, and for that I salute him. Chamberlain loved England too, but his was a quieter devotion. He lacked the odourful speech of a Churchill, but he was a great man, just the same, and I admired him very much.

You say you think America will be "in" soon. I don't think so, honey. Neither does anyone here. We've never expected America's entry into the War, unless of course, Japan starts her tricks. We are on the verge of War with Bulgaria now—still, what does War with another country matter? We're up to our necks in it now, we might as well step in right up to the eyebrows! I'm all for slamming hell out of the Bulgars, and all the other pettifogging little Balkan nations. The only reason I wish the Yanks would come in the War is because I think the Leaders of your Air Force might not be so soft-hearted as the Leaders of ours. I'd drape myself round the neck of any American pilot who'd drop a stick of bombs smack a cross the middle of Berlin, and not care whether it hit down a House instead of damaging a Power station.

Thanks so much for promising to send me the little things: I'm so grateful to all of you for all you do for me—Heaven knows, theres little or nothing I can do in exchange. I only wish there was. I'm writing you a shorter letter this time, because I shall try and write every so often, and trust to luck that some of the letters will get to you. At least Spring is coming, and we shall have the lighter evenings, and England is so beautiful in the Spring. Even London, never looks lovelier than she does in April and May. It seems awful that she, and so many other English towns should be punished so badly. Still, I'd rather have my London, with all her bangs and bruises, than Petain's Paris. Paris has still got her monuments, but she's got precious little else.

Wailing Winnie, or Moaning Minnie, as we call the Sirens, have just started, and I must get up to dinner in case the Germans drop a bomb in the Stew Pot! Write me often, Helen, and I'll do my best to answer everything, and once again, thanks for all you've done, and all you're doing for me.

Love,
Betty

I'm enclosing a clipping which made my Mother cry her eyes out. No more tragic picture of bombing could be imagined, than that poor man looking for his "darlings".

Mother also says that if she ever gets her hands on your Senator Burton Wheeler she'll skin him alive; and if she needs any help I'll be right there—The filthy swine should come over and live here for a while. He wouldn't be so smug, and safe & secure then. A bit of bombing will do a lot of 'em good.

B

### GREAT WESTERN RAILWAY.

Goods Department,
South Lambeth Station,
London, S.W.8.

May 5th. [1941]

Dear Helen,

Well! I've got a letter from you at last. It seems ages since I last heard, and I've written you on several occasions. If you ask me, the state of the shipping in the Atlantic must be pretty awful—much worse than the Admiralty tell us.[4] I used to get letters and things from the States every week—now its sometimes two months before anything turns up. I got the "Readers Digest" and the "Screenland" that you sent, and I also got a letter from New York about 3 weeks ago, but honey, I never got that parcel you sent me, and I can't bear to even think about it. All the things I wanted most are in it—I have to queue up for hours to get cosmetics, and chocolate, and from all accounts chocolate will shortly be a thing of the past, anyway. Its enough to drive a girl balmy. I *cannot* get stockings, only thick service weight and they're terribly expensive. Believe it or not, I'm still wearing the Nylon ones you sent me months ago, though they're all in holes at the top. If you ever have got any spare stockings, Helen, do try and send them over. I hate having to ask you, but I'm nearly going grey in the top-knot trying to find some thin ones. I think this Summer, if I'm still alive and kicking, I shall really have to start the stockingless fad. Trouble is the British climate's so chilly, the thought of bare legs at the moment, makes me shudder. Its been terribly cold for weeks—so cold, in fact, that my annual pests, chilblains, have returned in full force—and we're despairing of ever seeing the Spring. What a climate !!

Well! since I wrote you last, all sorts of things have been happening. I am allright, up to now, though I've been ill for the past two weeks with some sort of tummy trouble. I don't seem to have any energy at all. Actually, its not to be wondered at as my sleeping hours are irregular, and unrestful, and I don't care what the Government say our food leaves much to be desired. I don't say we're on the verge of starvation, because we're not, but we can't get the nourishment we need. The meat supplies are meagre, and of course, we have no fruit of any sort. Last week a cargo of oranges came in, but there was such a Battle for them very few people saw them at all. Eggs and fish are scarce and expensive. Cheese is rationed to one ounce per person per week, when you can get it. The foods we get shoved down our throats, potatoes by the ton, and

---

4. "The first peak in the Battle of the Atlantic came with the three months ending in May, when U-boats alone sank 142 merchant ships." Air attacks sank 179 merchant ships. In February–April, 1,600,000 tons of shipping was sunk. On April 14 Churchill ordered the Information Ministry to cease publishing the shipping losses (ibid., 267).

carrots almost eternally, may have some vitamins in 'em, but you get so tired of them. They're trying to introduce something into the new loaves of bread, but what it is, I can't imagine. I long for a nice juicy orange, an apple, or a banana, but like onions, and chocolate, they seem to be things of the past. Tomatoes were being sold at eight shillings a pound not so long ago, that's two dollars if you care to know. Hows that for super profiteering? Fish is anything from three to five shillings a pound. At one time we used to get cod for fourpence. Now on Saturday, they offered me a cutlet you could see through and asked me two and eightpence for it, thats just eight times as much. My income tax return arrived to-day, and the very look of it in its evil little envelope marked "O.H.M.S." makes me want to vomit. After they've demoted all the taxes they might as well take my salary, and just leave me sixpence to spend. Honey, don't you ever believe that the poor British people aren't being stung right and left to pay for this War. Its a wonder we've even got a couple of coppers left for a box of Matches by the time the Chancellor of the Exchequer's finished with us.

We've had some terrible air-raids since I wrote you last, and the one about two weeks ago on a Wednesday night I really thought was going to be my last performance on this earth. God! Helen, it was a nightmare! I've got pretty tough nerves, and I don't give way very easily, but by the time I'd stuck about four hours of it, I felt like having screaming hysteria. It started about 9 oclock, and the bombs literally rained down like hailstones—you could hear the swishes and crashes and the bricks and masonry crumbling all round you. I sat in the room while the house rocked, the windows smashed all round me, and the doors shook on their hinges, and every whistle and scream I Heard, I thought it was the end of me. Fire bombs fell all round, and the fire spotters and Firemen did a magnificent job extinguishing blazes that cropped up everywhere, while tons of high explosives fell behind them. Mother was on duty in a flimsy concrete shelter, with a woman whose nerves gave way completely. It was terrible! The Planes came over in droves, and circled above the houses. You can hear the monotonous buzz-buzz of their Engines way over your head, then all of a sudden the Engine shuts off, and you hold your breath and pray, because thats when the Plane comes down and dive-bombs. Everytime that Engine went quiet, I said every prayer I could think up, and then some more. I had no sleep at all that night, neither did anyone else for that matter, and when I looked out of the window at 6 oclock, the all clear had gone. The skies were blue, and everything looked lovely. I went wearily to work, and the havoc that met my eyes on the way made my eyes smart, as though there were tears behind them, and yet I couldn't cry. Land Mines had fallen all round our lovely main road.[5] Shops were masses of smashed glass and twisted windows, I picked my way gingerly over tons and tons of broken Plate glass while people tried to make a joke of it all, by picking up flutes and mouth organs out of the glass-less windows and playing them. On the way I passed Demolition Squads trying to dig people out of the wreckage of Flats and Houses. Going along the river Embankment I saw trees uprooted and thrown across the road, and railings twisted beyond description. One of Chelsea's loveliest old churches, built by Sir Thomas More, was nothing more than a pile of rubble. Destruction and desolation were everywhere, except on the faces of the people. It amazed me that after a night of horror like that, they could still carry on with their daily work, and smile as though nothing had happened. 3 night afterwards, on the Saturday, they gave us another pasting. I suppose by now we've got accustomed to it, but its dreadful while it lasts. Its queer, too, the different opinions people have about these things. We had a sort of symposium in the Office not long ago, and find that 50% of us instinctively run down below when they get scared, 30% prefer to stay on top because of the fear of getting buried. The remaining 20% liked being out in the Air rather than in a closed space. Actually there isn't much to choose between them. If you get buried in a basement you die of suffocation. If you stay on the top and the bomb falls you get killed by the blast. If you're out in the streets you can get sliced up by Bomb fragments or shrapnel. Whichever way you look at it, if the Bomb's got your name on it, you get it, whether you're up top or down below. It's a helluva life!

This week we are starting a series of Gas Mask Tests.[6] We have to work for half an hour every day in our respirators. We get stuffy and

5. Within ten days of the start of the Blitz, German bombers began dropping cylinders eight feet long and two feet in diameter. Tied to parachutes, they floated silently down at about forty miles an hour. They did not penetrate the earth, but their blast could throw thirty-five train cars into the air like shoe boxes (ibid., 198).

6. By June 1941, the carrying of gas masks by civilians had risen from none to 30 percent of people seen in the streets. By August, it had dropped back to 10 percent (ibid., 129).

tired, and hot, and breathing isn't so easy, but as it seems pretty sure
That Man will use poison Gas on us, we might as well prepare us for
that horror when it comes. The extra hour of daylight went on last
night, so that means we can stay out till ten in the evening at least. I
can now go to the Cinema, without wondering whether I'm going to
be blown out of my seat! As a matter of fact, I was in the Cinema when
Wednesday night's blitz began. The Guns were so loud they shook the
place, and the screen flickered as though it was doing a Jitterbug dance.
When I came out the sky was packed with searchlights, shrapnel was
tinkling down like the sound of fairy Bells, but wasn't half as pleasant as
it sounds, and about 10 minutes after I got home the Land Mine fell.
Had I been coming out of the pictures then, honey, I should certainly
*not* have been writing this letter. Those Land Mines are the most appalling things you ever knew. They can make mincemeat out of rows
and rows of houses, and as for human life, well, that gets mowed down
like a field of Corn.

I do hope that America will get going now, and really *do* something,
instead of telling us what she intends to do in a year or two's time. I
didn't expect anything more than we got in Greece, because it was impossible, and is impossible, for us to send the number of troops needed
to combat Germany's War Machine, but in spite of it, I think a lot of
terrible and costly mistakes have been made as usual. We could have
got Italy out of this War had the Bomber Command pursued the right
policy and bombed Italy unmercifully. They had magnificent Air Bases
in Greece, and yet they wouldn't do it. Many people here are completely
exasperated with the policy of the Bomber Command. This "military
objectives" only principle is getting on everyone's nerves. Its about time
we started to bomb Germany, and particularly Berlin, as indiscriminately and as mercilessly as she's bombed us.[7] And if the British people
have anything to do with it, they'll have to do just that, before long.

I am going to see "Dear Brutus" on Saturday. I saw Gielgud's film
"The Prime Minister" some time ago.[8] It was very good, and John was
marvellous. Olivier is in the Fleet Air Arm now, but he is given occasional leave to make special films. I saw a beautiful propaganda film

---

7. For seventy-six consecutive nights, with the single exception of November 2, 1940,
London was raided in heavy attacks (ibid., 184).

8. The story of Disraeli (1941; UK) was considered "dull."

made by the Ministry of Information last week, and Olivier spoke the commentary. It was very simple, just some pictures of England, and some of the lovely poetry written about the countryside and similar things. It was so sweet, it made me want to cry. Perhaps I'm getting unduly sentimental,—I don't know, I always was a bit patriotic, as you probably know, and it breaks my heart to see my lovely England bashed about like this, and her history of centuries vanished as though it had never been. Theres rather a nice song just come out now, it's first lines are something like this—"London will rise again, to greater glory,—telling a story, that cannot die!" It all sounds very nice, but it isn't much comfort to me. I hated to see the lovely Guildhall, just a mess of rubble after standing since the 11th century. Such wanton waste and destruction, and all for nothing. Still, I suppose its the fortunes of War, as they say in the best Books.

I haven't seen many good films since I wrote you last. I liked "Spring Parade" because it was light and frothy, and I simply loved "Little Nelly Kelly".[9] I remember when I was a small child in dancing class, we used to do an Irish dance to that tune, and as soon as I sat in the Cinema and they played it, I remembered the words even though its been about 14 years and more since I heard it. I love the Irish music, but I detest them as a Race. It seems a shame that a country with so much good in it, should have so much bad as well. I'm going to see a British film to-night, called "The Ghost Train". Its always good for a laugh though its been made and remade a dozen times. I saw a smashing British comedy last week, with Will Hay, called "The Ghost of St Michaels". All about a haunted Castle on the Isle of Skye. You probably wouldn't like it—its too British for words, but it made me double up with laughter, and thats what we need in these dark and dirty days.[10]

I hope you'll still try and send over little bits of chocolate or a tin of cosmetic, here and there—you know, nothing expensive or elaborate, but it will certainly be appreciated whatever it is. I never thought we

9. The musical *Spring Parade* (1940; U.S.) stars Deanna Durbin and Robert Cummings, and the musical *Little Nellie Kelly* (1940; U.S.) stars Judy Garland.

10. *The Ghost Train* (1941; UK)—about stranded travelers in a railway station who solve a mystery about a train full of ghosts and starring Arthur Askey, a vaudeville comedian and popular movie star—is a comedy/horror cult favorite. *The Ghost of St. Michaels* (1941; UK) is part of a popular series starring Will Hay, one of the most respected comedy actors in England and a flyer in World War II.

should run so short here, but still, even now, things will probably get much worse before they get any better. Its all very nice to look forward to, but you die if you worry and you die if you don't so what the heck's the use, anyway.

My brother is still up North, and I went up to see him about three weeks ago. He's in a terrible state because they can't get any cigarettes, but the famine is spreading all over the country. I'm blessed because I don't smoke,—its just as well now, what with the shortage, and the price of Cigarettes. He's coming down South again in a week or two, much to his joy. He says the Northern air doesn't suit him, and he isn't very struck on the people. I hope he will be able to keep out of the air a little while longer, but I suppose it won't be long now before he goes up, and then our worries start. Most of the boys in our Office are joining something or other, even the youngsters. It seems at last that the British boy, and man, are getting military minded.

I'm so glad that your friends like reading my letters. Some of them are a bit miserable, I know, and maybe you don't like reading anything gloomy, but I try to tell about things as I see them, and as you know things haven't been looking very rosy for us lately. Still, things are bound to improve sooner or later—we just can't go on having all the bad breaks, and until Hitler beats us in England, he can't win the War. And he'll *never* beat us here, so it all boils down to simple Arithmetic. Don't worry about me, as long as I am still on God's Earth, I'll write you, and if you don't hear from me for a long time, blame it on to Adolf's U-Boats. Take care of yourself, and don't forget to stick up for Britain anywhere and everywhere. I'm *relying* on you!

Love,

P.S. Jerry thanks Sultan for his kind invitation, but says that although he is severely rationed, and fish and milk aren't what they used to be, he is a British Cat, and is determined to stand or fall with Britain. I think, too he has a girl friend round these parts, and you know what Cats are in the Spring!!

P.P.S. Since writing you we have had another Hun "Hate" Raid. One of the worst yet. Many of our lovely Historic Buildings were hit, including my own Westminster Abbey. Some of the Architecture smashed up there dates back to 1074, and there isn't a single one of the magnificent stained glass windows left. The altar was damaged, and the roof fell in, but the Unknown Warriors Tomb stood up to it. I can't bear to go and look. The Debating Chamber of the House of Commons was destroyed and at first it was feared that Big Ben on his High Tower would topple, too, but somehow he was saved. Im sending you a picture of the end of St Clements Danes—Oh! the times I've sung, when I was little, "Orange & Lemons, say the Bells of St Clements". Now most of the Old Churches mentioned in the Nursery Rhyme are piles of rubble. At the height of the raid my brother, who was home on leave, put a record on the gramophone—it was "Silent Night, Holy Night". Ye Gods! What a mockery.

The talk of the moment here is the arrival of Rudolf Hess.[11] I think there is something rotten about it all, and God knows we have suffered so much at the hands of the Hun, that the common British man or woman should hardly make a hero of him. I cannot think that his visit is due to an uncontrollable desire to sit upon the bonnie, bonnie banks O' Loch Lomond! I'm all for shutting the Rat in Jail with a bit of bread & water to keep him company. Or chaining him to a Post or the highest Building in the City and making him do a bit of fire spotting. Nothing's too bad for him in my opinion. Probably little Rudy intended to land in Ireland, knowing how pally towards us those Shamrock scum are, but ran out of Petrol, and came down in the Heather instead. Well! he's doing well, now, partaking of a little boiled chicken, and an egg or so, while the average Britisher has a hell of a job to get a shillingworth of meat a week and has to queue up for hours for eggs. All they need to do now is give him an Orange, an onion and a Bar of Chocolate to finish me off altogether.

11. On May 10, during one of the last big raids, Hitler's deputy, Rudolph Hess, completed a solo flight to Scotland where he apparently hoped to convince King George that, since a German victory was certain, the British should accept Hitler's peace offer based on Britain's acceptance of Germany's free hand in Europe and the return of colonies lost in World War I. This "offer" was not tendered to the Churchill government. Hess denied that Germany was planning an attack on Russia and insisted Germany had no designs on America. By the end of May psychiatrists concluded that Hess was psychopathic and that little store could be put in anything he said. Churchill ordered that no mention of Hess be published in British papers (William L. Langer and S. Everett Gleason, *The Undeclared War, 1940–1941* [New York: Harper and Brothers, 1953], 528–29; Calder, *People's War,* 248–49).

I have to pay out two-thirds of my salary next week for Income tax. With the pittance I have left, I have to live for a week. Whoopee! Oh! and Helen, I am getting in a terrible state about cosmetics. The government are cutting down supplies of cosmetics & perfumes again from next week so if any of your friends have any spare lipsticks or small bottles of perfumes they don't want, and you could put in with your letter, they'll be doing a little private Bundles for Britain act just for me. I'm very blonde and usually use a light red lipstick, but we really can't afford to be choosy about colours now! I think I shall have to go about dressed in an old sack this Summer! Still, I suppose the first ten years are the worst!

Love,<br>Betty

*August 17*

East Anglian Sanatorium<br>Nayland<br>near Colchester<br>Essex, England

Dear Helen,

No doubt you will be surprised to see the above address, but since writing you last I have been very ill indeed. About the beginning of June I contracted Pleurisy and Pneumonia, and nearly passed out. I lost nearly a stone in weight and my temperature went nearly to 104! Lots of nearlys! Anyway its left me with a spot of Tuberculosis on the top of my right lung, and as a result I shall have to spend the Winter here, and be away from work until next March or thereabouts. Talk about bad luck the Doctors say I have not been strong enough to stand up to all the hardships of War conditions last Winter. Lying about on wet and cold stone floors of Deep Shelters, breathing bad air, getting no sleep, and not the proper food have all combined to break my resistance down. Still, I am getting better now, and gaining weight and am able to breathe properly except for the occasional gasp. At one time I couldn't take a breath without yelping with pain so I've got something to be thankful for! I am naturally bored to tears—I loathe the country life at the best of times—but the Doctor says if I go back to London to live for the Winter, the lung will break down rapidly and it'll be what you

Americans call "curtains" for me. I believe they're trying to frighten me into staying, because they know what a restless gal I am, but in any case I shall go home before Xmas. All you get here is the country air—the food isn't any better than you get at home.

Well enough of my cares and woes! I received your letter telling me about California. Aren't you lucky? My dreamland! Have a darned good time, and think of me when you see those Orange Groves. I am still coming to America, all being well, when this dreadful War is over, though when that will be, God only knows! I have the War to thank for all my aches and pains—and my poor Mother has gone grey with worry through it! Ain't it a hard life for a girl?

I am sending this very short letter by Air Mail, so you will know whats happened. I shall be writing you a longer one very soon. Keep on addressing your letters to me at the office, and they'll send them to me where I am. This is a very scrappy note compared with the sheets and sheets I usually write, but writing in bed is a darned awkward business, especially in ink. I'll do better next time. Don't worry I still have my chin up though I can't do much at the moment, I'm still going to help to whack Hitler when they'll let me.

Best love,
Betty

43 The Grove
Hammersmith W. 6
England

Dear Helen—

I do hope you will forgive me, dear, for scribbling in pencil, but it is so much quicker, and as I cannot go back to the Office and use the Typewriter until the New Year, my letters till then will probably be shorter—I have little or no patience to write in longhand—a complaint which seems to affect most typists—and when I do settle down, I usually fly to the Pencil rather than the Pen.

Well! as you will see I am now safely home again, after just over four months in the Sanatorium—four months which seemed like four years! The country is beautiful, when you are fit enough to walk around and enjoy it, but when you have to lie about and just gaze at it, it's plain monotonous. London seems like heaven in comparison. However, heaven or no heaven, if the raids start in earnest again, I shall have to pack up and go elsewhere—no more shelters for me! Its a case of you die if you go below, and you die if you stay on top so I think I'll take the top. I have been examined by a couple of specialists, who say the lungs are at present, quite clear, but the lining of the right one is still inflamed, and I have to watch my step. Of course, convalescence is made the harder and slower way nowadays, owing to the lack of most of the nourishing foods we could get in peacetime. The local food office have given me a special permit for 8 ounces of Margarine and 3 ounces of Cheese a week—two pints of milk a day, and a fairly good allowance of Cabbages and Carrots—but we are, of course, handicapped by the lack of fresh fruits, cream, chocolate and worst of all, eggs. We're lucky if we get one a month! I spent half an hour queuing up for half a pound of Chocolate last Sunday, and my poor mother goes grey-headed trying to get me something for dinner, when the meat ration for the week barely covers the Sunday joint! Think of me, honey, when you eat your next Steak, and thank your lucky stars that Hitler hasn't got around to you yet!!? Anyway, I understand we are to get some tinned stuff from the States next month, though the main problem is how to get the good old Christmas Pudd! Xmas isn't Xmas in England without a Plum Pudding, but though we've been saving our Dried fruits for 2 or 3 months, we still haven't amassed enough to make enough Puddings. As far as I can see, I've [*sic*] shall be sitting down to a Xmas dinner of tinned Beans and Rice Pudding, unless I can use my wiles on the Butcher, Grocer, and what have you! Still, leave it to little Betty to keep up Ye Olde English Christmas if possible.

Now, I almost forgot to tell you the most important thing of all—that is, I actually received the Box sent from Los Angeles, and it was simply lovely!! Gosh! was I grateful ?? Everything in it is scarce over here. The chocs were in perfect condition, and were eaten in about half an hour, I think! And the stockings, without coupons!! We've just been told that we're to get one pair each of fully fashioned silk stockings, and then no more until after the War is over; I am using the Powder, and it is just the right shade. Some of the Cosmetics put on the Market here now, are appalling concoctions, made mostly by Jews in forbidden factories from anything they can lay their hands on. The Government have just put a Ban on them. I'd rather go out with my face scrubbed and shining than use the stuff. Wherever you find any dirty work afoot, there you find the Yids, and if that sounds prejudiced, I really can't help it. I hate the sight of the Jewish people, and more than 50% of the Shirkers in this country belong to that Race. Anyway, enough of that. Many, many thanks for the Box. It was one of the most welcome gifts I have ever received in my life. I also received the lovely Silk hankie while I was in the Sanatorium and all the girls there admired it very much. I have been reading your letter about your trip and how I've envied you—California is still the land of my Dreams and if I ever come to the States, I shall be living in the East, and I'm going to save up if it takes me years, so I can see the West. I've often wondered if I could get a job further West, in Los Angeles or maybe even in your Kansas City—I wish to God this War was over so I could see it all and enjoy it, *now* while I'm young and healthy, so to speak. I believe, by the way, that they are going to publish a rather lovely coloured photograph of me on the cover of the New York Times Saturday Magazine. Grace, that girl in New Jersey who fixed up everything for me to come over, had the photo on her Table and one of the pals of the Editor, asked her for the negative, so that they could use it as a cover. I hope I can get some copies of it ever.

I've had a lot of Magazines from you this week, and am now going to pack them up send them to my very best boy friend, who went into Hospital on Saturday with one ankle broken and one sprained. He's in the Grenadier Guards—y'know the British Grenadiers—and a few months ago he went mad and volunteers for the Parachute Troops—now he's gone and done this for himself making one of the jumps. I saw him the day before he went into Hospital and he looked very bad—I spent my entire afternoon with his head on my lap—talk about acting like a mother! I had a terrible sore throat and he had a rotten cold, and I've naturally enough caught his cold, and I hope he's got my sore throat! I've been indoors three days sniffing, and he's in Hospital, so we're a pretty fine pair. Still, he should be alright with a week or two's rest, though it will finish his career in the Paratroops, thank God for that, say I. I would like to send you a photograph of the two of us together, but the censors won't allow a photograph of anyone in Uniform to go to the States.—Of all the balmy ideas! I'm going to try to find one of myself though, and enclose it. It must be quite a while since you had one.

I am listening in at the moment to the broadcast of the War time Lord Mayors Show—nothing like the old Pageantry of Peacetime when the Dinner was held in the Guildhall—This year there *is* no Guildhall and the Procession consisted of A. R. P. personnel as well as units of the Navy, Army & Air Force. I wish I could have seen it, but my cold is too bad and its raining, and Ted's in Hospital and I don't feel like going without him, so that's that! My pup is clawing like hell to get on my lap—he's been christened "Victory" and my Kitten is called Raff after the Royal Air Force, so both my animals are patriotic.

I hoped to send this letter Air Mail but I have written too much and it will be too heavy so must risk it by ordinary post. I hope you have both settled down to life in K. C. again and do write soon won't you. I should keep on addressing them to the Office. It's really much safer.

Best love,<br>Betty

P.S. I don't know whether you can help me in this direction. We can't get any Kirbigrips—you know, little clips to keep your hair back, so if you ever see anything like that in any of your shops could you send me over a card. They've absolutely vanished from the market here, and we gals are having a terrific job Keeping our hair back!

43 The Grove<br>Hammersmith<br>London W. 6<br>Dec. 30th 1941

Dear Helen,

Just received your Xmas Card for which many thanks—but I can't understand why you haven't heard from me as I've written you twice since I came home in October—Once in great excitement telling you that I had received a Box from Los Angeles—the one with the Powder and Chocs and (what a Heaven-sent miracle!) Stockings. I haven't had the Box sent from Kansas City—I suppose that's another lot gone to the bottom.

Well! before I start, let me apologize for the pencil scribble, and the paper. I have been trying to get back to work so that I can do my correspondence decently on a Typewriter but have been unlucky so far. I seem to spend the major part of my life going in and out of Hospitals and being prodded about by one Doctor after another, I've been away from work seven months now, and am sick and tired of doing nothing. The Specialist says that I can attempt work for six hours a day, but unfortunately just as I was about to take him up on his word, I came down with gastric influenza, about 10 days ago and am only just beginning to crawl about. I never felt so awful in my life!! I couldn't eat a thing without throwing it back, and ran a high fever of 103 degrees or so! I've lost about 7 lbs in weight, which will just horrify everyone; Of course in the middle of it, The Railway Specialist had to come along and examine me, and naturally enough he gave one look at me and refused to let me go back to work. Anyway, I'm going to try to get back in a month or two—All I longed for was fruit of all things!! Of course its practically unobtainable here, but my Mother managed to get hold of a small Bunch of Grapes. They cost 15 shillings & sixpence a pound, that's about 4 dollars in your currency—while a friend of ours scoured around and got one solitary apple. That was about all I ate for a week!

Well! here I am rambling on about my ailments, when I should be enquiring just how you feel now that you're an active ally of ours. To say I was shocked was putting it mildly. You know I was always extremely dubious about America's entry in to the War, although my mother has been prophesying it for a year. We both sat and listened to the Radio playing the National Anthems of the Allies, and when they struck up with the Star Spangled Banner I said "Well! I never thought I'd ever hear that!" Things seem to look pretty black in the Far East at the moment but when you're used to bad news as we are, you'll get hardened to it.[12] It seems such a damned shame that when we've got the Huns on the run in Libya and the Russians have nearly pulverized him in the U.S.S.R. the Japs have got to start off. Still, it's the good old Hitler strategy again. It seems dreadful that there isn't a place in the world where you can go for a bit of peace. I think I shall have to dig myself a nice little hole and pull the earth over me and come out in about 3 years time, when all this business is over. And giving it 3 years seems to be taking an optimistic view according to the "high-ups". At least we've been spared another winter of "blitzes" although, of course its too

12. During December 1941, Japanese forces moved against the British possessions of Hong Kong, Malaya, and Burma. Japanese planes sank two of the best ships in the Royal Navy, the *Prince of Wales* and the *Repulse*. On Christmas Day, Hong Kong surrendered (Calder, *People's War,* 305–6).

early to make any prophesies. I think last winter just about finished me off—I'm sure I shall never feel the same. I hope and pray for all your sakes that you wont have to endure the bombing that we have had, though I think it extremely unlikely. Whatever bombing of America the Japs do they will have to do it from Aircraft Carriers and that will eliminate the horror of having any of your Cities bombed continuously by 500 Planes as London was last year. The German bases are only about 30 or 40 miles from London, which is a vastly different matter.

We are sampling some of your tinned Meats now—indeed; several of our Comedians have thought up the most ingenious jokes about "Spam" "Mor" "Tang" "Treet" and what have you. I have tried "Mor" and found it very appetising. We are rationed on all tinned foods now—indeed its hard to find a commodity that *isn't* rationed I am still getting in a devil of a mess over my clothes, and if the Summer would only come, I think I shall have to start wearing a Sarong! My sister-in-law is having her first baby in February and we are having a heck of a job scraping up enough coupons to get it a Christening robe after we have expended 30 or 40 on napkins. What a life!

By the way, I had a charming letter from a girl working in Kansas City—a Miss Martha Warner, who had seen one of my letters to you (apparently it was passed around her Office). She wrote asking if I would let her send me Chocolates, Cosmetics, Stockings or anything, and if "I would do her the honour of corresponding with her"—What a fine, friendly, people you Americans are!!

I am sending you a couple of snaps I think you will like. It seems quite a time since I sent you one. I hope you get these. Let me know anyway.

I am writing this one practically the last day of the Old Year, so may 1942 bring your country and mine Victory and Peace. And a very, very Happy New Year to you, Helen, and to all those friends of yours who have enquired about me—

Love,
Betty

P.S. I am receiving Clippings and Film Mags and the Boy friend is tremendously interested in "North American Skyline!"

## GREAT WESTERN RAILWAY

Goods Department,
South Lambeth Station,
London S.W. 8

Dear Helen,

I have half an hour to spare at work, so I thought I'd write you. I haven't heard from you for a long time, except for Envelopes of clippings, so I suppose the Atlantic Mails are getting in the same state as they were in before. I have just managed to get back to work after eight months absence, and am feeling pretty pleased about it. It took half a dozen doctors a couple of months to make up their minds, but I eventually got round 'em all, and here I am—to stay, I hope.

The weather here is appalling—according to the papers we're suffering the worst winter we've had for fifty years. And to make matters worse theres been a shortage of coal and we've been sitting huddled over the dying embers feeling like Eskimos. As soon as one lot of snow clears away, another lot comes down. I am more fed-up with the English climate than ever—I tell you no matter what happens it'll be California or bust for me after this muck-up is over. England, home and beauty is no place for a Sun-loving baby like me. Even when summer comes we don't get enough of it to carry us on through the winter, and you have to fortify yourselves with enormous doses of Cold Liver Oil and Malt, a sticky concoction that makes me heave every time I take it. Honestly though, the amount of patent medicines the Doctors push down my throat must keep the Chemists of England in work for weeks. Calcium, Iron, Phosphates, Halibut Oil, Carrot Juice and the new Rose Hip Syrup which is supposed to contain Vitamin C. We get no fruit at all, so the Government is pinning its faith on the good old-fashioned Carrot. When peace comes I shall never be able to look a Carrot in the face again, having partaken of the darned things in Pancakes, Soups, Cakes and what have you. My soul yearns for the good old fashioned Onion, and all they offer me is a Carrot! Still with all the muck I take, I think if anything happens to me I'll will my body to the Government. They should find enough Iron and steel in it to make a good-sized Battleship. My boy friend is convinced that I am held together with adhesive tape! When he comes to supper he lines up all the bottles in front of my plate, and swears they fill up all the space on the table.

Talking of tables, and the stuff that fills 'em, we are having a rare treat on Sunday. Nothing more or less than a tin of Pears! We are getting out the best plates and Table Linen and polishing the silver spoons in anticipation of the great event, and I have ringed the date round on the Calendar with an appropriate remark "Ate a tinned Pear." This is the first tinned fruit since I-can't-remember-when, and we had to be up bright and early on Monday morning and fight off the competition to get it. Small supplies were released last week and you had to give up Food coupons—points, they call 'em over here—to get it. The months supply for my mother and I is one tin of Peas, one tin of Blackberries and the aforementioned tin of Pears. I queued up for half an hour on the way to work this morning and emerged with two bars of Chocolate which couldn't have tasted better if they'd been Golden Nectar, even though the Chocolate now is horrible compared to Peace time, when we were able to get all sorts of varieties of Milk Choc. Now its all plain and supposedly reinforced with Vitamins, which doesn't help the taste. Everything we eat is supposed to have had a couple of Vitamins dropped in the basin before we get it. They'll be putting 'em in our clothes next.

*And* speaking of clothes—are you any good at Arithmetic. I have 15 coupons to last me till June, and I want a new pair of Shoes which means 5. Some material for a skirt @ 2 coupons a yard, 2 ½ yards—sum total another 5. Some Angora Wool for a fluffy jumper one coupon for two ounces and I need eight, bang goes four—sum total 14 coupons, excluding stockings for which you have to fork out 2, and an occasion[al] brassiere for which you part with one. I fully expect to spend the summer walking about clad in nothing but a smile and a fig leaf. By that time I suppose they'll put fig leaves on the ration. The latest idea is soap and in England now if you run out of your months ration of soap after three weeks you stay in your dirt for a week until you can get the next month's supply! Life gets easier and easier all the time. Even if you had any money, theres nothing you can spend it on but War Savings and Income Tax, which, I suppose is the Government's idea in the first place. The moans that go up here when its Income Tax week are shocking to hear. I'm sure old Chinese Tortures could never produce such agony!

I suppose its no use asking you how you feel now you're in the War, or what you think of the whole damned mess. I've never been so disheartened in my life. All these months of War and it seems to me that we're a darned sight worse off than when we started. Our papers have been publishing bits of criticism from the American press about Singapore. Some Journal or other—probably the Hearst press—has been saying that Americans are only fighting to preserve the British Empire, a statement which seems ridiculous in the extreme. Its fairly obvious to everyone that Americans are fighting for their lives and their existence, just as we are. Also that you were actually as unprepared as we were in 1939. One of our journalists says that after Pearl Harbour Americans have no right to criticise anyone. It seems a shame that this sort of propaganda should be allowed to split up what everyone thought was a perfect understanding. I am certainly not excusing the British Government for the mistakes they've made. I think they've muddled everything theyve touched and what is worse their mistakes have cost us thousands of lives, money and material; I've got to the stage when I hate to pick up a paper and read about the Far East in any shape or form, and my mother, and the boy friend spend hours calling everyone names from the highest to the lowest, and making the direct prophecies of all sorts of disasters. My mother is a pessimist by nature, so I don't expect anything else, and I often get large chunks of undiluted gloom for breakfast. Personally, I was never a Churchill admirer, though I admit that he has a remarkable gift for oratory and has enough bombast to drive a train through a mountain, but he's certainly got a lot of things to explain, and whenever he makes a speech, he wraps it up in frills, hides the truth in the middle like the kernel of a nut, and finishes up by telling us we ought to be damned glad we're not even worse off. All very comforting, I have no doubt but in my opinion Churchill holds too many ropes in one hand. He wants to be Head Cook and Bottle Washer of the whole show instead of giving other, and probably better men, a chance.

*Thursday.*

Have just received your letter and was so pleased to hear from you. So you're a working girl now. Well! don't get too tired and if I don't hear from you I shall understand. The girl who wrote to me was a Miss Martha Warner. She read a letter of mine to you, and sent me a marvellous letter asking me if she could possibly send me anything or everything. I wrote back to her, very gratefully thanking her, and asking her if she could possibly get hold of some Angora Rabbit Wool in Burgundy, Ice Blue or Grey, enough to make a jumper, as I could not get any Fluffy wool in England, and in any case I hadn't the coupons. I told her to let me know how much it was, and I'd send her the money. I don't know if she's sent anything, as I haven't heard from her, but I'm glad to know that she's got a letter from me. It was very kind of her to offer, and I'm going to be as mad as hell if the stuff has got itself sunk. I have turned the shops upside down to try and get some in London, but of course, I've had the usual reply "There's a war on"—as if I didn't know—and "they're not making it any more"—which I don't know whether to believe or not.

I've been going to the pictures pretty regularly,—about three times a week, I should say. "This Chocolate Soldier" was here last week, but I didn't see it because I can't abide Nelson Eddy. I saw "Citizen Kane" though and thought it a most intelligent, and interesting bit of screencraft, though half the audience didn't seem to understand what it was all about.[13] I haven't been to the Theatre for ages. Gieldgud is doing "Macbeth" this season, and it will probably be his usual star-studded production, but I think it's a little too heavy for public taste right now. They need something a bit more on the frothy side, for which I can't say I blame them.

By the way, I am now a proud Aunt! My niece was born on January 31st. weight 7 lbs, name Pamela Mary, and she's a darling. Very pretty, and shows promise of being the 1960 "OOmph" girl. My brother has been married six years, and this is their first baby, and now poor Jack has been put on the Overseas draft, which means he may have to go abroad for anything from 1 to 3 years and see very little of his offspring. Still, those are the fortunes of War, I suppose. The boy friend has just come back from a longish stay abroad and is due to go again very shortly. Men are so scarce now, they'll probably suggest rationing 'em before long. Every time you have a date, you may have to part with a couple of coupons!

I am going to try and post this to-night, so it will get to you as soon as possible, always providing it doesn't get sunk on the way. Look after yourself and write to me when you have time, and don't feel too tired.

Love,

Betty

---

13. *The Chocolate Soldier* (1941; U.S.), starring Nelson Eddy and Risë Stevens, was nominated for three Academy Awards. Nigel Bruce, who plays opposite Basil Rathbone in Universal's Sherlock Holmes series of the 1940s, also appears in the film. *Citizen Kane* (1941; U.S.), considered by some the best film ever made, was directed by Orson Welles and stars Joseph Cotten and Agnes Moorehead along with Welles. The story is based on the life of publishing tycoon Wm. Randolph Hearst.

# V

## July 1942–February 1945

On November 15, 1942, bells rang in London to celebrate the victory of the British Eighth Army, under the command of General Bernard Montgomery, over Germany's Afrika Korps at El Alamein in northern Africa. Prime Minister Winston Churchill, who in July, after the surrender of British troops at Tobruk, had won a vote of confidence, told the war-weary nation: "Now this is not the end. It is not even the beginning of the end. But it is, perhaps, the end of the beginning."

But for Betty Swallow the conditions of daily life and her own health continued to worsen. Bombs destroyed her London apartment, her boyfriends were on active duty, rationing of food and clothing increased—three of her letters describe the rationing—and her health deteriorated. So much so that she spent July 1944–February 1945 in a sanatorium in Southport in northern England.

London, when Betty returned, was attacked by "flying bombs"—"doodlebugs"—starting in June 1944, and then, in February 1945, by V-2 rockets. "I celebrated last night," she wrote in her February 1945 letter, "by eating an orange—the first for about 10 months, and obtained after queuing up for about an hour. . . . Personally speaking, if this War will only end . . . after five and a half years of it, I've got absolutely weary."

## GREAT WESTERN RAILWAY

Goods Department,
South Lambeth Station,
London, S.W.8

Dear Helen,

I was so pleased to hear from you this week. I haven't had a letter for quite a time, though I had some magazines last week (Film Books too, quite a luxury in those parts) and joy of joys, I got those lovely Candies you sent! They were marvellous! And they caused quite a sensation here when they arrived. Thank you so much for sending them. I've been very lucky this week, because Miss Warner sent me a big box of stockings and cosmetics and that arrived, too. I feel absolutely the Queen of the City with two pairs of silk stockings in the drawer at the same time. My legs have been quite blue with cold on several occasions, as the summer has been far from warm up to now, and due to the lamentable lack of coupons, we have all been forced to adopt the stockingless fad, rain or shine. I have some liquid silk stocking make-up which should be applied to the legs to take off that "goose-pimple" look, but its such a messy job and takes such a hell of a time to get on, that I just can't be bothered.

Well! we have had another slice of bad luck in the house in the shape of a fire since I last wrote you. Burnt out our kitchenette, complete with furniture,—and left us with practically no china, cutlery, or saucepans, and minus all the Kitchen equipment from the Ironing Board downwards! I am convinced that we are jinxed, or something. In fact, I'm looking around for a couple of lucky charms to try and offset it—so if anyone should offer you a couple of four-leaved Clovers, or Horseshoes, you'd better send 'em over to me. I think my need is probably greater than thine! Anyway, You should have seen me sitting woefully among the salvage digging out the remains of our tinned food stock. I unearthed two tins as black as the Ace of Spades, and opened 'em not knowing what was in them, and discovered one was a tin of Pineapple—the first we've had for 18 months—and the other a Tin of peas. They were full of sooty smuts, and probably packed with germs, but I eat 'em regardless. No fire was going to do me out of my one and only taste of Pineapple. We get all tinned stuff on a "Points" system here. You get 30 points a month and to get a tin of fruit you have to give up about 24. All our stock went bust in the Kitchen Cupboard. Still, I suppose we were lucky. The Bedroom and living room weren't touched. As it is, the worst of it is that we shall have to move, as the place just isn't habitable. What a life, eh!

I have been seeing a lot of your boys mooching round London, and though they seldom have a good word to say for England, its food, its climate, or anything else, they seem to appreciate the English female of the species![1] One lad from Iowa practically proposed to me on sight, and it took the greatest persuasion to convince him that my heart belonged—even if only temporarily—to a common Englishman! Apparently this youth to use his own colourful lingo "was a pushover for blondes" and had promised his maw and paw to bring home an English wife! Cross your fingers, my dear, as if I see an Officer who suits me, and I happen to suit him, I shall grab him and hurl him on to the nearest Altar! Then I shall have to become a citizen of the States, without having an argument with my conscience! I went to Evensong in Westminster Abbey last night—it being Sunday,—and a lovely day—and went up to Hyde Park afterwards. There were literally hundreds of Yankees having the time of their lives. One U.S.A. Airman was lustily singing "Land of my Fathers" *in Welsh* at the Welsh corner. There are also large groups of young singers beating out the rhythm of "Deep in the Heart of Texas" and other similar ditties. I, myself, five minutes before I had joined in the chorus of "The Church's One Foundation" and "Come let us gather at the river" with the Sisters of Something or the Other. So you see how varied are my tastes!

I see Windbag Winnie has just returned again from another visit to the States.[2] Well! there was a lot of discontent about Tobruk, and the people are howling that something will have to be done to completely reorganise the High Commands of the Army, but I suppose Winston will come home, wave his arms about in Parliament, and make another

---

1. On January 26, 1942, two large transports landed at Belfast and unloaded 2,900 men. During succeeding months other GIs arrived and fanned out from Scottish and Irish bases to London and the Channel ports (ibid., 308).

2. While Churchill was in Washington urging that North Africa, not France, should be the Allied target for invasion in 1942, Tobruk, the British base in North Africa, after a long siege, fell to the Germans and 33,000 of the garrison were captured (ibid., 208–9).

of those grandstand speeches of his, and none of his critics will dare oppose him. He seems to be able to put the British Public in his pocket. Personally, I get so depressed about the progress of the War that I'm trying to stop reading anything about it. They're yelling their heads off for a second front, but the people who do the yelling don't have to go and fight in it. Believe me, we have enormous numbers of shirkers in England, too—men who take shelter in what are called "Reserved Occupations" mostly in Munition Works, and pull in large sums of money each week, while the soldier takes home two bob a day! Practically the whole of our Jewish population can still be found propping up the doors of the larger Dress and Fur Shops, or as Managers of other Establishments—and the remainder of their brethren do a flourishing trade in the Black Market. Those that do get pushed into the Army are usually experts at the gentle art of being invalided out—"Nerve trouble" is the usual excuse. Indeed, you would be amazed at the vast number of English soldiers who complain bitterly that they're fighting and dying to make England safe for the Yids to live in. The Government turns a blind eye to the anti-Jewish feeling in England. But the day will come eventually, when the people will take matters into their own hands, and something will have to be done about it. I hate Hitlerism, and everything it stands for, but I shall always be anti-Jewish, and I still consider that Hitler saved Germany from financial disaster when he turned 'em out. Trouble was, we got most of them and what we didn't get, was passed over to you.

The story of England expecting others to fight her Battles, seems nothing short of ghastly to me. The folks who say that might care to come and inspect our casualty lists—they hardly make pretty reading. The flower of our youth is going now, as it did in the last War—and when the second front eventually is started, it is Tommy Atkins who will be expected to bear the brunt of it. The trouble with our Government is that all along they have minimised the sufferings and spirit of the British soldiers and dished out all the praise to the Colonial troops—who, brave as they are, have done no more than our boys. As far as I see it, England has, from time immemorial been mixed up in other peoples quarrels and fought everyone elses Battles. I only wish it was possible for us to stick rigidly to a policy of Armed Isolation, but the people are too ready to help out a "pal" in trouble, and the Government take advantage of it. Fine pals some of them turned out to be, too. Nations like the French, and Rumanians—and the Turks. As I see it the only ones worth their salt are the Poles and the Dutch, and of course the Russians, though I do wish the British people would be a little more sensible in their fanatical hero-worship of Stalin and his Soul-mates.

Brother Jack is in India now—according to his latest reports. It has aged my mother ten years. The baby is a darling, and her mother is going back to work again. She will have to find a day nursery for Baby, and her home at night. Jack, of course, is in the R.A.F. has been for about 18 months now, and he's been stationed practically all over England. I don't know quite which boy friend you mean. If it's the one who is with me in the photo I sent you—thats my Ted. He's in the Grenadier Guards—went to France the day after War broke out, got out with the British troops at Dunkirk, and got himself shell shock in the process. He's somewhere in England now. He's been training for the Parachute Battalion, "Paratroops" we call 'em, Comes from Birmingham—which, in my opinion is England's dirtiest city. The other lad—the Sergeant I believe I told you about, has a Dutch mother and English father with pots of money—is in the Coldstream Guards, and has spent his time fighting in France, Egypt, and was in the last battle of Tobruk. Ted is the most pro-British youth I ever met in my life, and the other one—Jacques, his name is—thinks England's the lousiest dump ever. So you can't say I don't go in for contrasts. I have tried to "sell" America to Ted, by pointing out its many advantages, but he clings stubbornly to the idea that there is no Country in the world like the tight little Isle,—it's a proper case of "My Country—right or wrong", so I have given up in despair. Ted, I'm afraid, is as English as the sturdy Oak, just as immovable! Jakey, on the other hand, is convinced that whatever country he was obliged to live in, nothing could be worse than this one. I don't agree with either of 'em! Anyway, all my males are in one of the Services. I don't own a "Conchie" or a Civilian, amongst them.

I have to see the Doctor for X-ray, tomorrow—I believe I told you he wants me to be hospitalized again. I'm fed up with the whole business. If its got any worse, I shall have to go back in, I suppose. Anyhow, keep on writing to the Office, and wherever I am, they'll forward it to me. I am keeping my fingers crossed and saying my prayers every night. I really don't feel capable of enduring another six months on my back. Another thing, I have no faith in this "rest" treatment, and think the only cure for T.B. is by surgical means. They seem to believe in economy in England, however, and don't use A.P. or Phrenics or Thoras unless the cases are on their last legs.

No! we can't get American magazines, of any sort here now. The film Books you send are read by everyone at the Office and then sent on to the soldiers, who are mad about them. I used to give them all to Ted—indeed, when he was in Hospital just before Christmas with a broken ankle, I had to rack my brains to think up suitable literature for him so he had all the film magazines, and some of those "American Airways" books you sent. He was very keen on Civil Aviation, before the War and if he hadn't been a Guardsman in Peacetime and therefore automatically recalled to the Army on the outbreak of War he would have joined the Air Force. The Guards Regiments—there are five, the Grenadiers, Coldstreams, Scots, Irish and Welsh Guards, are usually composed of boys who were in the Peace-time standing Army, or new recruits with special qualifications. They have to be over 6 ft tall, and as straight as a ram-rod, and the discipline used in training them is appalling to think of. When their training is finished, however, they are typical model soldiers. Some men take kindly to the training, and some loathe it like poison. Jakey, my Coldstreamer, is one of the latter variety, and what he thinks of the life of a Guardsman could not be described in ordinary, lady-like language. He wants us to go to America after the War, where he says we should marry and live in a House called "Chatanooga" [*sic*]—the weird title being explained by the fact that he and I met at a Dance while the Band was playing "Chatanooga Choo-choo" and ever since then he has referred to it as "our song". Such sentiment! and what a song to pick!

Your piece about the patients always giving you Boxes of Candy makes me feel reel envious. I couldn't get any sweets at all last week, so I tried an American recipe for making Chocolate Fudge, which was written on a tin of Cocoa sent me by Miss Warner. With true British economy, however, I didn't quite use enough sugar, and as a result the Fudge didn't set properly, and resembled nothing more than a plate of thick, Mississippi Mud. However, it was sweet, and sticky, so I ate it with a spoon, having got to that desperate state when I'll eat anything as long as it will fill the holes up.

We had a terrific thunder-storm last night, and as a result the hot weather has vanished again, and to-day was quite cold and chilly. We've had very funny weather this June. Hot one minute and cold the next, and then the Minister of Health stands up and blithely announces that the Nations health is better than it was in peacetime. Did'ja ever hear such a tripe!!

I didn't know you had a shortage of wool over there. We have a good stock here, but of course, its strictly rationed and Angora Bunny wool which was what I was trying to get is unobtainable. The funny thing is, we *are* making large quantities of pre-War products, but they never appear on the Home market, and they're all exported abroad. F'rinstance, we haven't seen any of the Yardley Beauty Products for months, but they're still being made and sent to America. We can't get a bottle of Perfume for love nor money, but most of the manufacturers of our perfumes are distributing their stuff over your side. It makes me wild to think of it.

I hope you won't be bored with this trashy letter—reading it through it doesn't seem a very intelligent epistle Maybe I'll do better next time.

Once again, thanks for the candies, and don't work too hard. Not so hard that you won't find time to write me, anyway.

Love,<br>Betty

## GREAT WESTERN RAILWAY

Goods Department,<br>South-Lambeth Station,<br>London, S.W.8

My dear Helen,

This will be quite a short letter, but I wrote to you some months ago, and now read in the paper that all letters posted to the States about the time of mine were lost by Enemy action. So thats that! Anyhow, I am taking a chance on this reaching you before Christmas, but whenever it gets to you—if it ever does—I wish you all the best of the festive season and a happy New Year as I always have done ever since I first knew you, before Adolf started to interfere with our mail.

I have been very busy in work, and with the winter and the early black-out upon us I get very little time for attending to my own correspondence. I expect you are in the same position as I know how busy you must be, but I always know when I don't hear from you for months that something or somebody is fiddling about again. It was a dreadful summer here, cold and wet, and now the winter set in earlier than ever before. I have know[n] Octobers that have been quite mild but last month was quite frosty and November is living up to its name in a series of wonderful, thick, foggy fogs, which only cease to allow the rain to come down in the proverbial buckets. My chilblains—the bane of my life—have started very early this year, and I have lost about eight pounds in weight in the past two months. The latter is probably due to the fact that I am continually hungry and can't get anything I want, to eat. It wouldn't be much news to tell you anything about the English rations, as if I do the Censor accuses me of giving away secret information or something, but the times I long for a good, juicy steak, with fried onions!! Oh! my,—still we have one meat dinner a week, on Sunday, which is about all our ten-ounces per person meat ration will allow, and I've been filling myself up lately with chipped potatoes—when I can get the fat to fry 'em. The Government is always yelling at us to eat potatoes instead of bread, but very few people can go on eating 'em boiled, and you can't get the fat to fry 'em. Seems silly to me. I'm getting accustomed now to the three-ounce a week sweet ration—indeed I can walk past counters of sweets and stop my mouth from watering, if I don't look directly at them. My mother, though, is frantically wondering how to make a Christmas pudding out of half a pound of sultanas which is about all the dried fruit we possess! We are trying to store a couple of pounds of apples and are jealously guarding a pot of preserved plums done in the summer, and marked up with great gusto—"not to be opened till Christmas." The old sweet ration should provide two bars of Chocolate and if somebody's spare hen will only wander into our back yard we may yet have some sort of a Christmas dinner. Anyhow, I hope if you have anything decent to eat out there, you'll eat an extra one for me while you're at it! And my brother, mark you, wrote from India this week and asked my mother what about sending him a Christmas parcel! In any case, I suppose Xmas won't be Xmas with everyone away, so who cares about their old Puddings, and Mince Pies. The first peacetime Christmas, I'm going to eat till I'm sick, and then get drunk to celebrate. I've never been canned in my life, so it's about time I tried! I always shock my mother by telling her that on Armistice night I'm going to take off all my clothes and stand on my head in Trafalgar Square!!

Well! we heard the Church Bells last Sunday, ringing away for our victories in the Middle East.[3] They were the loveliest sound ever, I can tell you, although it seems funny when we think about how we've prayed that they wouldn't ring. I've always though it silly to have the Bells as an Invasion warning. Theirs is such a joyous sound, and it seems so out of place to ring them to tell us that the scum of the earth have landed on Blighty! Still, it is tremendously heartening to hear of the Germans in full retreat, and I'm so glad that the British Army after all the slurs and insults that have been hurled at it, has proved to be what we always said they were—the finest fighting force in the World. They're a marvellous lot, those boys, and nothing's too good for them—in fact they could even have my precious sweet ration if they wanted it. And thats some sacrifice for me!

One of my boy friends has just rung up to say that he's just going on Embarkation leave as he's going overseas in a fortnight. He's a Lancashire lad, from Blackpool, and my mother and I have a hell of a job to understand what he's talking about sometimes. He's one of a family of four brothers who were at Dunkirk and he's the only one who came home, so I think his mother, more than anyone I know had done her share of providing cannon fodder for the preservation of the British Empire. My sister-in-law is up in London to-day, too, to broadcast to Jack. He's been ill in hospital in India for five months and hasn't heard from her at all, though she writes every week. Anyway the B.B.C. have invited her to come up and broadcast to him in the Overseas Service, so I hope and pray he'll be listening in. I always love to hear the soldiers broadcast to their families, although I always want to cry pints all over the Radio.

I hope you aren't working too hard, and wearing yourself out, also that things are alright with you. I have received several lots of film magazines which the current boy friend takes to the Barracks to give to the Soldiers when I've finished them. They love the pictures of the glamour-gals and stick them on the walls above their beds. Much to the disgust of the Sergeant, no doubt. Anyway, I shall miss this Lancashire

3. On the night of November 4, 1942, the BBC announced that General Bernard Montgomery's Eighth Army had defeated General Erwin Rommel's Afrika Korps at El Alamein. On November 8, in Operation Torch, Allied troops landed in Morocco and Algeria and moved toward Tunis. On November 15 church bells rang all over Britain to celebrate the victory (ibid., 304–5).

boy; he was good fun and grand company! Still, thats how it goes in War-time, I guess. You know each other a little while and then the War Office up and moves him away somewhere. Ships that pass in the Night! Although my mother is beginning to grumble at the number of "ship"s" that I manage to harbour on our Doorstep, and I can't convince her that its only my patriotic duty!

This letter is very badly typed, and is very scrappy I know, but I want to get it away as soon as possible so that you'll know that I am thinking of you this New Year. I am being very nice to the Yankee soldiers here, because the people in the States have always been so very kind to me, even though my kindness has to stop at the pleasure of my company—the family rations not being in a fit state to stand the provision of Hot Dogs and Hamburgers In any case, the American soldiers have christened our sausages "Bread rolls" which is a very apt description. Oh! to live in a country where there is unlimited supplies of "Spam", "Mor", "Prem" and all the rest of it. You lucky people!

Write me soon, God bless and have a very happy Xmas,

Much love,
Betty

## GREAT WESTERN RAILWAY

Goods Department,
South Lambeth Station,
London, S.W.8.

Dear Helen,

I have been trying for weeks to write to you, and have eventually [lines deleted by censor] in a Munitions Factory—she'll certainly notice the differences. She will have to work from 7.30 am. to 6.pm. where she is now, with only half an hour for dinner, and the wages aren't so very marvellous. About three pounds a week—thats about 15 dollars in your currency. And the income tax will take ten bob of that, so she'll get about twelve and a half dollars a week. Not exactly magnificent is it. Wage s over here seem to be very low compared with yours. I earn about two pounds twelve shillings after deductions, and my mother earns about the same. The Coal Miners in your country who decided to strike for higher money should come over and take a dose of the average

British Miner's medicine. He goes down the Pits day and night, often with only a meal of Bread and Margarine, and gets the princely sum of about 20 to 25 dollars a week for doing it. Your miners get that amount per day, practically. We occasionally have small strikes—fiddling affairs, usually—but I'd like to remind all strikers that they'd be in a pretty fine mess if the fighting forces laid down their arms and decided they wanted more dough. The British soldiers pay is three and a half dollars a week, if he's single and three dollars if he's married—Wonderful isn't it? That's counting the dollar equal to five shillings. I'm not sure of the rate of exchange now. Our prices have been stabilised pretty well, but we have a 50% purchase tax on practically everything we buy, and theres not an article that doesn't cost three times as much as in Peacetime. Clothes have gone up to extortionate prices, although with the coupon restrictions there isn't much chance of buying 'em, even if we had the money. I have given up the problem [lines deleted by censor] and shoes—I need about twenty-five [line deleted by censor] book to last till the end of August, and all my efforts to secure a couple of "spares", including agonised pleas to my grandmother, and attempts to vamp any man left in the Office, have proved completely futile. Therefore 25 into 10 won't go and I am left with minus 15. So I either have to do without pants, or stockings, or underwear of any description, or go out barefoot! What a life for a gal in the prime of her youth!!

I have come without stockings to-day, and feel a wee bit chilly at times, although it is just as well to get yourself used to it. We don't have very warm summers, but you always find that when you start your "stockingless" season you feel a bit cold, even when the temperature is above average. "Average" in England is about 60 degrees. When it reaches 80, the perspiring populace collapse from shock, and the Papers come out with large headlines about a heat-wave. Trouble is in England, the climate is so very variable, that you can never go out with perfect confidence, without a coat, and an umbrella is never out of place, even on a balmy sunny day. Last week, on Monday, we were so cold we had to sit huddled round fires, and type with our Outdoor Coats on—this state of affairs continued until Wednesday—[line deleted by censor] and awoke on Friday morning to sunshine and blue skies, and the hottest day of the year. Naturally we were all in our winter "undies" and nearly boiled, as a result. Friday night, we had something approximating to a Cloudburst and were nearly washed away.

[Lines deleted by censor] Anyway, what with one warning and another, I got about three hours slumber, which isn't enough for anyone, and don't feel any too bright in consequence. Thats one thing you Americans can count yourself blessed with—immunity from Air attack. The Japs and Germans may hurl threats at you but you're much too far away for them to do anything about it, and I doubt very much whether New York will ever hear the thud of the "plonkers" as we have. I can imagine the panic it would cause if a thousand-pounder fell on top of the Woolworth building! Or the Empire State! I shall never forget the days on the London "blitz" as long as I live—You dreaded the approach of night, and were never able to make arrangements for even a day ahead, as you didn't know whether you would be alive to keep them. When I used to see the dawn every morning, I always said my prayers of thanks to the Almighty that I was still there in one piece. And it was ghastly to go to work each morning, wondering who the next absentee was going to be. And when you got there more often than not there was no Water to wash with, and no Gas or Electricity to cook the food. The Manager of the Canteen here used to light a fire in the Goods Yard and boil a pot of Stew over it. The windows were out, and we used to work with our coats on, and later on the windows were boarded up and we had to work in artificial light all day. It was a nightmare! Add to that the fact that we lived in daily dread of our lives, and had about one hour's sleep nightly and you get some idea of what is known as "Total Warfare' Some existence.

*Wednesday.*

[Lines deleted by censor] I suppose these are reprisals for our big raids when we knocked out the two big Water Dams in the Ruhr. What a marvellous stroke that was! Probably hinder War production for months and sent to Eternity another couple of thousand Huns that the world can well do without. I have no sympathy for anything German, dead or alive, and what they are getting now, and what we hope they'll get in the future, they richly deserve, believe me.

Our casualties in the N. African campaign are 220,000—somebody's son, sweetheart or husband, everyone of 'em. The collapse in Africa was quite unexpected though. I expected the Germans to make a long, wearying stand at Cape Bon, or at least try a "Dunkirk". But we *fought* at Dunkirk. Our boys fought without weapons, or supplies, but this Army had everything—yet they folded up. I think it should put an end to the fable about the undying courage of the German soldier. They're alright when they're winning but when they know they're beaten, they give in and squeal for mercy like the Rats they are. The Tunisian victory has had a tremendous effect on the people here—it's given a great "flip" to production, if it needed that, and it showed that we are at least beginning to see Daylight after three years of Set-backs, trials and tribulations. Hero worship of General Montgomery has reached unheard of levels here—I think if "Monty" wanted it, he could have the whole of Britain wrapped up in brown paper and presented to him—gratis. Although, I think it's a pity that people don't remember that there was a First as well as an Eighth Army, and that Montgomery and the "8th" boys had things pretty much their own way including 1500 miles of flat country to fight on, and Lady Luck on their side. The "1st" boys under Anderson and Alexander had all the difficult, hilly, terrain to conquer and most of the "bloodiest" battles of the Campaign to fight—and their casualties are much heavier than those of the 8th. I, personally, think no more credit is due to Monty than Alexander and Anderson and to the Yankee boys who took Bizerta and the French who fought at Mateur. The names of the Regiments taking part in the Campaign have been given this morning—some of our oldest and best fought there. My boy friend's Company did some heroic work on one of these dratted Hills that kept holding up operations. He's in the Brigade of Guards—remember, I told you. And he's been in Tunisia sometime now. I haven't heard from him for weeks and I hope he's alright. Ted is still in London, though he's anxious to get out and see some action before the War ends. The one in Tunisia is Chris—I'd better get you straightened out about these males or you may get them mixed up. Ted is the one in the photo I sent you. Chris is a slightly newer acquisition, but a very nice one at that.

I have to see the Doctor again on June 11th. Apparently I'm not doing so well. I have now developed fluid on the left lung, as well as the right, and they are still dickering with the idea of shoving me back into Hospital again. They can't attempt surgical interference because of the adhesions on both sides. I am still at work and feel pretty well, though I wish we could get some decent food. I don't seem to lack energy, however, as I dance twice a week and feel perfectly fit. The "Doc" says I have no active symptoms—it's just the X-ray that keeps on letting me down. Jack is in South Africa—and is having the time of his life. Plenty of fruit, food and sunshine, and he's doing fine. He's rather apprehensive about coming home to rationed England and if he's wise I think he'll try and stay there till after this is over.

I listened to those Programmes about America and thought them very interesting, but there, I've never visited the States and wouldn't know the difference. Did you hear the one of ours about Lancashire? The accent was pretty rich. I love a North Country brogue though— think it's fascinating.

Did you get my last letter when I asked you to try and get in touch with that Martha Wagner for me. Remember she wrote me after reading a letter of mine to you. I do wish you could get hold of her for me, Helen. As I told you she sent me a parcel at Xmas, and she'll think I'm no end of a worm for not replying to her. I've been quite worried about it. If you ever can get hold of her do thank her for me, and ask her to write again and let me have her address. She was so nice and thoughtful, and I should hate her to think I was ungrateful.

I hope you are able to send those film Mags again; I used to love to read them and afterwards I always give them to Ted to take for the Soldiers in the Barracks to read. Our film Books are tiny fortnightly affairs—about twenty pages if you're lucky, and then you have to order it. The shipping position in the Atlantic seems a bit better now, and most of the stuff gets here when it's sent. Chris said he was going to send me some Oranges from Tunis, but he's probably been so busy saving his hide that he doesn't even know where to get 'em. I do wish they'd send him home, but from all appearances, they'll probably be sent farther afield, to Burma, or some such place to fight the blasted Japs.

I must close now, honey, as I've a lot of work to do, and this will never win the War. All my love to you, and write me soon.

Yours,
Betty

## GREAT WESTERN RAILWAY

Goods Department,
South Lambeth Station,
London, S.W. 8.

Dear Helen,

Just a few lines written while I have nothing to do—in other words, for the first time for weeks I am at a loose end. I have done all my work and in British Railway language am "up straight"! Sounds more like Irish, doesn't it? I don't suppose in a Hospital you ever get to that stage! Anyway, I might as well type a couple of lines while I have the chance.

Well! we've all been tremendously excited here by the downfall of Mussolini—at last, after all these years.[4] What ultimate effect it will have on the War is problematical at the moment, though. There is a lot of speculation one way and the other and opinion is sharply divided—one section thinks it's a good thing and the other, that it's not so good, and definitely smells "fishy". Personally, I'm ready to wait and see. My own bet is that the Italians—who are yellow to the core, anyway—are thoroughly fed up with being on the losing end and are hoping for Peace of some sort to save their own extremely sensitive skins. It is obvious to them that Badoglio will be more acceptable to the Allies than would Musso, and I think that Italian diplomats are well aware of the notorious soft-hearted attitude of the British government who persist in adopting kid-glove methods with these greasy little Wops and are banking on a more than lenient Pearce offer. I only hope that Stalin and Roosevelt will be able to introduce a stiffening-up atmosphere into the proceedings, for if its left to the British Government I guarantee that Musso, and the whole Italian race will get off scot-free. The British passion for being fair to the other fellow will get them well into the Soup one of these days if it hasn't already. The majority of the folks here are disgusted at the fuss and bother which preceded the raid on Rome. We dropped leaflets humbly apologizing for the liberty we were taking and assuring the citizens of the Wop Capital that we would only bomb in daylight so as to be sure of hitting Military objectives. I, and

4. On July 25, 1943, King Victor Emmanuel II replaced him with the former Italian governor general in Ethiopia, Marshal Pietro Badoglio, who began sending peace feelers to the Allies (Calder, *People's War*, 606).

many million other Britishers, have fond memories of the "Blitz" days
when the Italian Air Force asked to be allowed to join in the "honour"
of bombing London! British history and civilisation—her Cathedrals,
her monuments and everything else that was dear to us, and to the rest
of the World, was completely shattered and no-one bothered to send
us leaflets or bomb us solely in daylight. St. Paul's, Westminster Abbey, Canterbury Cathedral, the Pump Rooms at Bath—and so many
other things—all these beloved things belonged to the great things
of the World as much as the ruins that grace the City of Rome. Yet
we allowed all that military activity to take place there for three years
and would not touch it, for fear of knocking yet another piece off the
Coloseum [*sic*] or more than probably to avoid sending that worthy
gentlemen—his Eminence the Pope—scuttling to his Air Raid Shelter. We have given Rome *one* raid, in three years, and I'd like to bet
my weekly salary that that's all they'll get. The Roman Catholic ele-
ment among the "high-ups" will see to that. Also that "shadow" ruler of
Britain—the Archbishop of Canterbury had his usual bit of "flapdoodle" to say, all about the Raid being a crime against Civilisation
and Christianity. Strikes me we're fighting this war, not to save democracy, but to save Rome! I am a Churchgoer myself, and count myself
as good a Christian as the next best, but I have no patience with the
constant interference of the Church of England into the affairs of War.
The church complains that it is losing it's hold on the young and that
they no longer believe in the ideals that Religion has stood for all these
years, but how *can* you convince youth that God is a just and mighty
being and that the Church's attitude is right, when Youth itself is in the
middle of the biggest Blood bath of all time, and the Church makes it
its business to do everything to hinder the speedy finish of that Blood
Bath. I think the prosecution of a War should be left to those who
know about it, and the Church should stick to it's own "métier" and
what it's paid to do, which is preach the Gospel to all and sundry. I
wonder though, if the Vatican had been situated in England whether
we should have been regarded as so sacred by the Huns and Wops!

Jack arrived home in England a month ago, and is now endeavour-
ing to find himself a place to live in—which is some job in England
nowadays. Houses are practically unobtainable and a Flat isn't so hot
with the baby running up and down stairs all the time. He looks very fit

and well and had a wonderful time in South Africa by all accounts. The climate here doesn't suit him at all, however, and I dread to think how he's going to dislike the winter. I dread the thought of the dark nights and the cold. Let's hope that this will be the last winter of War, anyway, although I can't see the darned thing ending for a year or two yet. Jack had a perfectly awful time in the Burma-Assam jungle, according to him fighting the Germans is a picnic compared to fighting the Japs under jungle conditions. His baby is a pretty little girl, but unfortunately she screams when he comes near her, which upsets him very much. I'm afraid though, there'll be a great many babies who won't recognize their fathers when this War is over. Some of our men have been in the Middle East and India for the past three years and the Government offers them no hope of getting home before another two or three—it's only natural that the men feel a bit "browned-off" about it. In fact while all this yelling about the falling Birth rate is going on, they usually omit to mention that the most important factor to consider is that the majority of the young potential fathers are thousands of miles away!

One of my boy friends in Tunisia—Jakey, the Coldstream Guard I used to tell you about—has been wounded, pretty badly and is now in Hospital. He writes to say how much he is longing to come home— and when he was in England he was longing to get out of it! He was knocked out on the last day of the campaign so whether he will be kept there or sent home, I don't know. I doubt the latter course, as they are patching up most of the men and sending them back into action, and in any case I don't suppose they've got the shipping space available. Chris is with the Eighth Army and Ted is also out in North Africa with the First. The majority of the troops over here are Americans and Canadians. By the way, thanks for sending the Movie Magazines. I send them all out to N. Africa when I've read them, and the boys cut out all the pictures of the Hollywood beauties and paste 'em up in their Billets. They were the first decent Film Magazines I've seen for ages.

The general situation here stays much the same. There are the unusual queues for this that and the other. Recently it's been for Cherries, Tomatoes and the inevitable Fish. The first of the year's apples were on sale last week and there were long queues for them, but they're getting plentiful now and aren't so hard to get. Plums are beginning to be seen now, too, and later on we shall have some of the big Victoria Plums that are so good for preserving. I only had one taste of Strawberries this year and no Raspberries—most of the soft fruit went to the Jam makers, although the Jam now is nothing much to write home about. The fruit content never goes above 30% and the rest is made up of Pectin. I am feeling very blue because the Government have put a ban on the manufacture of Nail Polish I have always like[d] to tint my nails with nice coloured Polishes—usually the Cyclamen and Clover Shades—and as I have long narrow nails, they used to look quite nice, and now with this new order it looks as if we're not going to have anything at all. Although it's been practically impossible to get anything decent in that line for ages. Most of the stuff is Nail Lacquer, which peels off as soon as you put it on. Similarly I get heart-aches when I read that we are still exporting Perfumes, Grossmiths, Yardleys, Cotys, things the British girl hasn't seen for two years. I am simply mad on perfume, and even now I haunt the shops to see if there's anything going. You can sometimes get a bottle, but it's nothing more than coloured water and the prices are terrible. Still, it seems a bit hard that the gals in the other countries can get the stuff which we should be having. But there, I suppose we should be content to trade our Scent for "Spam"! Hard as it is to have to go around without a whiff of "good smell", it's so much nicer to have a full tummy, I suppose.

I saw the Doctor last week. I don't think he's very pleased with my X-rays and I have to see him every month which is a monotonous business, and is really getting me down. The truth of the matter is they haven't got the room in the Hospitals and Sanatoria for half the people who are suffering from T.B. and they can only take the bad cases. So I shall be reprieved for months, probably. I don't want to go back in at all, but I'm fed up with this eternal "watching and waiting" policy. T.B. has become a real menace over here, and more and more young people are going down with it every day.

I went to see "Hello, Frisco, Hello" last night and thought it was pretty good. Usually, though, I get fed up with Technicolour films because they will persist in showing us plates of lovely coloured food! I shan't forget "Happy Go Lucky" in a hurry—with a big plate of Chops, Mushrooms and Green Peas and so on in Technicolour and Banana Splits and so on, as Dessert, the audience got thoroughly fed up with thinking of their own humble Sausage and mashed—and until you've eaten a British sausage you have no idea of how awful it tastes.[5] The clothes too, are a source of great envy to me. To see Betty Grable trailing about in yards and yards of chiffon, when I have to surrender five coupons for enough for a blouse, just isn't Cricket.! I'd like to see la Grable look glamourous on a supply of 36 coupons a year, which a little bird whispers is all that Hugh Delton is going to allow us for the year. Thats nine for each three months, and stockings run at 3.0 coupons a pair. A Coat takes eighteen, which would practically be your year's supply, and no provision is made for underclothing or mere incidentals like that. The aforementioned Master Mind, Mr. Dalton, has issued a pamphlet for Expectant mothers telling them how to dress their babies on the supply of coupons he allows them.[6] He says blandly that a baby doesn't need hats or gloves, or rubber knickers, or flannel binders or anything else that a baby used to need in peacetime—and as for the poor mother, well! she doesn't need any clothes at all! He says she should cut up two frocks and make herself one out of it. Frocks are seven coupons a piece, so out of the dozen coupons which you now get to last you three months the future mamma has to spend fourteen on one frock. Mr Dalton, I believe, is childless, and has very little idea of what mothers or babies need. The more he cuts the coupons down to a minimum the prouder he gets, but he forgets the important fact that the Black Market is flourishing for that very reason. We are all prepared for sacrifices, and we all make do as much as possible with our old clothes, but his ideas are beyond the realms of possibility and its no wonder that when people are offered stockings and material, with no coupons, they jump at the offer even though they are charged double and treble the value of the stuff!

I shall have to close now after that delightful moan—which, after looking at my wardrobe I can assure you is perfectly justified—and go

---

5. *Hello Frisco, Hello* (1943; U.S.), a musical comedy starring Alice Faye, includes the Oscar-winning song "You'll Never Know." The musical comedy *Happy Go Lucky* (1943; U.S.) stars Mary Martin, Dick Powell, Betty Hutton, Rudy Vallee, and Eddie Bracken.

6. Hugh Dalton, president of the Board of Trade and a member of the Labour Party, was identified in the public's mind as "Austerity." His ministry issued regulations for clothing, household goods, and furniture, as well as food rationing (Calder, *People's War*, 318–26).

on to my sumptuous repast in the Office canteen. I hope that you are keeping your head above water and not worrying about the rationing of coffee. We have two pound tins in our Cupboard which we never touch! They've been there for about a year or more! They're probably as hard as bricks now. Write me when you have time, and look after yourself.

Love,

Betty

## GREAT WESTERN RAILWAY

Goods Department,

South Lambeth Station,

London, S.W.8

[February 1945]

Dear Helen,

It will probably shake you, hearing from me, after so long—seems ages since I wrote you anything like a proper letter, and equal ages since I heard from you. Guess you must be working pretty hard, still at the Hospital, are you? Anyway, as you will probably guess by the fact that this is typewritten—I've started work again, believe it or not. After eighteen months! It's about time.

Many things have happened since I wrote you last. The flying bombs commenced last June and nearly blasted us all to Kingdom Come.[7] I developed pneumonia again and the Doctors decided that London was no place for me and so in July, they shifted me up to Lancashire—to a lovely seaside place called Southport. I was very happy there, and it got quite like home to me—got friendly with loads of people and managed to get back a bit of energy I'd lost while spending my nights and days in Shelters. I had eight weeks of flying bombs before they sent me out of it, and they nearly drove me to drink. The Germans are now using their V.2's on us (poor old London seems to be their chief target every time) but I think the Londoner has got so used to living among ruin

---

7. By the end of August 1944, 6,725 V1s had been sent over Britain. Only 2,340 reached the London target area. The bombs killed 5,475 people and severely injured 16,000 more (Calder, *People's War*, 648).

and destruction that he is now impervious to it.[8] The rest of the country can have no conception of what the Cockney's have had to endure for the past four years, and between you and me they don't seem to care, either.

Our place caught a packet in August, and all the roofs caved in and practically ruined the furniture. Luckily Mum was in the Shelter at the time, but the place looks awfully shabby now, and it's made us so weary of it all we'd like to shift out of London altogether. I love the place, but it doesn't seem to hold many happy memories, not this past couple of years anyway. The Doctors in Southport played merry murder when I came back, but the plain unvarnished truth was I darned well had to! The Railway had stopped my money, and it's practically impossible (or so I've found) to live in other people's houses with no funds. My job was in London and in these days of strict Government control, I couldn't get my release, so back I had to come. I admit that it isn't the healthiest, or the safest place to work, but that's how it had to be. I must say, though, I don't feel so well down here as I did up North. There doesn't seem to be so much air to breathe.

We're all terribly excited at the Russians approaching Berlin—by the time you get this God knows where they'll be.![9] I've always been one of those who wanted the Russians to get to Germany first, because I honestly believe they'll use the right methods with them—ruthless methods, the only sort those swine understand. If we get near them, we'll start our usual Milk and Water, strictly cricket, tactics and we'll all be ever so matey and forgiving in a few weeks. The British High Command never seem to have heard of the "Eye for an Eye, and a tooth for a tooth" principle. They believe firmly in letting Bygones be Bygones and not being beastly to the Germans, or anyone else for that matter. Rudolph Hess is treated like a Lord and the Italian prisoners are handled

---

8. The first attack of the V2s began on September 8, 1944. By November, an average of four to six attacks were made each day. A V2 was forty-five feet long and weighed fourteen tons. It traveled so fast one could not hear it before it exploded. Only 518 V2s reached London, but nearly 3,000 people were killed in these attacks, not all Londoners. On March 27, the last V2 fell in Kent (ibid., 649–52).

9. On January 12, 1945, the Russians launched a new offensive, and by the beginning of February the Red Army was forty miles from Berlin. By the end of April 1945 the Russians had encircled Berlin. Hitler and his new wife, Eva Braun, committed suicide on April 30 (ibid., 653).

with kid gloves and given more care and consideration than anyone in the country, the dirty Wops. They even send the clothes needed badly by our own kiddies to children in Occupied Europe—and ladies clothes to Paris. Well! from what I've seen in the papers and heard about the Parisiennes they're a darned sight better clothed than we are! Coupons are tighter than ever over here now. We get 24 to last us seven months and it takes eighteen of those to buy a Coat and two for a pair of stockings. I have just bought a new Coat, so that leaves me half a dozen coupons to play around with until September. What a life. I often wonder why the President of the Board of Trade doesn't ask us to walk around naked and have finished with it.

I celebrated last night by eating an orange—the first for about 10 months, and obtained after queueing up for about an hour. I think it must have been one of the new dehydrated ones, as it was singularly lacking in juice and seemed to consist entirely of pith and peel. Still, it was a change. Our diet is so monotonous and stereotyped now. Everything we eat seems to be either rationed or on points—and when you've cooked it, it just doesn't look appetising. They've promised to improve the Sausage (and by heck, the War-time sausage certainly *need* improving) and our Bread is slightly whiter, but apart from that the food situation seems to stay pretty much the same. I remember one letter you wrote me last year you said you were preserving Peaches—it sounds amazing to me that anyone could get enough peaches to preserve. Here they cost 5 shilling each for small ones—thats about a dollar and a quarter—and an ordinary water melon costs 5 dollars for the smaller variety. Black grapes are thirty shillings a pound—about 7 ½ dollars, so you see luxuries are out for all but the wealthier folk. However, we as a nation, are quite used to it and as we've been warned that its likely to continue for a long, long time after the War, its just as well that we don't get any illusions about going back to normal living. Personally speaking, if this War will only end, I don't give a damn what I go without—After five and a half years of it, I've got absolutely weary.

My boy friend is still fighting like mad in Italy—he's been overseas about two and a quarter years now. The conditions over there have apparently to be seen to be believed—snow a few feet thick and frozen over and bitter cold. He's with the Eighth Army in the Mountains somewhere. Poor little devil, I feel real sorry for him.

I suppose whatever we have to put up with at home, its nothing compared to what those poor lads are going through out there. And what they're having is probably much lighter than the difficulties of the Germans, although as I've said before whatever happens to them they richly deserve and I have no sympathy at all for them.

It's been wickedly cold over here—the severest winter for about 50 years, snow and burst pipes and chilblains and all the rest of the things that go with dat ole debbil Winter I am a Summer baby, I love the sun and the long evenings so I just exist from October to May and live the other four months. They say a hard winter presages a warm summer—Let's hope so. I always think the Sun puts a different complexion on things. It was lovely in Southport in August and September—I used to go and sit on a Seat on the Promenade and take in great gusts of the Sea Air. For once in my life I got a suspicion of a Sun-tan!

I haven't been able to go to many Shows—having been out of London. I've seen some good films though—most of them British. Saw a grand one last night called "Waterloo Road" with a new British romantic star, Stewart Granger—Watch out for him, he's going to be the current rage over here. I also paid a visit to see an old French film: called "Carnet du Bal"—Ever see it? I think it is the most perfectly acted picture I have ever seen![10]

My mother wishes to be remembered to you. She's looking much older and greyer after all the bombing, but manages to stay pretty cheerful. Looking through this letter, she seems to be more cheerful than I am. Still, I'll do better next time. I just wanted you to know that I was still in the land of the living and to know how you are.

As always,

Betty

10. *Waterloo Road* (1945; UK) stars John Mills and Stewart Granger. Granger, who was classically trained in the British theater, appeared in West End productions and was England's top box office star in the 1940s. He was wounded while serving in the British Army during World War II. The drama *Un Carnet du Bal* (1937; France) is still highly regarded.

# VI

## August 1945–1947

In July 1945, in the first national election since 1936, the Labour Party and its Liberal allies polled more than 14 million votes to the Conservatives' 9 million. Betty welcomed the result, even though more stringent rationing of food and clothing resulted in pneumonia, weight loss, and another prolonged stay in sanatoriums. "Have just had my lunch," she wrote Helen in 1946. "Potatoes, Cabbage and Gravy and a slice of Vegetable Pie—no meat—and some sort of Sponge Roll, tasting exactly like pulped cardboard."

Under orders from her doctors, Betty left London and moved to Southport, twenty miles from Liverpool, where her mother, Gladys, joined her. Betty, wrote Gladys thanking Helen for her packages of food and clothing, was "a wartime casualty." Chris, Betty's fiancé, returned from India and ended their relationship.

Betty, unlike many girls of her age, did not become a GI war bride.

## GREAT WESTERN RAILWAY

District Goods Manager's Office,
11, James Street, Liverpool, 2.

My dear Helen,

I was so very pleased to hear from you—seems like ages since I did and I've been wondering how you've been getting on. So much seems to have happened since our last letters—the end of the War in Germany, and the approaching end of the business with Japan. As I sit here, we are hourly awaiting the news of the Jap surrender and it seems hardly believable that once again the world will be at Peace. To us the end of the German war—apart from stopping the bloodshed and killing our boys, meant that we—in London at any rate—could go to sleep and be reasonably sure of waking up again! The last few months of the V2. menace were horrible. You never knew as you were walking about, when death would suddenly drop on you, without warning. I came back to London in January, and between then and the end of the Rockets in April, I lost about a quarter of my crowning glory. That's serious! I developed a big bald patch on the back of my head. The Doctor put it down to nerves, and told me to thank my lucky stars that I had a thick head of hair, so it didn't notice so much.

Apart from being able to go to sleep safely, theres very little difference in the general situation here—unless it's for the worse. Food is getting tighter than ever—our fat ration having been cut again and trying to get a decent dinner out of the week's meat ration—25 cents worth in your money—is enough to drive you mad. We have one meat dinner a week, on a Sunday, and the rest of the week we manage on Potatoes and Vegetables, with some Onion to cheer it up, or Chipped Potatoes, or Fish, when you can get it. As for clothes—we've just been told the sad news that our next issue of coupons—24—has to last us for *eight* months—a Winter Coat is 18 out of that and stockings 2 a pair. Oh! my Gawd, we shall all be walking about in fig leaves. Apparently, they say we must take our share in clothing Europe, and there is a shortage of cotton and woolen cloth here. Still, I guess we expected it. They warned us some time ago, that we, in Britain, couldn't expect a return to even liveable conditions for a year or two after the finish of *both* Wars, and we don't have the vast resources that you have, or the ability to turn our industries over from War to Peace. I always think the Americans are streets ahead of us in that respect, seem to have more initiative and drive when they're tackling a problem. It says in the paper this morning, that American women are going to be O.K. when the War with the Japs ends, their stockings and their Household goods, and textiles, should be back with them before Christmas. So you're a little luckier than we are in that respect. I'd like to be out there when the first hundred pairs of Nylons get into the Shops—I bet millions of females will be killed in the rush. I don't think I'd be able to get a silk stocking on my leg now, I'd be too scared the thing would ladder. I've been managing without wearing stockings for the best part of the Spring and Summer, but I usually have to go back to them about October. I'm too cold a body to go with my legs uncovered in Winter and they won't allow us to wear slacks in the Office—think it's undignified, or un-feminine, or some such tripe.

By the way, I shall probably be leaving the big City within the next few weeks. I didn't want to do it, but the Doctors have yelled so much about London being unhealthy that I'm going back up to Southport, maybe the Seaside air will have a better effect than that of the Gas Works. I shall be working in Liverpool, and traveling back and forth each day—about 20 miles. I feel awful blue about leaving London, though. I've been here 10 years, and the place has a hold on you. Yet it really doesn't agree with me—the air, I mean. I have to go up alone at first, and then look around for rooms for my mother—some job. Getting rooms or a flat is practically impossible here now—the housing situation is appalling, and what it's going to be like when all the lads come back and set up house I can't imagine. They're always talking about big Housing Drives, but I don't see much sign of it starting yet. All I ask out of life is a two or three-roomed pre-fabricated bungalow, and I shall be a happy woman, but my prospects are far from rosy, believe me. Anyway, keep on writing to me at Lambeth, and then they will send it on to me wherever I am, and as soon as I am definitely settled in, I'll let you know. It will be a big wrench leaving this Office, too. I've been here so long and everyone has been so kind to me.

Since you wrote, we have changed our Government, and as you prophesied—Churchill is out of the picture. Not through ingratitude— oh! no—although I still insist that it was the men and women of the fighting forces and the Home Front who won the War, not any one man—but because England needed a change of policy and we, with the rest of the world, are showing a Left-ward trend that has always been there really. I am a rank Socialist, and the Conservative party never had a single constructive thing in their programme—all they had was Churchill, and they played him up like a Clown in a Circus. I don't know how much you understand about our politics, but England has been ruled by the Conservative party from Time immemorial—they are supposed to be our "betters" the big boys, with the money, and the family tradition, and the big business men who yell about the stifling of private enterprise when they are only concerned about the effect it is to have on their own pockets. It was a battle of the "haves" against the "have-nots" and the boys in the Forces were determined that there should be no repetition of the 1918 fiasco, when they came back to unemployment, sweated labour, and practically starvation, instead of the "Land fit for Heroes" that they were promised.[1] Labour have never had a fighting chance in Parliament, they've never had a big enough majority, but now they have got their opportunity and I hope they will use it to advantage. Tomorrow is the State opening of Parliament and I hope it will be a Peace Parade as well—there won't be all the old Ceremonial, but it will be worth watching, nevertheless.

We were all very grieved about the passing of Mr. Roosevelt—it seemed so tragic that he had to go just when the War with Germany was drawing to its close.[2] He was a great man, and he had done his work well—it's a pity he wasn't spared to see the end of it. We thought of him V-Day when we stood in our thousands outside Buckingham Palace waiting for the King and Queen to come out on the Balcony— London that night, was a sight to behold—everyone seemed to have gone completely crazy, but I was so tired after all the celebrations I wanted to sleep for a week! They are making great plans for celebrating again now, when the end of the Jap War is official—everything seems to be "up in the air" at the moment.

1. In June 1945, 4,531,300 men and women above twenty-one years of age were in the armed services. Many were overseas. Only 1,701,000 votes were cast by the military. The results could not be announced for three weeks (Calder, *People's War*, 671–72).

2. Roosevelt died on April 12, 1945, in Warm Springs, Georgia. "The shock in Britain was stunning; the mourning sincere" (ibid., 653).

I should have loved to have seen Chris's letter to you (his name's "Chris", not Ted, honey—you've got them mixed up) If you still have it, I wish you'd send it over to me. I'll return it without fail. I have a very sad story to tell about it all. He came back to England last April, but we've had such trouble with him since. He deserted from the Army on May 24th. and is in London somewhere—I don't know quite where, but they haven't picked him up yet. He seems to be a different man—went completely mad—you know, wine, women and song—the old story. I was terribly grieved over it, and so are his mother and family, but however much we try to influence him for good there are always so many others trying to use their power for evil, and we are completely helpless over it. He had such a fine, military record, too, and it's awful to think of him acting up like this. Funny, the end of the War to me always meant that he would be home safe and well, yet now it's come it's the very thing that has taken him from me. It's quite taken the gloss of[f] my Peacetime celebrations, still, I guess that's a selfish view to take—others are getting their men back and it's wrong for me to fret because I lost mine. Anyhow, I'm afraid that's the end of my dreams for the two of us—his, too, because I wasn't the only one who did the planning. After three years, it's quite a big break. He told me that he had had a letter from you and that he had written to you to thank you. Chris's trouble is the old one, Helen. He's a very good looking man, and has got a heck of a swelled head in consequence. Women chase him around like Moths round a Candle, and he likes to sit down and hear them flatter him—I've never done it, and I won't—which is one of my failings, I suppose. Still, I hope they'll be able to get him back and then he can at least take his punishment and come out and walk down the street with his head up. It seems awful that a man who has gone through as much danger and discomfort as he has should have lost his head so completely.

I haven't read a Movie Book for ages—I used to send them all out to him when I used to get them. It wiled away many a weary hour for them. I guess the Post Office won't be so fussy now about accepting things. They don't even censor the stuff now, and its gets here much quicker, and the shipping position will be getting easier, anyway.

You were certainly lucky getting all those dresses given you. I am the most devout admirer of American clothes that ever was—especially the shoes which seem to be the smartest ever. Ou[r] stuff is all Utility now—the costumes aren't bad—though they're 18 coupons and beyond me—but the Shoes are very drab, and the leather isn't much good. We used to get a few pairs of American styled shoes here in Peacetime—some of those lovely low Wedgie type—but haven't seen them in the Shops for years. We can only get one or at the most two pairs of Shoes a year anyway. They're rationed out there aren't they? I think I read it once. How much butter and meat do you get on your ration, now? We get two ounces of Butter and 25 cents worth of meat a week—do you get more or less? We were getting two ounces of lard a week, but they cut that a few months ago, and we only get an ounce now—but they increased the Tea ration to 2 ½ ounces, which was one blessing over here. I'm a non-smoker myself, but the last time I saw Chris, he was very nearly reduced to smoking cardboard, because he couldn't get any "fags" and that, for a Chain-smoker like he is—is hard going.

I've been getting thinner again—Can't seem to keep the weight on me. I'm trying Cod Liver Oil and Malt now, to see if that will do the trick. I'm also trying to eat "filling" foods—plenty of bread, and an occasional Suet Pudding. My boss has just brought me over three slices of Bread and Dripping from the Canteen, and has showed me something which I always used to love in Peacetime, but which I haven't seen for a long while—a tin of Corned Beef! God knows how many points he's given for it, I can't bear to think. It's grand with a Salad, though. I always develop passions on stuff you never see. I love Salad Cream—mayonnaise I guess you'd call it—but there's a world shortage of that owing to the Olive Oil in it. I thought if I could get a Doctor's certificate for a Priority bottle of Olive Oil I might make some of my own. Goodness knows what it would turn out like, though.

I seem to have rambled on and on in this—I really must close. I hope by the time this reaches you that the world will be at peace again, and you won't be working so hard. Don't forget to write to the old address and they'll forward it.

All my love,
Betty

P.S. I can't remember if I sent you the enclosed snap last year. It was taken in Southport, Sept '44, and I don't know why I was looking so pleased with myself!

## GREAT WESTERN RAILWAY

District Goods Manager's Office,
Accounts and Rates Dept.
11, James Street, Liverpool, 2.
[April 1946]

Dear Helen,

I haven't heard from you for an age, and am wondering how you are all this time. I guess you must be busy. I wrote to you about three months ago, I think—did you ever get it? telling you all about my leaving my lovely London, and coming up here—"for the benefit of my health" the doctors, say, but personally, I don't think it's made much difference. I am still as thin as a Barber's Pole and the English climate is so indescribable that as fast as you build your resistance up, something happens to pull it down. We had a bitter cold spell early January ice inches thick, snow and everything that goes with it—and now it has rained every day steadily for twenty three days—gallons & gallons of it—the earth is soaked and the clouds perpetually grey. To-day is appalling. There is thick fog over the river and the rain is pouring down—indeed, if there is anyone else more sick of winter than I, I should like to find them. It seems to me that when the sun is shining your troubles take on a lighter aspect, but on days like this I can understand the mentally unstable committing suicide!

I've just recovered from my third bout of tonsillitis and a bad cold, and the Doctors are now nagging me to have my tonsils out. Trouble is it means three weeks in the hospital, and they won't let me have chloroform, so the prospect is far from appealing. On the other hand, I keep getting these bad throats, so maybe it's better that I pluck up my courage and get the job done. I say that once they've got my tonsils, they can't take any other part of my anatomy and still leave me alive. I'm beginning to feel as if I'm kept together with Adhesive tape, when they keep taking little bits of this and little bits of that. Still, maybe the summer will effect an improvement. Where I'm living—Southport—is very pleasant in the summer—the main street looks like a wide boulevard, with trees on either side, and we have a lovely Promenade where you can stroll on Sundays. And when the sun *does* make an appearance we can bathe in the Swimming Pool and sit on the Sand. A bit different from my old London, where my Sunday outing was to go to Hyde park to hear the speakers, and precious little else, apart from my Church service at Westminster Abbey. I still go to Church every Sunday, but in a little tin affair called St. Simons and St. Judes—what a difference to the old Abbey, although I guess the Pomp and Circumstance don't mean so much, after all.

My mother has been ill and has to go for X-ray in a fortnight's time if she doesn't improve—tummy trouble, a complaint which seems to run in our family along with the inevitable Weak chests. She is still in London, it being practically impossible to get rooms up here yet awhile, and it's very worry[ing] her being so far away. There are something like three thousand people waiting for houses in this town, and only thirty will be up by May. The housing problem here is ghastly, and it gets worse and worse every day with so many Servicemen being demobilised. I am beginning to despair of ever finding even an empty Barn—there has been much talk of "pre-fabricated" temporary houses, but it remains, as so many other things do, in the talking stage. They may not be ideal dwellings but at least they are something to live in—some sort of a roof over people's heads, and that's better than nothing. The only houses available to-day are those that you buy, and you now have to pay four and five times the value of them. A house built in 1939, and put up for sale at £400. now fetches something like two thousand pounds! It's criminal—because they aren't worth it.

I can't understand why they won't get on with the idea put forward of converting Army Nissen Huts—there are thousands of those scattered over the country and they would make comfortable accommodation for three or four people. Something will have to be done, anyway. The returning Warrior isn't going to be very pleased when he sees the chaos he has to come back to and I say that even though I am a loyal Socialist and an ardent supporter of our present Government.

We are in the middle of a storm now over the new food cuts. It was a bitter blow to us to have the fats rations sliced again—we get so little now, and Doctors have warned them time and time again that our present nutritional value is the lowest we should and could ever endure. They have also stopped the import of dried egg, and as we get little or no Shell Eggs, that has upset the weary British housewife who is just about fed up to the teeth with managing on near starvation rations. After all, Helen, we get no fruit, precious little meat and no vitamins at all—and it's bound to tell after six years of such a diet. Our resistance is so bad we can't stand up to anything. I've had six colds this winter up to now, and each one worse than the last. Think it must be due to something lacking in the diet—fats, mostly, I suppose. I've started taking Cod Liver Oil and Malt now, to see if that will do the trick. I loathe the stuff, but it's better than nothing. I always have to avert my gaze though when I take it. If I gave one look, I'd never have the courage to swallow it.

The papers are full of the stories of the G.I. Brides, who are now going off in bunches to their husbands in the States. They've come for a lot of criticism in a lot of quarters, but I feel that they've got a heck of a lot of courage to put an Ocean between them and all they know and start their lives so far away. Although, I guess if you think enough of any man you'll face life in Timbuctoo if its necessary. I wasn't bothered where I lived when I was "courting" as they call it here. By the way, Chris's young cousin, Barbara Howard that was, and Barbara Neumeyer that is—is married to a G.I. from Kansas, which is your neighbouring State, I believe. She's coming over to join her husband in a month's time and I'm giving her your address in case she is ever round your way, so that she can call on you. She's only 18, and is far from an advert for "starving Britain"—she's like a Barrel, some gland trouble, I should imagine. Her father is Chris's mother's brother, if you can sort it out. She's going to live on a Ranch, twenty miles from nowhere, so I imagine she'll find it slightly different to life in Southport. I know her parents very well, and she's an only child, so they're going to miss her very much.

Chris is "demobbed" next week, I believe—so what he will be doing with his future I haven't the faintest idea. I haven't seen him since September, and only hear vague rumours of his activities from this that and the other local source. Don't suppose I shall ever see much of him, even though we live in the same town.

I won't write any more now, Helen. I should like to hear from you if you ever get the time. Don't you start getting anti-British on me, will you? I hear that most Americans are that way now, though I can't think why.

Best love,
Betty

## GREAT WESTERN RAILWAY

c/o Accounts and Rates Dept.
District Goods Manager's Office
G. W. Rly. Liverpool, 2

My dear Helen,

How glad I was to hear from you and to know that you are still very much alive and kicking. I have put my new address on the top of the paper—I hope you can decipher it. The District Goods Manager's Office is in two sections—one lot up the Street in James Street, and we down in Irwell Street—right by the banks of the Mighty Mersey. Sitting at my desk I can watch the big liners come down the River— although they are conspicuous for their absence this morning, as the country is in the grips of a paralysing Dock Strike. It started in Liverpool and spread all over the country in less than no time—worst of all it's holding up our food supplies, which are bad enough at the best of times. I know what I'd do with every damned docker they gave me to deal with—apart from wringing his Neck—I'd shove every manJack of 'em in the Army and bring the other lads back to do their work— perhaps then they wouldn't grumble so much. I disapprove heartily of Strikes, unless they have genuine grievance and the whole thing is backed by their Unions—which this one isn't. As it is they're fighting against the very Government they fought to put in—and the Labour Party has enough on its plate to deal with as it is.[3]

Today has nowtturned [*sic*] fairly sunny—although it started off with a dreadful fog. I am getting more used to living in the North now—although it s a lonely life with my Mother in London and me up here. I have been trying everywhere to get rooms, but it seems an impossible task—there isn't any accommodation to be had anywhere, and there seems to be no prospect of any Houses going up for the next six months. Everything seems to be so slow and taking such a time to get going. Plans are afoot for the erection of a few hundred Prefabs in Southport—to me they resemble Chicken runs, but they are nicely fitted inside and to get a roof over my head I'd live in an empty Barn. My

---

3. The dock strike, not supported by the unions, was against the new Labour government (ibid., 672–73).

name is about seventeen hundredth on the List in Southport, and there will be about two hundred houses which doesn't seem too hopeful. The only solution seems to be to take furnished rooms for a while and let our Flat in London furnished, but I am one of those folk who like to have their own things about them and don't take kindly to living among other people's. Still, beggars can't be Choosers, and thats how things will be for some time to come.

Southport is a very nice, clean Seaside town—most of the G.I.'s who've been there say that it is the nearest approach to an American town they've seen—you know tree-lined Streets, and white and green Houses—it's really a very wealthy-town too, has quite a number of Big Business Wallahs on its list of residents, but like a lot of other English towns in many ways, it's as backward as hell. Mixed up with it's shady Boulevards, Rose Gardens and Luxury Cinemas is the strange fact that 50% of the Town's Houses are still lit by Gas and have practically no indoor sanitation and no Bathrooms! I was evacuated here last year when the Flying Bombs were on, so I know a lot of the people. They're friendly folk, far more so than those of the South, but they have the usual small-town fault, they know the inside story of your life in five minutes, and what they don't know they invent, just so they can have something to talk about over their "coop of Tay", which seems to mean more to the people in Lancashire than it does in London even and that is certainly saying something. I guess it must be healthier than London, but part of me will always stay down there with the fog and the dirt. I'm not a Cockney born, but my heart always belonged there and always will till the day I die. There's an indefinable something about London that will always "get" you. I was down there for my week's holiday a week ago and strange to say, though I've lived there all these years, I found there were so many things to see that I hadn't seen. Every inch seems to have it's own history. I spent hours in the Cloister at Westminster Abbey where all of the great—and small, sometimes—of our Land are buried—from 1350 onwards. I was always passionately fond of History in School and it still fascinates me. The most amazing thing about the Cloisters—to me anyway—are the names carved in the Walls of the people who've visited there. Theres a Richd Parker who carved his name in 1610, a Charles Collett who carved it first in 1650, and then came back in 1700 and wrote his name again—and Francis Drake, who must have stood right where I was standing, and chipped his moniker in the stone—How I wish you could come over here sometime so I could show it to you. I love historical Novels, too—have just finished reading two very good ones—"Swan of Usk" and a grand Novel by Phyliss Bentley called "Take Courage" both about the Civil War in 1642—the first written from the Royalist and the second from the Puritan Point of View. I can always enjoy those sort of Books, where the light Love stuff gives me a chronic pain in the neck!

Thanks so much for sending Chris' letters. He and I are washed up now, finally—and I think it's the best and most sensible thing to do. No-one in this world has thought more of him than I have but you can forgive and forget once too often—and I have had just about enough. He was grand when he was away and I really thought that he intended to wash out the past, and make a new start, but it seems that he only had to get back to the old temptations and he was as bad as ever. As I've told you Helen, he's an extremely handsome man and has that attraction for women—often, unfortunately, the wrong type—that leads to all sorts of things, usually wrong things. I have tried with him, but I've lost heart now. I am giving you his address, because I know he'd be happy to hear from you—he was very grateful to you for sending him books. He loves those Film Mags—and when you know Chris like I do, you'll realise that his three ruling passions seem to be Women, Cigarettes and Movie Magazines—and when I used to send them to him I always knew that he would pass them on to the other lads wherever he may be. His address at the moment, or when I last knew of it and I don't think he's been moved, was L/Cpl. Owen. H. 2613374. Att.14th. Grenadier Guards, Caterham Barracks, Surrey, and if you write to him—and I hope you do, because as I say, he was always grateful to you—you'd better say you asked me for his address, which will adjust things from my angle. Chris had everything in his favor to be a good, decent member of the community—he's a good soldier, and he knows no fear of anything or anybody—but this passion for women simply will not subside, and it's that that has split us up after four years of sticking together through an awful lot. He and I are on opposite sides, Helen, and it doesn't work out. I wish he would try keeping straight for his mother's sake—he's worried her to death this past few years. And she's been such a brick to him.

I have had to change typewriters, so excuse the appalling typing. Have just had my lunch—Potatoes, Cabbage and Gravy and a slice of

Vegetable Pie—no meat—and some sort of Sponge Roll, tasting exactly like pulped cardboard. How I envy you your fruits and your Meat and your Butter!—Things are getting worse than ever here. The monotony of the diet is enough to drive you mad and we live in hourly anticipation of more cuts. Bacon is the next foodstuff threatened—we get three ounces weekly of it, now and it will probably be cut to two. Lendlease, or the finish of it, is the main topic of conversation here. We know it is going to make a terrific difference to us in everyway, but 95 per cent of the British people are definitely against a big loan from America and say they would rather do without than beg from any nation. We've been cut to the lowest possible level now, but we'll pull in our Belts even tighter to stay out of debt. Poor England has had a hell of a time in this War—All her resources, her manpower, her wealth, went in to save the World for Democracy, and its going to be a hell of a pull to get back to normal. Personally, I think it will be ten, or even twenty years before we even get back to a comfortable standard of living, much less to luxury. As for all those who are yelling for them to cut our meagre rations to give to "starving Europe"—and we have thousands of them right here in our midst—should shut their damned silly mouths, and realise that Britain cannot do any more than she is doing—it's impossible. And from what I've seen of Europe, from the Newsreels and the papers, it's far from starving! I, personally, am sick of the eternal queueing for this that and the other—even for a piece of Soap to wash in, and if they're going to cut us down any more they may as well kill me off and finish it quickly. I have to see the Doctor tomorrow, by the way, and am shaking in my shoes at the prospect—I've lost about eight pounds in weight since he saw me last. I do *try* to gain weight, but I don't seem to be able to put on an ounce!

I have received one envelope of Magazines, which were very welcome and were read all round the Office—the others may come soon. I share Chris's passion for Movie Magazines—they are grand reading I think. By the way, when I was telling you about Chris's deserting the Army, I think it best to tell you that with his usual luck he's got away with it. He walked out on May 24th. went back in on the 24th. August, and hasn't got a day's punishment for it! Something to do with his good, fighting record, I believe.

As for the thought of the Nylons—my Gosh! I shouldn't know I was born. I've been doing without stockings for months, due to the lack of coupons, but I shall either have to get some or try wearing Slacks this winter. I much prefer the latter—even though they do cost 6 coupons a pair—but they aren't very keen on Slacks for Office wear. I don't know why, because I have a slim sit-me-down, and a pair of Slacks looks quite decent and respectable on me—but men are funny that way, I suppose.

As for Olivier and Leigh. Well! Larry and Ralph Richardson have been given early release from the Army to start a sort of National Theatre project at the New—mostly Shakespeare and the old Classics—they're doing Henry IV, now with Richardson as Falstaff. Gielgud is in India, touring with some plays for the Troops, and poor Vivien Leigh has developed T.B. and was in University College Hospital, London, up to a few weeks ago—where she is now, I don't know. They recommended treatment in Switzerland, so even with all the difficulties of transport I expect she will be able to get there, where the ordinary person suffering from the same thing can't go. All the same, I'm sorry she had to be stricken so—I'm sorry for anyone with this blasted complaint. It hangs like a shadow over my head, day in and day out. While I was in London I saw Emlyn William' new play "The Wind of Heaven"—it was grand!

I've seen several movies this week "I'll be Seeing You"- absolute trash, "Three Caballeros" not much better, and I usually love Disney, and a grand British film "Dead of Night" all about Ghosts so not for the squeamish.[4] I was so scared I ate the whole of my week's Sweet ration—two ounces—just to keep my nerves in shape, and slept with a Candle lit!

I must close now, Helen. Do write when you can, and let me know how things are. I am always so pleased to hear from you. I'm sending this Air-mail, because Surface Mail takes so long.

As always,<br>Betty

---

4. *I'll Be Seeing You* (1944; U.S.) with Shirley Temple is a patriotic Hollywood movie with a twist: Ginger Rogers plays a convicted murderer on Christmas furlough and Joseph Cotten a shell-shocked war victim released from the hospital. *The Three Caballeros* (1944; U.S.) was the first Disney film combining live action and animation (Donald Duck); some critics consider it the best film Disney ever made. *Dead of Night* (1945; UK), considered one of the best "horror anthologies" ever made, includes Mervyn Johns, Ralph Michael, Basil Radford, and Michael Redgrave, some of the best English actors of the time.

# GREAT WESTERN RAILWAY

Rates & Accounts Office,
2, Irwell St.
LIVERPOOL, Eng.
[Spring 1946]

My dear Helen,

I was so very pleased to hear from you this week, and to know that you are still in the land of the living, although you are working so hard. We are terribly busy here—indeed the work wears me out at times—and the atmosphere in the place isn't as cherry and friendly as it was at Lambeth—probably because they're all so busy they don't have time to think of anything else but Trains and Railways. However, I am swiping the time from the Great Western to write this, and they can all go to the Devil for all I care. I am not the slightest bit interested in my work—never was—I've hated it all my life and longed to get out of it—but my health prevents me from taking any risks. I have to have some measure of security and some from of employment that will pay me something when I have to take one of my frequent trips into this that or the other Sanatorium. People with my sort of lungs can't afford to be independent and do the work they want to do!

The winter here has been long and appallingly hard to endure. Funny, I used to take them in my stride—but this one has seemed the longest I've ever known. I seem to have had everything the matter with me all through it—Colds, half a dozen of them one after the other—three bouts of Tonsilitis, Bronchitis, and the latest—an attack of Pleurisy on the left side—which upset me a bit because my left side has always been the best one. I am getting somewhat weary of it. The colds, though, are not to be wondered at. The weather's been dreadful, wet, cold, windy—all the things that make the British clime the world's worst. And of course, after six years of war-time diet— particularly the present fat ration—our resistance wasn't what it was. Then theres the inevitable clothes trouble—particularly the Shoe situation, which in this country has to be seen to be believed. You have to give seven coupons for shoes and then queue for hours to get them— which automatically cuts out the working gal, who had to be at business in the morning and doesn't have time to stand outside a Shoe Shop. And when you get them the leather is rotten. Just as it is when you have your shoes mended. My feet haven't been properly dry all though the winter, I don't think. Gosh! How I've longed for the days when you could go in and buy those lovely Fleece and Fur Lined Boottees—it seems almost incredible that at one time we could walk into a Shop and buy things of that sort without any difficulty at all. Those were the days! I look at the girls often with their bare legs, rough and red and blue with cold—and wonder how they ever manage to escape rheumatism and other like things. I can't manage without stockings in the winter—my chilblains are that bad and disfiguring—but I leave them off during Spring and Summer, which saves coupons a bit. We have been allotted 14 coupons to last us from April to September, which is a dreadful blow—because it isn't really enough to buy anything—but then austerity has become part of our lives here—but I am an ardent supporter of our present Government, I think they are overdoing it a bit. The people are weary of it, and you can't blame them. After such a long time of scrimping and saving their wardrobes and cupboards are threadbare, and they are sick and tired of the whole business. We feel, over here, that we have been called upon to sacrifice enough and that it is adding Insult to injury to ask us to suffer anymore. I could put up with the monotony of the food, and the holey condition of my clothes, if I was ever given any encouragement that things might be different say in a year from now, but when you pick up your papers as I did this morning, and read that Sweet rationing will not end until December, *1949*, and Clothes rationing will not end for five years, together with other gloomy prophecies, it's enough to dishearten even the cheeriest of souls.

I was so interested to hear of your G.I. Bride as we call them. I was mistaken about Barbara's destination, though. It's her mother's fault not mine—she told me it was Kansas. Now it seems that Jakeys folks are in Kansas, but Barbara will be in Montana—which probably explains about the ranch. She hasn't gone yet, although there are a lot of girls from Southport who have gone, or are on their way over. As for the little W.A.A.F.'s. preference for the cut-away-toes and wedge heels. Please Helen, don't argue with her over that. You've got no idea how we English girls simply crave after those very things that you despise so. Ask any G.I. Bride what she's looking forward to most in the States, and I guarantee she'll answer "The Shoes"! Come and take a look at the severe, austerity stuff that we have to put on our feet, and you'll not wonder why we hanker after the lovely American styles, and lovely they

are, without a doubt. In fact, I've been thinking of writing and asking
you if it was possible for you to get me a pair of white ones—with the
despised cut away toes, and a low wedge heel, (I'm too tall unfortunately for the very high ones). I've scoured London and Liverpool and
Southport—and theres nothing like 'em to be got anywhere. Trouble
is the American sizes, of course. I have a 10 inch foot and I believe
my American size is a 7 ½ - A or something like that. Your sizes are
different to ours. Mine is a 6 in an English shoe. I bought a lovely
pair of American sandals once—many months ago, but the size has
worn off the bottom—and the Shoes have nearly worn off my feet, as
I've practically lived and died in them. I don't know the rulings about
sending Money to the States, but if I ask at the Post Office if it's possible to send you out some money by the International Money Order
Method, and you could get some Shoes for me, of any sort, I should
be grateful. They have a very clever dodge here for avoiding Customs
duty—they pack one shoe in each box, and mark it "Sample" and you
don't have duty to pay on them. They undo the tackings in skirts and
other garments, and they come duty free. They pack like pairs of stockings in letters, magazines, and in between pieces of Cardboard marked
as "Photos" and they also escape duty. My mother, who works in the
Post Office, often tells me about it. I have no qualms of conscience
about cheating His Majesty's Customs—they have more money than
me. One of the girls at a Dance last week whose fiancé is a G.I. was
queening it in an American Corselet waisted skirt of Powder Blue and
a White Peasant blouse, and white wedgies that her boy friend had sent
to her and to say she was the belle of the ball was putting it mildly. And
oh! boy did she know it ??? She made the rest of us look like drabs and
didn't hesitate to remind us of the fact!

I am sending you a photo I had taken a month or two ago—for a
Fancy Dress Dance. Don't look at my skinny arms though—they spoil
the effect. The flowers are made of white tissue paper, and the whole
thing was improvised out of nothing. I hope you can recognize me—
I'm the blonde one!

I was also tickled pink to hear about the Oil that maybe someday
someone will find on your land. Gosh! I wish something could come
of it, for your sakes. Still, if I wish anything it never seems to happen,
so perhaps I'd better keep my mouth shut. I'd do you more harm than
good.

As for the coming to America—that's another dream I'm beginning to have to relinquish. It's a country I've always longed to visit—but the difficulties of getting anywhere but England seem to be well nigh insurmountable nowadays. Except the big bugs like Churchill, who can, of course, sneeze once or twice and get off to Florida to recuperate.

You and I, I'm afraid we disagree about Churchill—but definitely. To the rest of the world he may be a grand old man—a great fighter—but a great many of us in this country have seen the other side of it. We call him a great Showman—and a born actor. In the limelight he must be—and the Big boss of everything he must be too, otherwise he acts like a small child and sulks. Whatever may be anyone's feelings about Soviet Russia, this is hardly the time to embarrass our present Government by starting a lot of ill-feeling and international bad-fellowship. Russia is a great and mighty power—who fought well and nobly in this War, and while the War was on Winston was full of this flapdoodle of "our great and noble ally, Russia" and so on and so forth—the damned old humbug. I am, I suppose, politically opposite to you—I am a member of the British Labour Party—The Party that rule England at present,[5] and our Prime Minister is a Mr. Clement Atlee, not a Mr. Winston Churchill, but the latter gentleman doesn't seem to take easily to relinquishing his former high rank and if he can't hold the stage completely in England, he'll do it in America. Winston, of course, is leader of the Conservative party—the party that's had more to do with fostering the legend of the capitalist and Imperialistic England than anything else in the world. If he is speaking as a private individual, then of course, he has every right to do so, but not as the Voice of England—a certain section of it, maybe, but not all of it.[6]

Chris was demobbed about five weeks ago, and is causing a great stir among the females of the town. I have spoken to him on one occasion—for about five minutes, during the whole of which time he never looked at me once—just spoke with his shoulders hunched up and his

5. On July 26, 1945, the BBC announced the results of the general election, the first since 1938. Labour gained 212 seats, giving them a majority of 393 in Parliament. The Tories (Conservatives) and their allies won 213 seats. Fifteen million votes were cast against Churchill's government (see Calder, *People's War*, 670–74).

6. Betty seems to be referring to Churchill's famous Iron Curtain address at Westminster College in Fulton, Missouri, in March 1946.

face turned the other way. It was just like speaking to a stranger—not a man I'd known for four years. I was beginning to wonder if my face was pock-marked or become so distasteful that he couldn't look at it!! I see him fairly often at dances, and he ignores my existence as completely as I ignore his—such a strange end to so long a friendship. I have given up wondering and puzzling about such things. I only regret the loyalty and thought I wasted on him, which was obviously so little appreciated. It really doesn't seem like him at all—almost like someone else had taken his place. Unless, of course, I was seeing him though rose-coloured glasses, which often happens. Anyway, it's over and done with, now, and I have settled down to it better than I thought I would, although I would have preferred it to have ended on a friendlier and less bitter note, and known a little more of the reasons.

From what I can gather, he seems to be going from bad to worse as far as Women are concerned, and the lies and yarns he tells are fantastic. Seems to be living in a world of his own. I'm honestly beginning to wonder if he knows when he's telling the truth, and when he isn't.

I've just been served up with some Jelly—made of weak Lemonade mixed with Gelatine Powder—and it's dreadful. I've wasted all my Dinner hour searching Liverpool for some White Angora Bunny Wool to make myself a jumper and have come back with some wretched stuff in Moss Green—which is a colour I'm not at all keen on—and it isn't Bunny wool, and why I bought it, I'll never know, and I shall probably have to sell it again. Why do we women do such silly things.

I'll be writing you again shortly—this is an awful rambling affair— God bless, Helen, and write me when you have time.

Love,

Betty

GREAT WESTERN RAILWAY

District Goods Manager's Office

11, James Street, Liverpool, 2

Dear Helen,

Have just received your Note and thought I would drop you a line whilst I have a few moments to spare. It's such a wretched day—grey and depressing, and the sight of the pile of work in front of me makes things even more so. How I hate Railway Offices, and the dullness of the work—still, I suppose everyone gets like that about their jobs—and weather like this doesn't help the general atmosphere. Neither do the newspaper headlines which, this morning announce "Less Bread, No Breakfast Foods, Plainer Cakes, Less Beer"—it makes me wonder when the poor long suffering British public are going to read on their morning news "More Something or other". The Less Beer doesn't worry me, and the rationing of Bread was expected, but the Cakes are vile enough now, looking and tasting like mouldy cardboard—how they can be plainer is beyond me. We haven't had a fancy cake since 1940—only plain Buns and Scones, and Utility Sponges. As for the Breakfast Foods, I loathe breakfast, and am usually dashing out of the house in the mornings with an empty tummy apart from a Glass of Milk, but its going to come hard on mothers of big hungry families, when theres nothing else to feed them on. We have little or no Bacon—three ounces a week isn't much—and no eggs, and even Preserves are rationed to a pound a month, which limits the conventional bread and marmalade. I used to like an Apple or a Banana for Breakfast in Peace time—I used to love Fruit—but we've hardly had a bit of fruit in our mouths all winter, and the Food Minister doesn't seem inclined to spare shipping for the purpose of bringing any over. Oh! for the days when we could nibble apples all day, and throw Banana skins over the pavement, and have Coconut in our Cakes (Coconut, I am ashamed to say was a passion of mine, even though it had no vitamins!) A G.I. writing in the paper this morning compliments the English girls on the beauty of their complexions, and says he doesn't know how it is done with the Fruitless diet on which they are forced to exist. My Mother cooked me some Spinach on Sunday and I thought I'd be smart and drink the water it was cooked in, but regret to report that all I got for my intelligence was a badly upset tummy. Probably my poor old inside is not used to vitamins. Still, with Summer coming, there's a faint hope of a bit of Rhubarb, and maybe an English apple or two later on. We shan't see any Strawberries, or Raspberries, or anything like that because the Government has earmarked most of the crop for Jam, and what is left over will go to those folks who can afford to buy it, just as the Hothouse Peaches and Grapes do. Peaches are ten shillings each—thats about two and a half dollars—and grapes five dollars the pound. What hope have the poorer people got of getting things like that.

I am so delighted about the shoes, Helen, believe me. You have no idea how hard it is to get shoes here—it means queueing for hours, and I have longed so much for a white pair. Ours, you see, are all Utility models and we have no white ones, and I love white shoes in the summer. But it seems terrible that you had to send me a pair of your own stockings. One of my friends works in the Customs and has told me some very useful tips, which have come in handy. You don't have to worry, for one thing, about the clothes actually *being* second-hand. All you have to do is *declare* it was worn, and if it is very new, usually undo a hem, or a seam somewhere. Often it isn't even inspected by the Customs Folk, especially if it isn't packed amongst food. A man friend of mine in New York sent me somethings some months back—they were brand new, but declared as worn, and I didn't have a penny duty to pay on them. Unfortunately, knowing my favorite colour was blue, and being a man and naturally contrary, he sent me a Jacket and Blouse in *Green,* a colour I am vaguely superstitious about. (My mother always says I would live and die in powder blue and white, my favorite combination!) Still, I was eternally grateful to him. The Customs bloke also says that with shoes, it's a very wise plan to pack one shoe separately—sending the pair in two boxes instead of one—and mark each box Sample. That lessens the risk of pilferage, and eliminates duty, as it isn't payable on one shoe. And with hose, Helen,—the best thing to do is to put them in with a letter, and send them over—another dodge to avoid pilferage, which is rife over here at the Ports and in the Clearing Depots. An American Shoe shop in Liverpool, says my size is 7½ B.—the "A" size is supposed to be a little wide, but don't worry a shade too wide won't hurt me. I am hoping and praying that they will arrive before summer ends—knowing the time these things take, and I am so very grateful to you for going to so much trouble. But if you could see the state of my wardrobe—or of any working gal in this country to-day—I'm sure you'd think your efforts weren't wasted.

You don't say whether you had the photo or not, but I suppose you have. Aren't my shoulders and arms thin, though I Do wish I could get some fat on 'em. My legs stay fairly well plump but whereas five years ago I used to have a back and shoulders to be proud of, I am now ashamed to exhibit them in a bathing suit.

By the way, I have my mother in Southport with me now. She was very lonesome in London on her own, although she was very upset over leaving. I'm hoping it will only be temporarily. I managed to get a flat, after a devil of a job, but it's very expensive and in a strictly aristoocratic [*sic*] quarter, too "posh" for words. I'm used to the more working class areas, and I think I was happier there. Still, it's a case of getting where you can—the housing situation is appalling in this country, and we shall have to look out for something cheaper later on. This town is very pleasant in the summer, but I miss London, just as much as my mother does, even though the air seems fresher up this part of the world.

I have tried to bang this off while the Boss isn't looking but must really stop now. I just wanted to send you my grateful thanks, and will write again soon, when I hear from you. Do remember me to the G.I. Bride and wish her luck for me in her new home, and when her baby comes.

All the best for now, Helen, and do write me again soon.

Love,

Betty


## GREAT WESTERN RAILWAY

District Goods Manager's Office,
11, James Street, Liverpool, 2.

My dear Helen,

You will really have to forgive me if this letter is badly typed, short, scrappy, and everything else, but I wanted to get it off to you, Air Mail, as soon as I could and time is very limited. We have two typists away here and I am trying to cover their work as well as my own, and it's no easy job and my colleague has just had a phone message that her boy is home from India and has got herself the day off to go and see him. I can't begrudge her that—bless her—but it doesn't ease things for me. She is quite pale from excitement, and I can appreciate it. When Chris landed home last year I had such a shock it upset my inner workings and I couldn't eat anything for a week! Anyway, at least Joyce got warning and could make herself look something before she went round to see him—I had just gotten out of the bath, had a towel wound round my head for a Turban and a pair of shabby slacks and no make-up! And after planning for months what I should say and what I should wear, that's how I looked and the only thing I could keep on saying was "I'm so glad to see you!", which wasn't very original, after all. I certainly hope that Joyce will put up a better show, also that she'll be able to hold her man a bit longer than I did!!

The main thing is, Helen, that the package arrived quite safely yesterday—it had only taken seven weeks, which is very good, I think, and oh! I am so grateful to you. The shoes were simply marvelous. I really love the white shoes and I can't get any over here at all. Even if we could they wouldn't be the ankle-strap and peep toe styles. I know you may think I am exaggerating the shoe position over here, but it really is very bad indeed. My feet have been practically on the floor, because I simply haven't the time to queue for two hours in the morning, which is what you have to do to try to get anything of the day's quota, and then it takes seven coupons. I don't think I have ever been so poorly off for footwear in my life. My mother was worried to death over it—she swore I was catching innumerable colds because of not having decent shoes, and when we take them to be mended they take about three weeks, so you [can] tell how delighted I was with the white ones. I nearly covered the Postman's embarrassed face with kisses when he brought the package in—reckon the poor man will be frightened of me—and of course, all work in the Office was completely held up while the girls "ooh'd" and "ah'd" with delight. The clothes were grand, Helen,—the vest is going to be put away for Medical Exams and X-Rays, of which I have plenty of as you can imagine and my underwear is literally full of patches. Poor old Mum picked up a pair of my unmentionables the other day and remarked sadly that there was nothing left to patch! I was going to take a tuck in the yellow blouse, but before I even got a chance to suggest it, my mother grabbed it, so I've had it—in British Army slang! As for the stockings—I am now struggling to do my usual summer session of going without, but my legs are a vile colour—purplely red—and the scars of the winter's chilblains are still visible. Very much so, so it will be grand to have a decent pair of hose for a special "date".

The tinned fruit, of course, caused a minor sensation. The only trouble is I cannot bring myself to eat it! I've put it in the Cupboard, and am almost stroking it reverently—the last time I tasted Pineapple was in 1941—believe it or not. Anyway, we've decided to open one tin on Victory Day, which also happens to be my birthday—June 16th. and the small tin on Mum's birthday, and hoard the other one for Xmas, which seems to be the best solution, after a lot of concentrated time and thought! So think of us on the three celebrations, eating your tins of fruit.

I had an Exam last week but the Doc wasn't very pleased—says I'm losing weight and looking "peaky" and run down, also that that the last bout of pleurisy didn't help. He told me that he knows I can't get any of the food that's needed, fats, Chocolate, fruits and stuff like that, but I'm to eat as much green cabbage and vegetables I can, and salad stuff, so I'm trying to push down the Cabbage, and make meals of lettuce and water cress and the only fatty substance available, Cod Liver Oil and Malt, which unfortunately makes me throw up everything I eat, but I really must persevere and get myself to take it.

They say it's also a good tonic for the hair, and mine hasn't been up to par lately. My hair really used to be my crowning glory, but it seems to be getting very dry and breaking off at the end and not so shiny as it used to be. I suppose it boils down to the old National Diet again. Must be something lacking. The new load they've put us on is almost black, and after keeping it a day it's like a brick and tastes like cardboard. Talk about unappetizing! Our cheese ration was cut to two ounces weekly last week, and everyone seems determined to cut rations as near to the Starvation level as they can. Don't believe the stories that your Press put out about Britain having more than adequate supplies of food, Helen. It's not true. The food situation and indeed the clothes situation are very, very bad. A few weeks on our diet and I guarantee you'd be sick to death of it!

I shall be writing to you again soon—more of a newsy letter than this, but I did want you to hear that I'd got the package alright. My mother wants to put in a little note for you, so I'll shut up now. With many, many thanks.

Best love,<br>Betty

P.S. There was no duty at all to pay on the package, in case you were wondering how that angle got by!

P.P.S. Joyce has just come in sporting a great big diamond ring which was just put on the third finger of her left hand at quarter past 11 last night! So *she* obviously had what it takes even if I didn't!

28–5–46

Dear Helen,

I feel I must write you a few lines to thank you for your great kindness to my daughter, who, as usual with girls of her age, loves pretty things, but unfortunately owing to the state of things prevailing in England now is unable to indulge in anything.

Your parcel's arrival caused great excitement and even I was thrilled to bits and I am quite sure you would feel quite satisfied without expressed thanks if you could only have seen both of us. The yellow blouse is a little large for Betty so I have had it and I can assure you I have thoroughly appreciated your kind thought. As for the white shoes, well, ecstasy is the right word to use as we are starved here for anything smart.

Still, we are hoping for better times to come, but perhaps by that time we shall have forgotten what a good Steak or a tin of fruit looks like. So I do hope you will take this letter as an expression of my deep gratitude to you.

I really feel this, as Betty is really one of the war casualties. She was a lovely healthy girl before the war, but life in shelters and lack of variety and quality of food caused a breakdown that we have never been able to pull up and that is why I want you to know how grateful I am to you for your many kindnesses to her.

Again, thanking you
I am
Yours very Sincerely
Gladys

c/o D.G.M.O (Rates)
2, Irwell St
Liverpool. 2.
[September 28, 1946]

Dear Helen,

You will no doubt be surprised to know that I am writing this in bed, propped up with umpteen pillows, having really nearly kicked the bucket this time. I was taken ill about 3 ½ weeks ago, couldn't breathe, couldn't move, went a peculiar bluey-grey colour, & had a temperature of 104 or there abouts! The Doctors diagnosed Pleurisy & Pneumonia,

& put me on M. & B. Tablets, which, though they made me pretty sick, I'm sure saved my life. I was transferred to Hospital in the middle of it, & sent home because I was lying awake all night what with women dying next to me & another Woman going mad & rushing round the Ward as though she was on a Horse! Anyway, here I am still alive & kicking—though only feebly. I don't think anyone expected me to get over it, so I thought it only fair to surprise them! Actually, I'd been feeling off-colour for a few weeks before I was actually taken ill—we've had the most appalling summer within living memory, nothing but rain beating down every day since the middle of May, & terrific gales & no sun at all—I kept getting my feet wet—our shoes are rotten, anyway—& its bound to wear your resistance down, & make you liable to anything that comes along. We were relying on a good summer for the Harvest, & its been absolutely disastrous in every way!

Anyhow, I now have eight weeks in bed to face—which isn't a very amusing prospect, or one that I'm looking forward to—I get some grand luck don't I?

You never [saw] anything looking more like a Skeleton with Skin on at the present—it puzzles me where all the Flesh goes to!

I wore your White Shoes doggedly through the Summer(?) & they caused admiring glances wherever I went—the Battle for Shoes here gets worse & worse—even to get them repaired takes a month! I never thought the Day would come when I would get so fed up with England, but the eternal shortage of everything is getting everyone down.

I won't write anymore Helen—I wanted to let you know how things were—I'll write you again when I'm able.

All my love,
Betty

# GREAT WESTERN RAILWAY

District Goods Manager's Office,
11, James Street, Liverpool, 2.

c/o D.G.M.O.
Great Western Rly,
Claims Dept,
PIER HEAD DEPOT.
Liverpool. Eng.

My dear Helen,

This is a belated letter—darned if I can remember if I've written you since I was taken ill, and it seems ages since I heard from you—or perhaps it is this winter has seemed so endless to me. We are very busy, too, and it's difficult to even get ten minutes to type a private letter. And for the past ten weeks the Offices have been so cold and unheated that our hands were blue and quite unable to function properly.

As I write this, it is raining outside and I never thought I should be pleased to see it rain. But this has been the worst winter for us since 1814—nine weeks of snow, ice and Arctic conditions. It's been appalling and I wonder how I've ever survived it. I've been crippled with chilblains and could only hobble about—and I've had three bouts of influenza which have left me with a racking cough and a badly infected throat and a fit of the blues the like of which I can't remember. Worse still was the effect of this dreadful winter on the economic state of the country. What luck we've had! The worst summer for years, which ruined our harvest and now this winter which has set Agriculture back for at least two years, and now the aftermath of all of it—the worst floods the country has ever suffered and all the hardship and ruin that go with it. We have lost a million sheep in the blizzards—transport was chaotic—trains held up by drifts for days—some dug out weeks later, completely frozen. People have died of cold sitting marooned in their Cars and fifteen were killed in the terrible Gale that blew over the country three nights ago, bringing all this rain and flood havoc. The factories are going back to work now—due, mainly to the heroic struggles of the Miners who have worked like Titans in impossible conditions to try to bring the Coal to the top. It is easy to criticize this Government, and to shriek at their so-called mistakes, and be wise after the event, but they *are* a Worker's Government and they do try to do their best for the people who are the backbone of this country and who have suffered so much in the past by the administration of our so-called "ruling class". To a certain extent, you know, Helen the feudal system still reigns supreme in England. You are expected to curtsey to the Squire of the Manor and to bob up and down if a Duchess passes you by, because the poorer folk of England have been reared for centuries in the belief that this was the Class that were born to rule—nowadays, the big business man, the Landowner, The Colliery Owner, and men of their Ilk from what is known as the Opposition, or the Conservative party of this nation. They will, I can assure you, use every dirty trick at their disposal, and they are considerable, to oust any Government that helps the Workers. Their expressed view is that the best way to make the Britisher work is with "a whip at his back and hunger in his belly". The British aristocracy both in past years and now was no better than their French counterparts in the days of Marie Antoinette—the only difference is that the average Briton hasn't got the courage, or the energy, to revolt against it.

The ready moan now seems to be that we are giving away our Empire.[7] Well in the first place, it isn't ours to give—India deserves her freedom, and if she is able to rule herself then this Government is determined that she shall quite rightly do so. I have read some of the American press and it seems strange to me that America—always so ready to call us "Imperialistic" in the past, should now bemoan the passing of our Empire because one great nation is getting her independence. Canada, Australia, South Africa, New Zealand—they all govern themselves—have done so for years but they are bound to us by ties of blood and sentiment, and from what I have seen, heard and read of Colonials, those ties are as strong as ever. I know they would be ready to help us in any way—far more so now that we have used up all our energies and money fighting a War, than when we were rich, powerful, and a World leader. It has always been my opinion that the strength of

7. King George VI's cousin Lord Mountbatten of Burma, the new viceroy of India, arrived in Delhi at the end of March 1947. To avoid a civil war between Muslims and Hindus, the date for independence was moved from mid-1948 to mid-August 1947, and its basis was a partition into the separate nations of India and Pakistan (Peter Hennessy, *Never Again: Britain, 1945–1951* [New York: Pantheon, 1993], 232–35).

a country is in her people, and I would back ours against anyone. Few nations have suffered as consistently as we have, or sacrificed more in the past six years with so little reward and so little thanks. We face an even worse time now. We have little food, and are shabby and living the most threadbare existence of any nation in Europe, but I believe we shall come through it, and the Obituaries written by the American nation will look a little silly in the years to come. They are always telling us what Americans think of us—but no journalist has yet had the courage to reverse the picture. All sorts of campaigns and Propaganda is suggested to get the Americans to see our side of the situation, but I guarantee that if you came to England today you would find more anti-American feeling than has ever been. The British are a proud and stubborn race and they dislike being put in Uncle Sam's pockets—What is more the average British worker is not as violently anti-Russian as his American counterpart, and he dislikes intensely the tactics of that old Mountebank Churchill and his crew, particularly Winston himself, whom they firmly believe is itching for another War—and for the glory that will come to him, personally, through it. I have no use for Winston Spencer—he is, of all the men in the world, a ranting hypocrite—a man who uses his gift of oratory to mesmerise the masses, whom actually he has no use for.[8]

Enough of politics anyway—How are you doing all this time?? I often think of you, and wonder how things have gone with you. I have been back at work since the end of December but last September's "do" of Pleurisy and Pneumonia nearly finished me off altogether. I was in bed three months and they want me to go away to another Sanatorium now—at least when there is a vacancy, which may not be for months. I don't know what to do about it. I'm worried about my work—they won't keep on putting up with these continued absences, and even when you're in Hospital you don't seem to get on very rapidly. The Diet is so poor—and you can't seem to pick up. The Doctor told me last week that lack of fats and lack of sugar in the diet is causing all the trouble—people can't keep warm, and I have developed a craving for

---

8. In a Gallup poll taken in England in the days after Churchill's Iron Curtain speech in Fulton, Missouri, 89 percent of respondents had heard of the speech, 39 percent disapproved of its anti-Russian theme, 34 percent approved, and 16 percent had no opinion. Betty was one of the 39 percent (ibid., 363).

sweet stuff that baffles me. I was never a Sweet-tooth before the War. I bought a lot of Candy, of course—but it was more habit than anything. I've tried to pin it down to the fact that I'm a non-smoker, they say people who smoke heavily rarely bother with sweets—but with my Chest ailments I don't think it wise to take up smoking now. Anyway I'm a hopeless mess at it—never could do anything but chew the Tobacco and give myself watery eyes. Cigarettes aren't easy to come by here, either—in fact, nothing is easy to come by and we have forgotten what so many things look like we're getting used to the lack of everything. Austerity rules us—we get nothing pretty or fancy either in clothing or food. I used to love frills and fancies, but like most of us, I have put even moderate luxury behind me, and now concentrate on things plain, and practical.

I had a package of papers from you this week, but the envelope was in very bad condition and looked as though it had been opened. There were two Newspaper clippings and two Newspaper mags in it—so you will know better than I if anything had been removed. It was nice to see you writing again after all this time. I thought you were lost, or that you'd come into money and forgotten your old mates.

I am still living in Southport, though Mum hates it and wants to go back to London. Chris is now part owner and driver of several Taxis in Manchester, so I don't see him from one year's end to another. He is very much the prosperous business man and floats all his gals round in a brand new Car. What luck I get! When I knew him he didn't have the price of a Taxi ride! Not a Bus ride—in fact, we used to walk! I think I must be fated in that direction.

I am sending you a snap of myself taken on one of our two summer days last year, wearing the shoes you sent. I hope you admire the beautiful background of my pal's husband's working shirt—very much worse for wear but still on active service!

I must close now, or you'll be fed up. Do write me if you get any time—I am always pleased to hear from you at any time.

Best love, Betty

# VII

# May 10, 1949–December 1950

These letters are the last that Betty wrote to Helen. From September 1947 to June 1948 Betty was hospitalized in another sanatorium outside London where her tonsils were removed and her diaphragm "hoisted" to improve her breathing. But now, after twenty months away, she is back at work in Liverpool.

Betty says she is "an ardent Socialist and a great supporter of our present Government—the only one we've ever had that ever gave the workers of Britain a square deal. I am not, too, as anti-Russian as you . . . To me, no difference of opinion . . . is bad enough to cause any more armed conflict . . . We feel that if there is an other War with Russia it will be America's war . . . I don't think I could endure another six years like '39–45 again." Rationing is easing, but "at least with rationing the poorer people get their fair share," she writes.

A short handwritten note dated September 24, 1949, and posted from Ireland indicates that Betty has not heard from Helen in more than six months. Betty's last correspondence, a Christmas card dated December 12, 1950, reports that she is now married and living in the north of England.

## BRITISH RAILWAYS

The Railway Executive
London Midland Region

D.G.M.O.
11, James St.
LIVERPOOL. 2.
England.
[May 10, 1949]

My dear Helen,

It does seem ages since I wrote to you, and it must be Xmas since I had your letter. Indeed, so much seems to have happened I hardly know where to begin, but I have waited to come back to work and get near a Typewriter. I should never have had the patience to perform in Handwriting. They say that's a complaint that afflicts most typists, or those professing to be typists.

Anyway, to get down to brass tacks. I started work a week ago after a year and eight months away—what a spell this time! Don't know if you've heard from me since I went off duty last time but I went into yet another Sanatorium in September, 1947, and came out in June last year. During that time, they tried to give me an A.P. but it flopped so they gave me what they call a P.P. which consists of hoisting my diaphragm up about six inches, thereby letting the lungs rest on it, and sort of semi-collapsing them. Needless to say I was pretty sick of the country life after 9 months of lying around looking at some very uninteresting railings with a flat expanse of green field beyond it. The place was very strict, too—no little outings anywhere—you were just shut in like a Gaol. Anyway, when I came out last June, they promised me I should start work in six months, but winter came, as winter has a habit of doing, and I got three bouts of tonsillitis one after the other, whereupon they decided to remove the offending Organs, which have been septic for years and should have been taken out long ago. This started a three-month argument as to whether the lungs were tough enough to take an anaesthetic, the Lung Doctor refusing to give his permission to have me put to sleep and the Throat man refusing to use a local. In the end, after reducing me to a nervous wreck between them, they carted me into the local Hospital, placed me in a private ward, shook my hand and wished me luck, and gave me Pentethol. I was out for three hours and 20 minutes and when I woke up still alive no-one was more surprised than me! Anyway, it held up my going back to work for quite a time. I lost a lot of weight and have had an awful job to put it back on again, but I am beginning to feel a lot better now, and am certainly much brighter since I started work. I may have to go back in to have the Phrenic nerve crushed and thereby help the old diaphragm to stay hoisted, and after that I hope they'll leave me alone for a while. I go to the Clinic every ten days for refills of air and parts of my midriff are beginning to resemble a much-used Pincushion. I have come to the conclusion that this battling with T.B. is a great life if you don't weaken. I have done pretty well, but I think I am beginning to show signs of Battle Scars. I really am getting pretty sick of it, one way and the other. I seem to have been ill pretty much all my younger days. Indeed, I'm beginning to wonder if a short life and a gay one isn't the best way to look at it!!

However, to get off miserable subjects—how are you all this time, Helen. I have wondered so often how things were with you. I always counted you, and one other American girl I know, as very dear friends of mine, and I often speak to people of your kindness to me. I always hope to hang on to individual friendships, however many international differences crop up, as crop up they will—even among allied nations. I know there is a lot of things we do that irritate Americans intensely, just as there are things in their characters utterly alien to our way of thinking, but I have always spoken of people as I found them and you, and Gwen (the girl in New York) were very good to me, and I am not likely to forget it. Politically, I think you and I differ Helen—I am an ardent Socialist and a great supporter of our present Government—the only one we've ever had that ever gave the workers of Britain a square deal. I am not, too, as anti-Russian probably as you—in fact I don't think the masses of Britain are violently anti-Soviet at all. I am no admirer of the Communist doctrine in its entirety, though there are many things in it, which had the party stuck to the ideals laid down by Lenin, would have made the world a pleasant place for the poorer people, but I have a mortal horror of War—having suffered quite enough through the last one—and I cannot conceive of anything bad enough to cause nation to rise up against nation. To me, no difference of opinion, and no hatred, however great, is bad enough to cause any more armed conflict, and I swear that if there *is* another War, with Russia, or anybody else, I'll have no active part in it, and neither will any one belonging to me if I can possibly prevent it. We in Britain had a shocking time in the last lot—and we'd be wiped off the face of the earth should it happen again. And there you have the hard core of the disagreements between British and Americans. We feel that if there is another War with Russia it will be America's war, and we shall be dragged in as a buffer state for Russia to drop the bombs on. People can call me a coward, or a pacifist, or anything they like, but I don't think I could endure another six years like '39–45 again and there are an awful lot of British people who feel the same way, and who can blame them?

Conditions are certainly easing a bit here—Clothes are off ration although they're pretty dear, and there are still things we can't get—Cotton stuff, for instance is very scarce because most of it is for export—Nylons, that dream so dear to a British female's heart, are absolutely unobtainable and will continue to be so, as every pair we manufacture goes overseas. We are said to be the only country in the world whose women can't wear Nylon, which seems ridiculous when you can go abroad anywhere, if you have the money, and see the famous articles with "Made in England" stamped all over 'em. Most of us still go stockingless through the summer—if such a season ever comes in England—although I must say it's a fashion I'm not keen on, as unless you can acquire a perfectly smashing suntan, bare legs look horrible. I rarely suntan because I am a blonde, and we never get enough sun, anyway. Sweets, too, came off ration this month, but the Government have had to warn people that they will have to put them back on unless the mad rush stops. Folks have gone absolutely mad, and are buying up Chocolate in pounds at a time, and there aren't sufficient stocks to warrant it. So would it be with food, if they let it go on to a free market. At least with rationing the poorer people get their fair share. I am all for it, myself. Meat, of course, is a sad story here, at the moment. We get—in value—eight pennyworth a week each—that's about 6 ounces of steak, or one Chop, and getting a dinner every day is an absolute nightmare! Still, rather than pay the colossal prices demanded by the Argentine, I'd cheerfully become a Vegetarian. I'm very nearly one now, anyhow. Ive given up trying to gain weight—on the food we're getting it's impossible!

I am sending you a snap or two—one of them was taken in the Office last week. I hope you'll remember which is me—I'm the blonde one of the gang. The other one is taken in the garden with the current boy friend. The latter isn't very good of me, because there are a few scratchy marks on the negative and it looks as if I've got 'specs on, which I haven't. It's very good of Bob, though. He has corn-coloured hair and I was always devoted to dark men. It just shows you!

I shall have to finish now, and will tell you more of the family history on my next letter. Do write me soon, Helen. I was so pleased to hear from you, and I hope we may keep in touch with each other now.

Love,<br>Betty

H7, Queens Rd
Southport
Lancs.

24/9/49

My dear Helen—

Thought I would drop you a line from the Emerald Isle. We are over on holiday for the second time this year and the food is so good, I have broken out in spots with the unaccustomed richness of it; and the Boy friend looks as if he's gained a stone!

How are you doing, anyway? Seems ages since I heard from you! I wrote you about three months ago!

Hope to hear from you soon

Betty

[Christmas Card]

December 17, 1950

Helen—

I don't even know if you are still at your old address, but I thought I would send you a Xmas wish just in case.

I do hope everything is well with you—Haven't heard from you for so long!

I am married now, but still living in the North of England!

All my best wishes always —

Your old pen-pal—<br>Betty

# VIII

## Helen Bradley to Betty Swallow,
## August 18, 1969

Dear Betty,

Yesterday I finished re reading all your letters to me. I had saved them all and I surely wish I had read them long ago. I was filled with sorrow and guilt. I quit writing to you because I could not take any more of your criticism of the U.S. Now after reading again of all you had been thru I know I should have forgiven you anything. I am writing after 19 years, with not much hope of finding you to tell you that I am giving your letters to the Churchill memorial in Fulton, Mo. Where he gave the "Iron Curtain" Speech. They are so good they should be published.

There is so much I'd love to tell you if you are still alive—I am now 78 years old and still enjoying an old lady's life. I went to Europe four times, three times to England—I loved it so much—I am so sorry now that I didn't try to reach you.

I'm hoping that this letter may find its way to you—not likely after all this time—

Affectionately, Helen.